SHURI

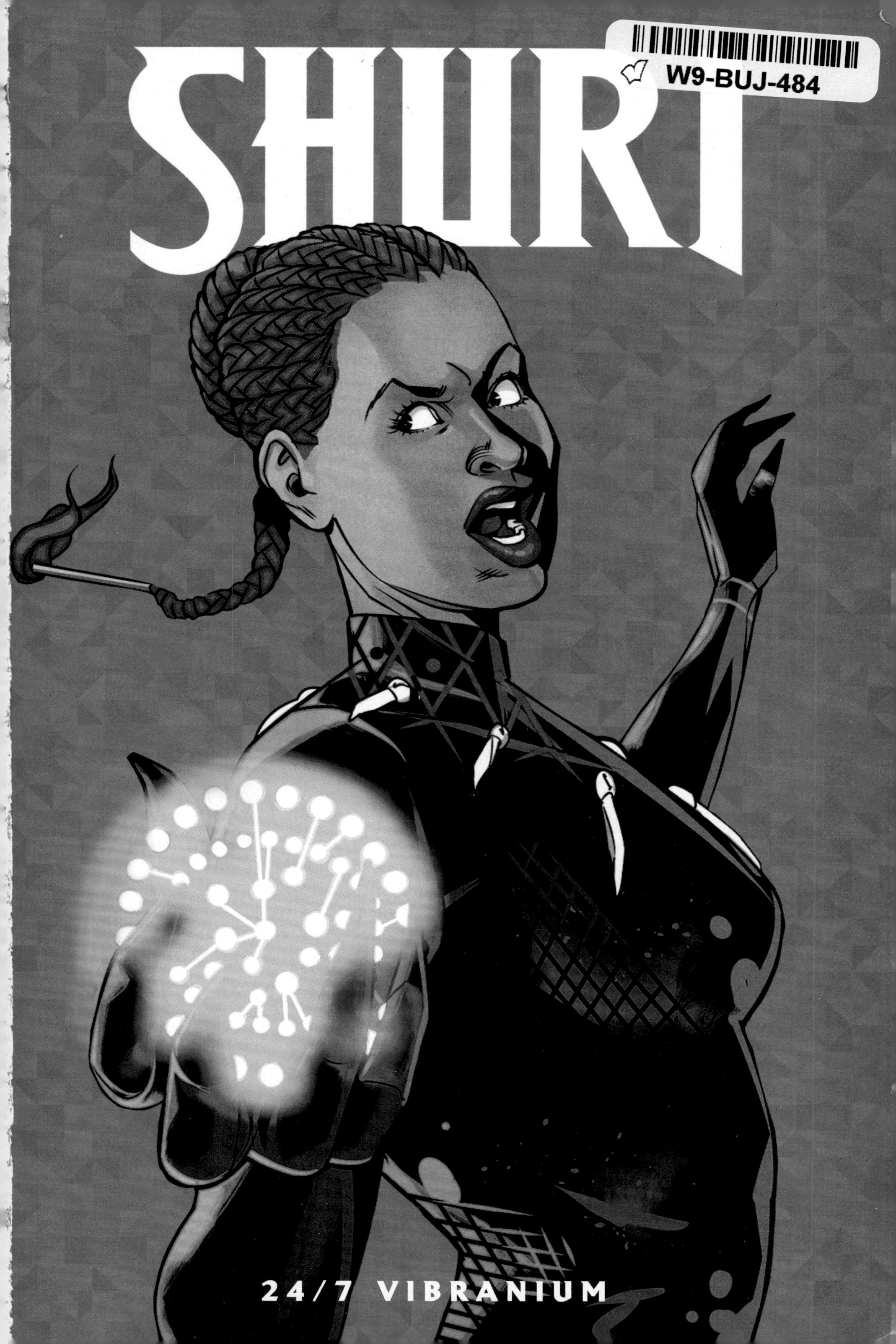

24/7 VIBRANIUM

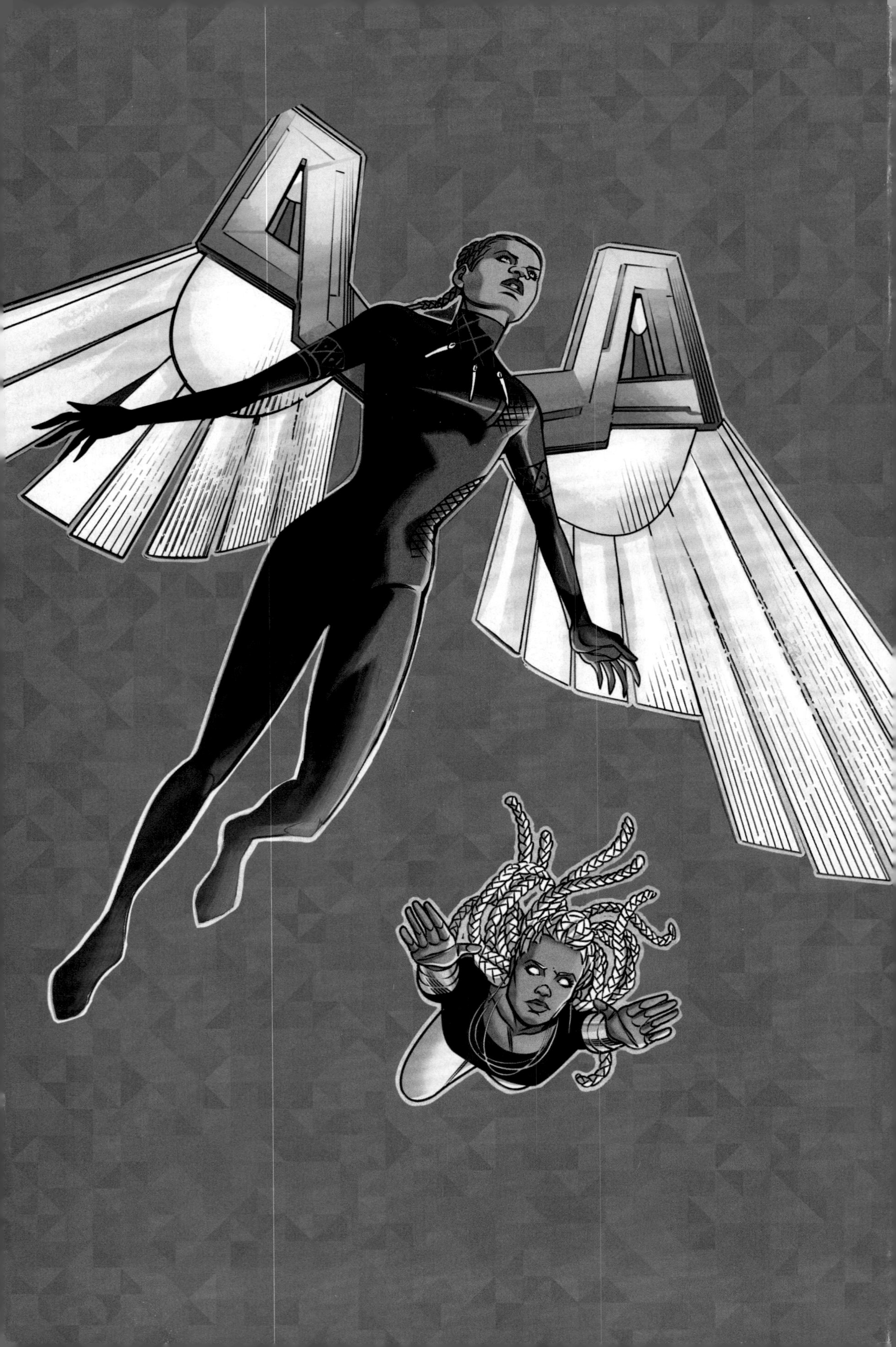

SHURI
24/7 VIBRANIUM

ISSUES #6-7

Vita Ayala
WRITER

Paul Davidson
ARTIST

Tríona Farrell
COLOR ARTIST

ISSUES #8-10

Nnedi Okorafor
WRITER

Rachael Stott
ARTIST

Carlos Lopez
COLOR ARTIST

Leonardo Romero & Jordie Bellaire
RECAP ART

VC's Joe Sabino
LETTERER

Sarah Brunstad
ASSOCIATE EDITOR

Kirbi Fagan
COVER ART

Wil Moss
EDITOR

COLLECTION EDITOR **JENNIFER GRÜNWALD**
ASSISTANT EDITOR **CAITLIN O'CONNELL**
ASSOCIATE MANAGING EDITOR **KATERI WOODY**
EDITOR, SPECIAL PROJECTS **MARK D. BEAZLEY**
VP PRODUCTION & SPECIAL PROJECTS **JEFF YOUNGQUIST**
BOOK DESIGNER **STACIE ZUCKER**

SVP PRINT, SALES & MARKETING **DAVID GABRIEL**
DIRECTOR, LICENSED PUBLISHING **SVEN LARSEN**
EDITOR IN CHIEF **C.B. CEBULSKI**
CHIEF CREATIVE OFFICER **JOE QUESADA**
PRESIDENT **DAN BUCKLEY**
EXECUTIVE PRODUCER **ALAN FINE**

SHURI VOL. 2: 24/7 VIBRANIUM. Contains material originally published in magazine form as SHURI #6-10. First printing 2019. ISBN 978-1-302-91854-5. Published by MARVEL WORLDWIDE, INC., a subsidiary of MARVEL ENTERTAINMENT, LLC. OFFICE OF PUBLICATION: 135 West 50th Street, New York, NY 10020. © 2019 MARVEL. No similarity between any of the names, characters, persons, and/or institutions in this magazine with those of any living or dead person or institution is intended, and any such similarity which may exist is purely coincidental. **Printed in Canada.** DAN BUCKLEY, President, Marvel Entertainment; JOHN NEE, Publisher; JOE QUESADA, Chief Creative Officer; TOM BREVOORT, SVP of Publishing; DAVID BOGART, Associate Publisher & SVP of Talent Affairs; DAVID GABRIEL, SVP of Sales & Marketing, Publishing; JEFF YOUNGQUIST, VP of Production & Special Projects; DAN CARR, Executive Director of Publishing Technology; ALEX MORALES, Director of Publishing Operations; DAN EDINGTON, Managing Editor; SUSAN CRESPI, Production Manager; STAN LEE, Chairman Emeritus. For information regarding advertising in Marvel Comics or on Marvel.com, please contact Vit DeBellis, Custom Solutions & Integrated Advertising Manager, at vdebellis@marvel.com. For Marvel subscription inquiries, please call 888-511-5480. **Manufactured between 7/19/2019 and 8/20/2019 by SOLISCO PRINTERS, SCOTT, QC, CANADA.**

10 9 8 7 6 5 4 3 2 1

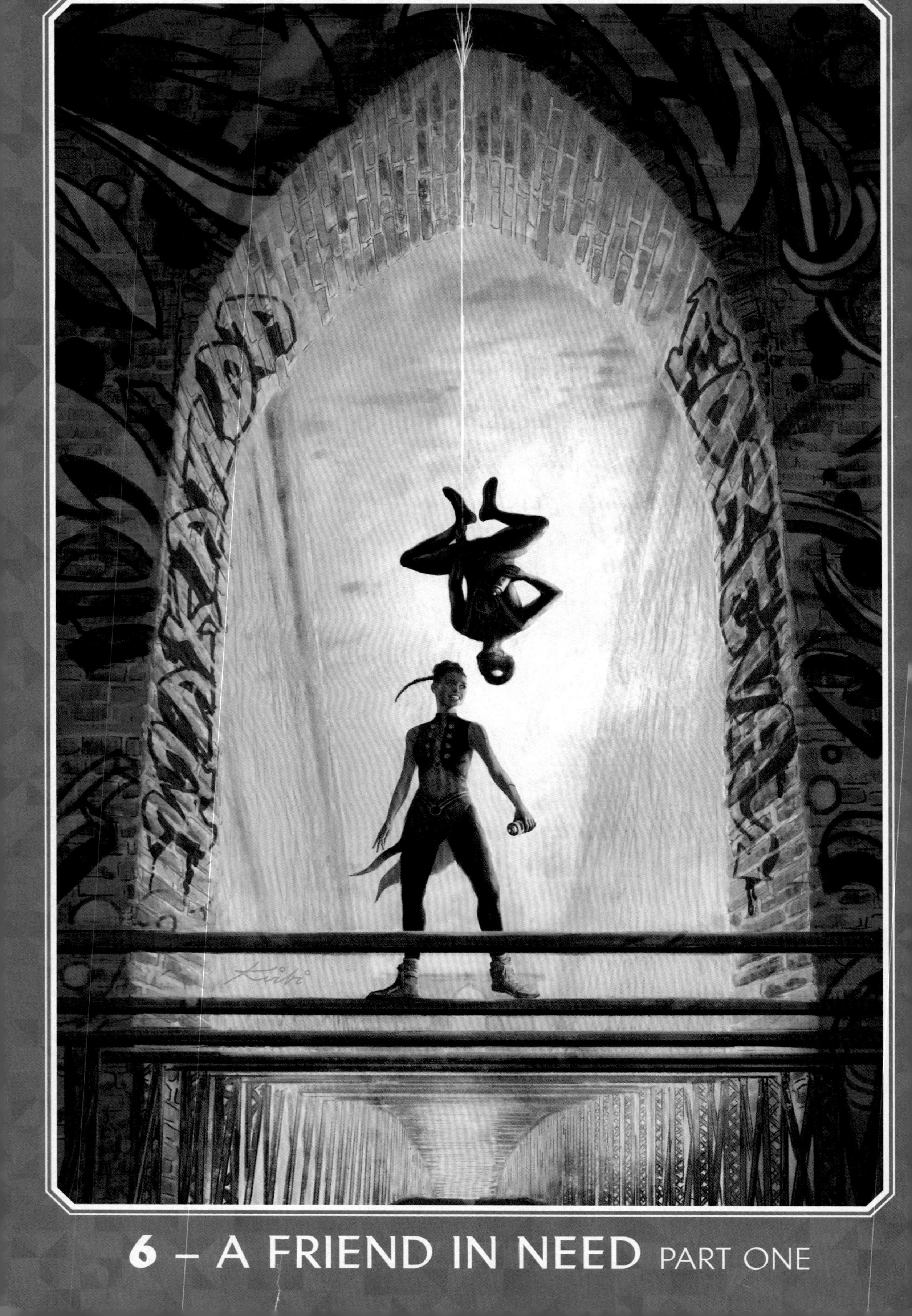

6 – A FRIEND IN NEED PART ONE

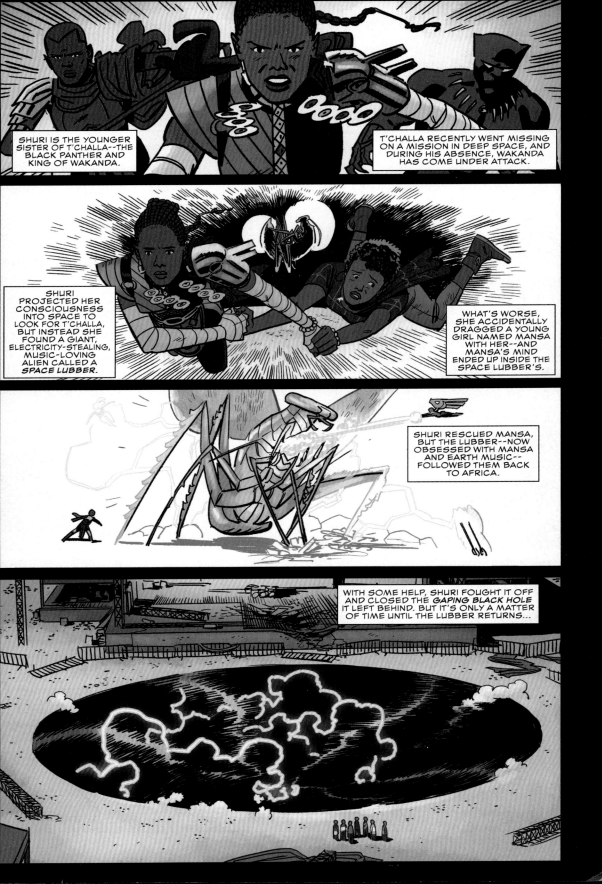

SHURI IS THE YOUNGER SISTER OF T'CHALLA--THE BLACK PANTHER AND KING OF WAKANDA.

T'CHALLA RECENTLY WENT MISSING ON A MISSION IN DEEP SPACE, AND DURING HIS ABSENCE, WAKANDA HAS COME UNDER ATTACK.

SHURI PROJECTED HER CONSCIOUSNESS INTO SPACE TO LOOK FOR T'CHALLA, BUT INSTEAD SHE FOUND A GIANT, ELECTRICITY-STEALING, MUSIC-LOVING ALIEN CALLED A *SPACE LUBBER.*

WHAT'S WORSE, SHE ACCIDENTALLY DRAGGED A YOUNG GIRL NAMED MANSA WITH HER--AND MANSA'S MIND ENDED UP INSIDE THE SPACE LUBBER'S.

SHURI RESCUED MANSA, BUT THE LUBBER--NOW OBSESSED WITH MANSA AND EARTH MUSIC-- FOLLOWED THEM BACK TO AFRICA.

WITH SOME HELP, SHURI FOUGHT IT OFF AND CLOSED THE *GAPING BLACK HOLE* IT LEFT BEHIND. BUT IT'S ONLY A MATTER OF TIME UNTIL THE LUBBER RETURNS...

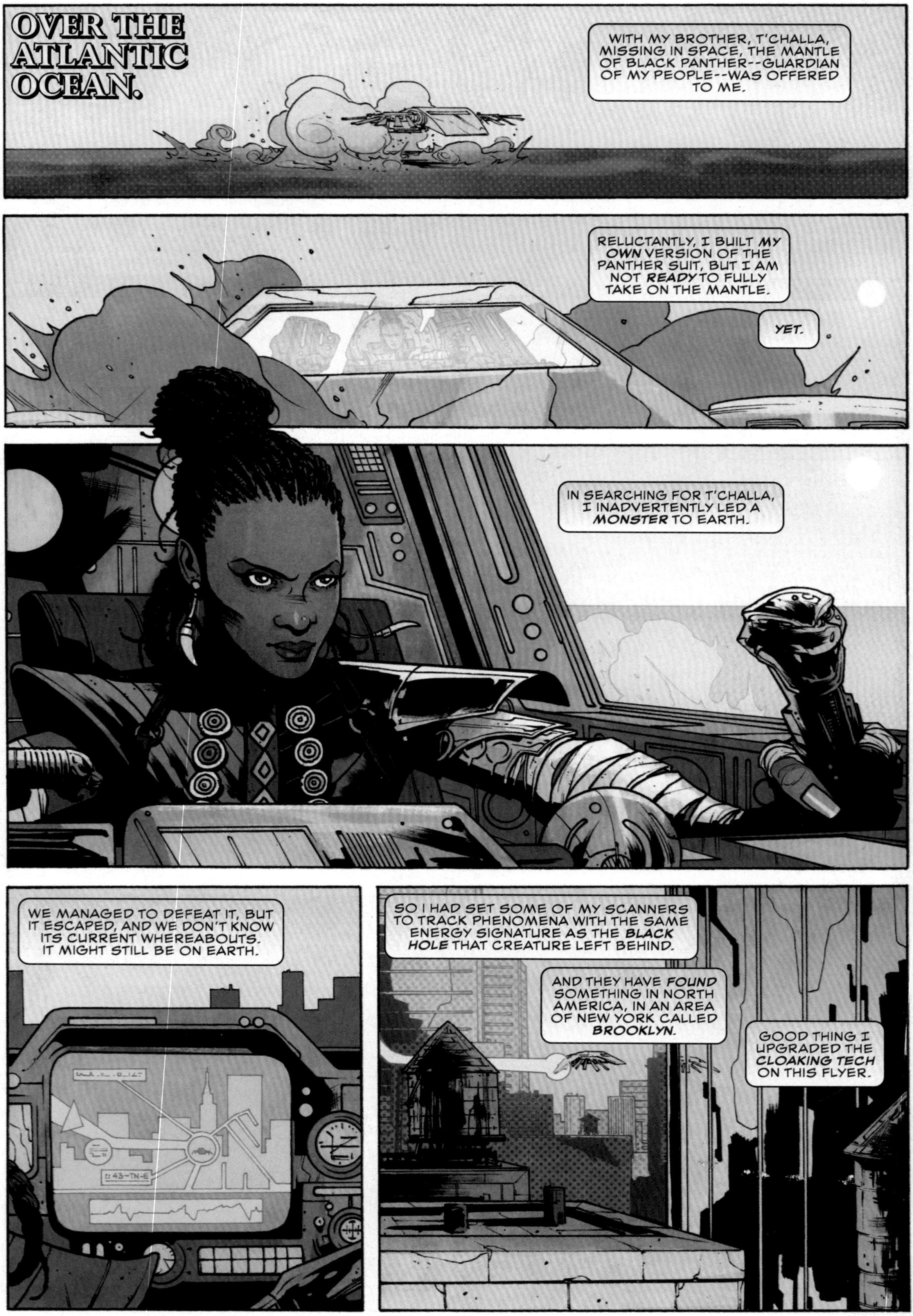
OVER THE ATLANTIC OCEAN.
WITH MY BROTHER, T'CHALLA, MISSING IN SPACE, THE MANTLE OF BLACK PANTHER--GUARDIAN OF MY PEOPLE--WAS OFFERED TO ME.
RELUCTANTLY, I BUILT MY OWN VERSION OF THE PANTHER SUIT, BUT I AM NOT READY TO FULLY TAKE ON THE MANTLE.
YET.
IN SEARCHING FOR T'CHALLA, I INADVERTENTLY LED A MONSTER TO EARTH.
WE MANAGED TO DEFEAT IT, BUT IT ESCAPED, AND WE DON'T KNOW ITS CURRENT WHEREABOUTS. IT MIGHT STILL BE ON EARTH.
43-TN-E
SO I HAD SET SOME OF MY SCANNERS TO TRACK PHENOMENA WITH THE SAME ENERGY SIGNATURE AS THE BLACK HOLE THAT CREATURE LEFT BEHIND.
AND THEY HAVE FOUND SOMETHING IN NORTH AMERICA, IN AN AREA OF NEW YORK CALLED BROOKLYN.
GOOD THING I UPGRADED THE CLOAKING TECH ON THIS FLYER.

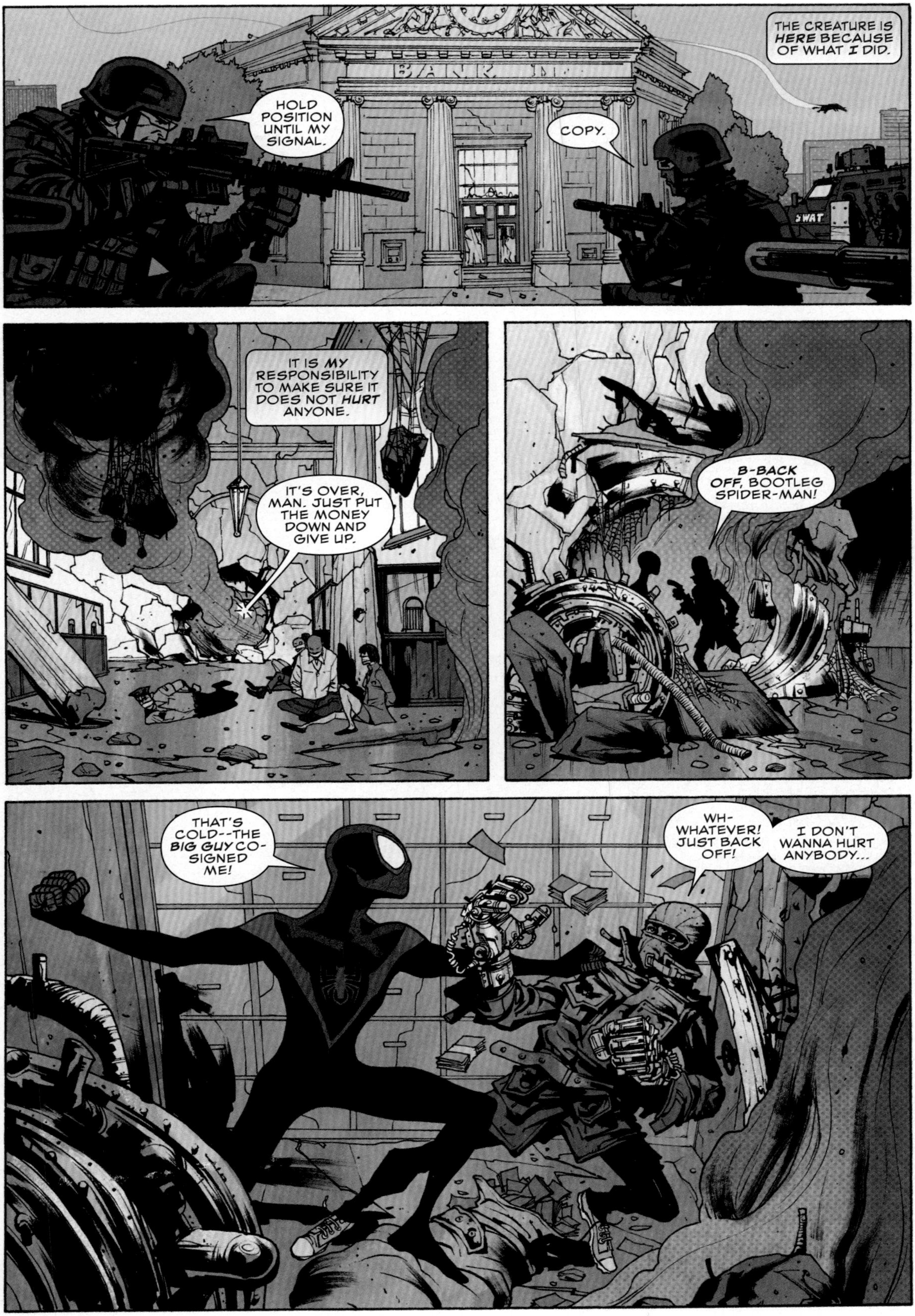
THE CREATURE IS HERE BECAUSE OF WHAT I DID.
HOLD POSITION UNTIL MY SIGNAL.
COPY.
BANK
SWAT
IT IS MY RESPONSIBILITY TO MAKE SURE IT DOES NOT HURT ANYONE.
IT'S OVER, MAN. JUST PUT THE MONEY DOWN AND GIVE UP.
B-BACK OFF, BOOTLEG SPIDER-MAN!
THAT'S COLD--THE BIG GUY CO-SIGNED ME!
WH-WHATEVER! JUST BACK OFF!
I DON'T WANNA HURT ANYBODY...

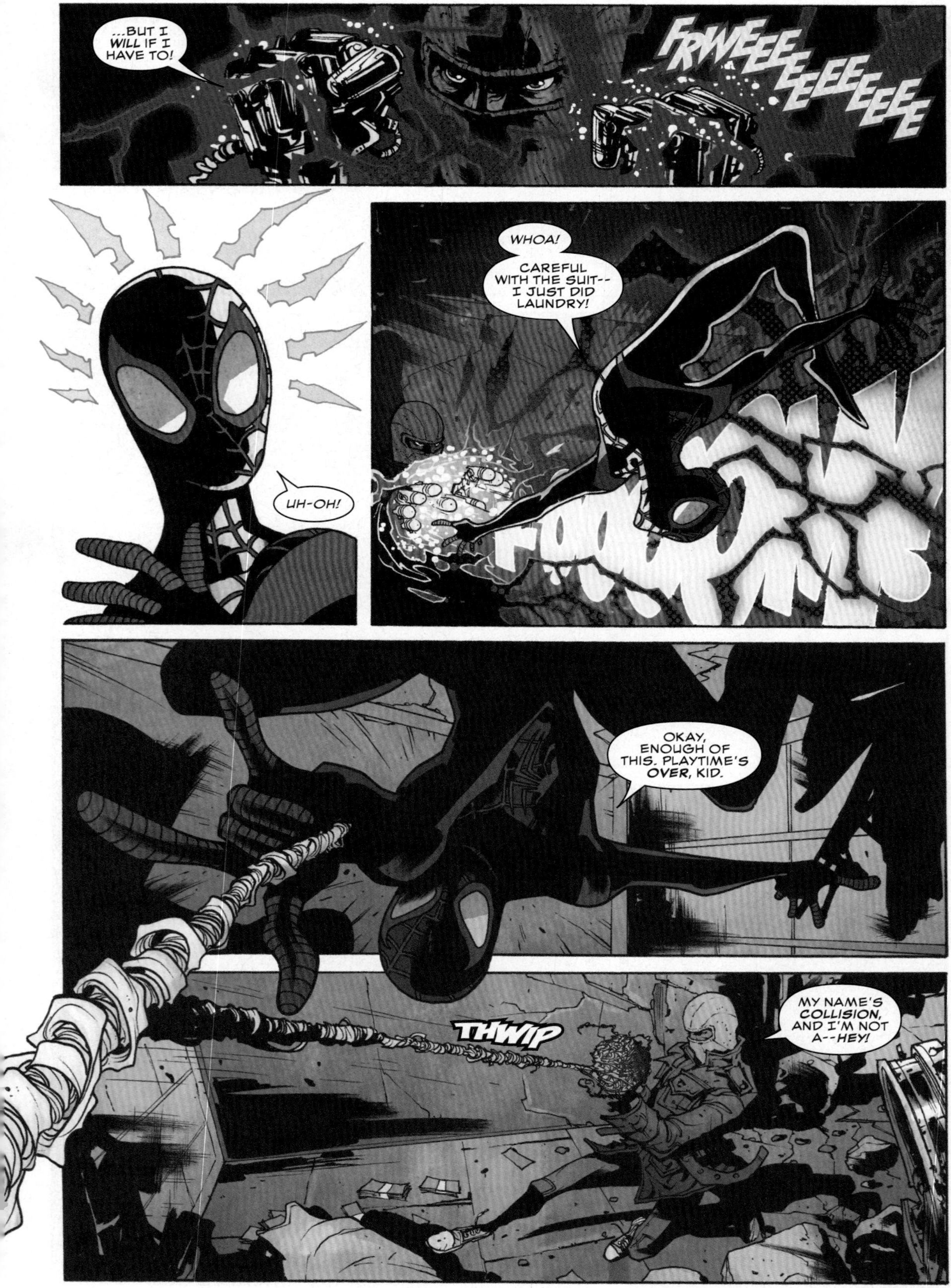
...BUT I WILL IF I HAVE TO!
FRWEEEEEEEEEEEE
UH-OH!
WHOA!
CAREFUL WITH THE SUIT-- I JUST DID LAUNDRY!
OKAY, ENOUGH OF THIS. PLAYTIME'S OVER, KID.
THWIP
MY NAME'S COLLISION, AND I'M NOT A--HEY!

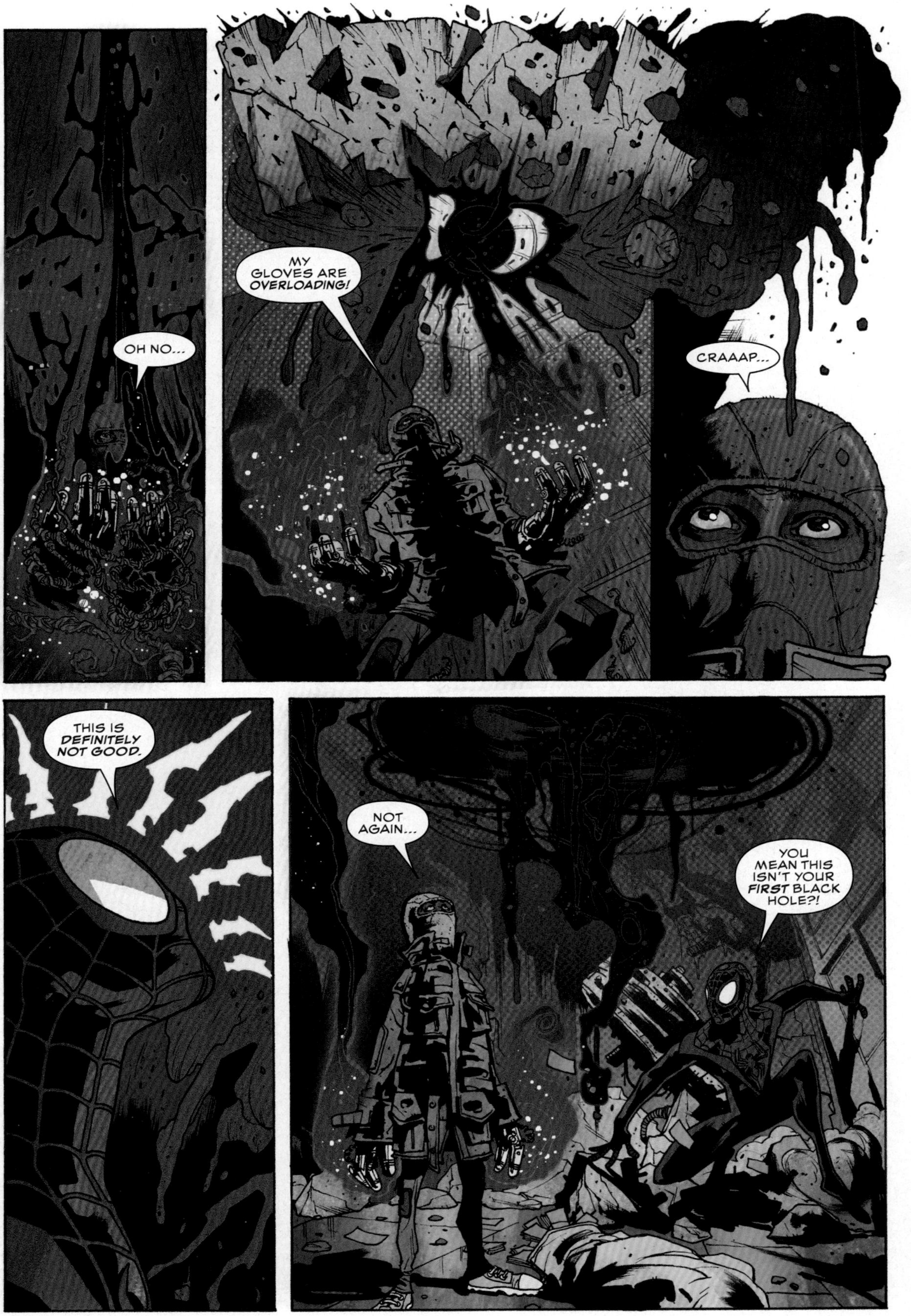
OH NO...
MY GLOVES ARE OVERLOADING!
CRAAAP...
THIS IS DEFINITELY NOT GOOD.
NOT AGAIN...
YOU MEAN THIS ISN'T YOUR FIRST BLACK HOLE?!

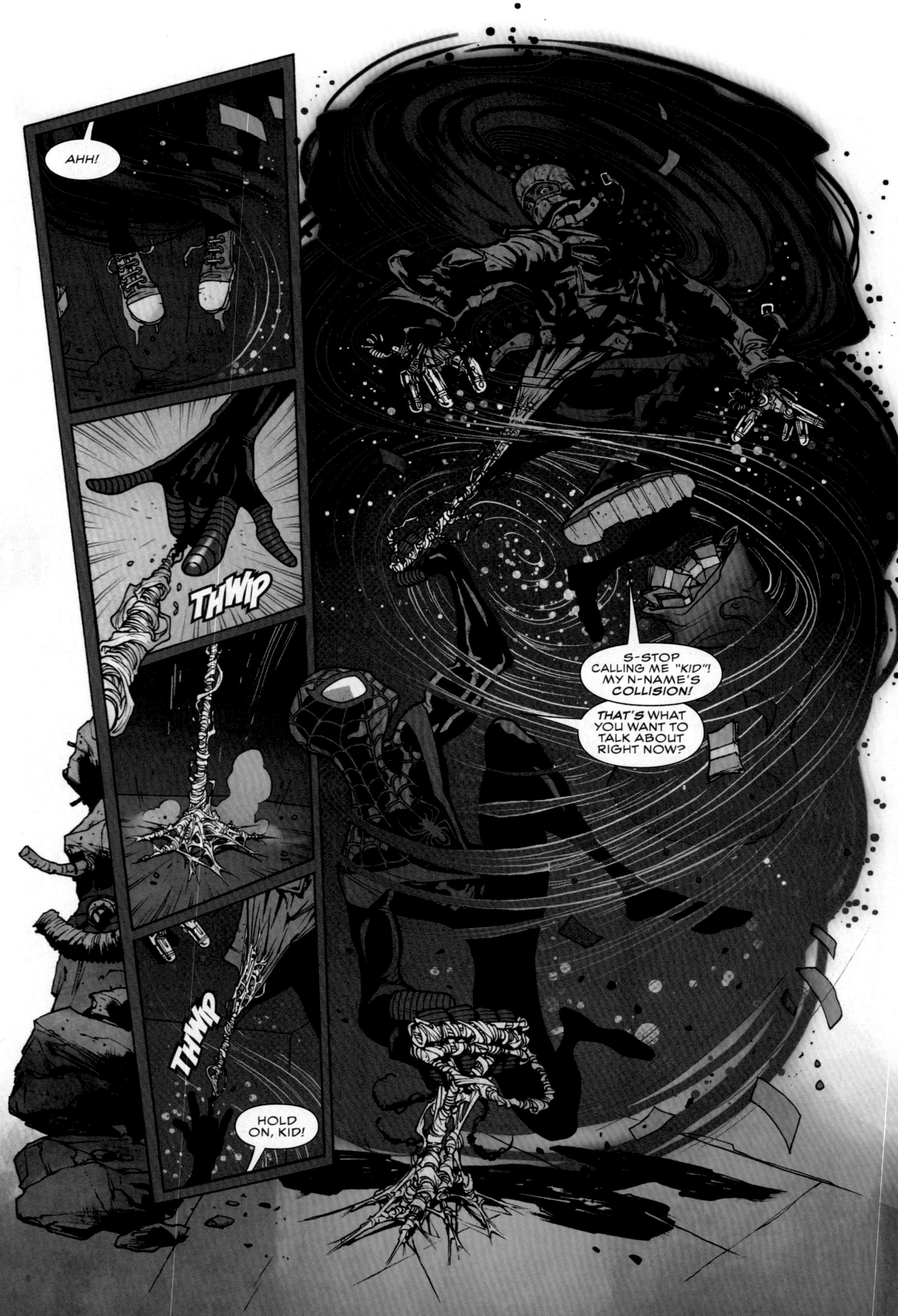

AHH!
THWIP
S-STOP CALLING ME "KID"! MY N-NAME'S COLLISION!
THAT'S WHAT YOU WANT TO TALK ABOUT RIGHT NOW?
THWIP
HOLD ON, KID!

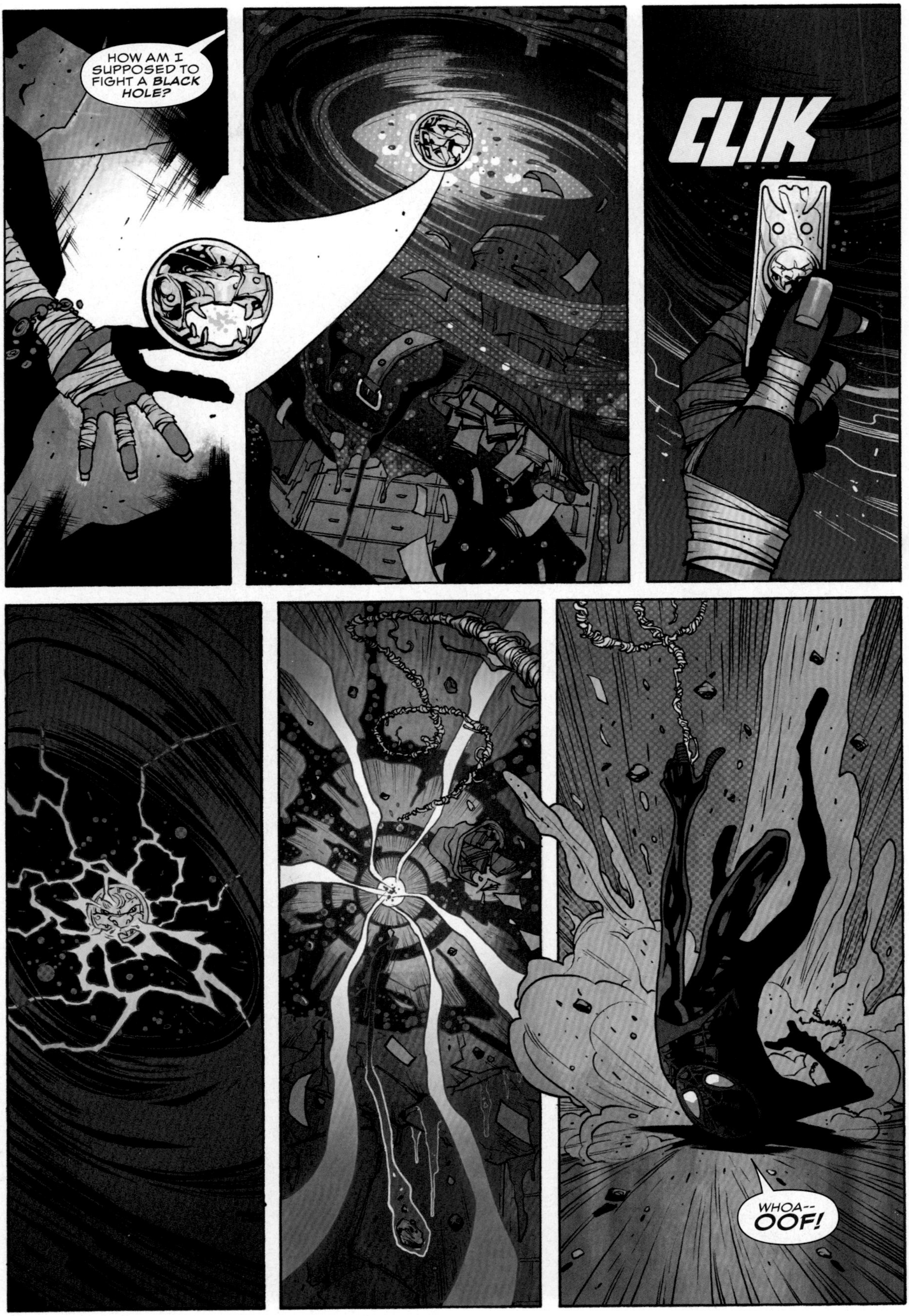
HOW AM I SUPPOSED TO FIGHT A BLACK HOLE?
CLIK
WHOA-- OOF!

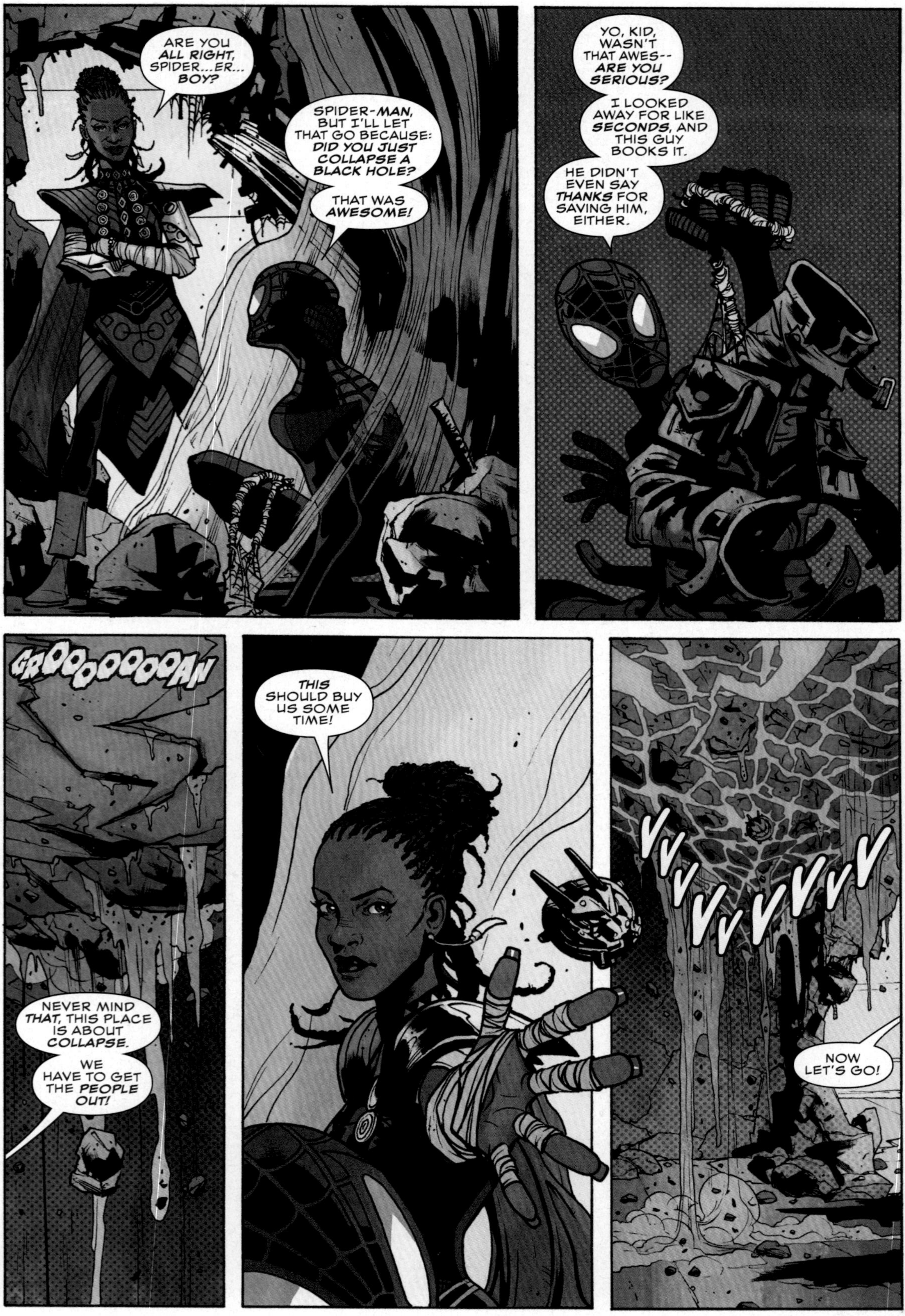
ARE YOU ALL RIGHT, SPIDER...ER... BOY?
SPIDER-MAN, BUT I'LL LET THAT GO BECAUSE: DID YOU JUST COLLAPSE A BLACK HOLE?
THAT WAS AWESOME!
YO, KID, WASN'T THAT AWES-- ARE YOU SERIOUS?
I LOOKED AWAY FOR LIKE SECONDS, AND THIS GUY BOOKS IT.
HE DIDN'T EVEN SAY THANKS FOR SAVING HIM, EITHER.
GROOOOOOOOAN
NEVER MIND THAT, THIS PLACE IS ABOUT COLLAPSE.
WE HAVE TO GET THE PEOPLE OUT!
THIS SHOULD BUY US SOME TIME!
VVVVVVVVVVVVVV
NOW LET'S GO!

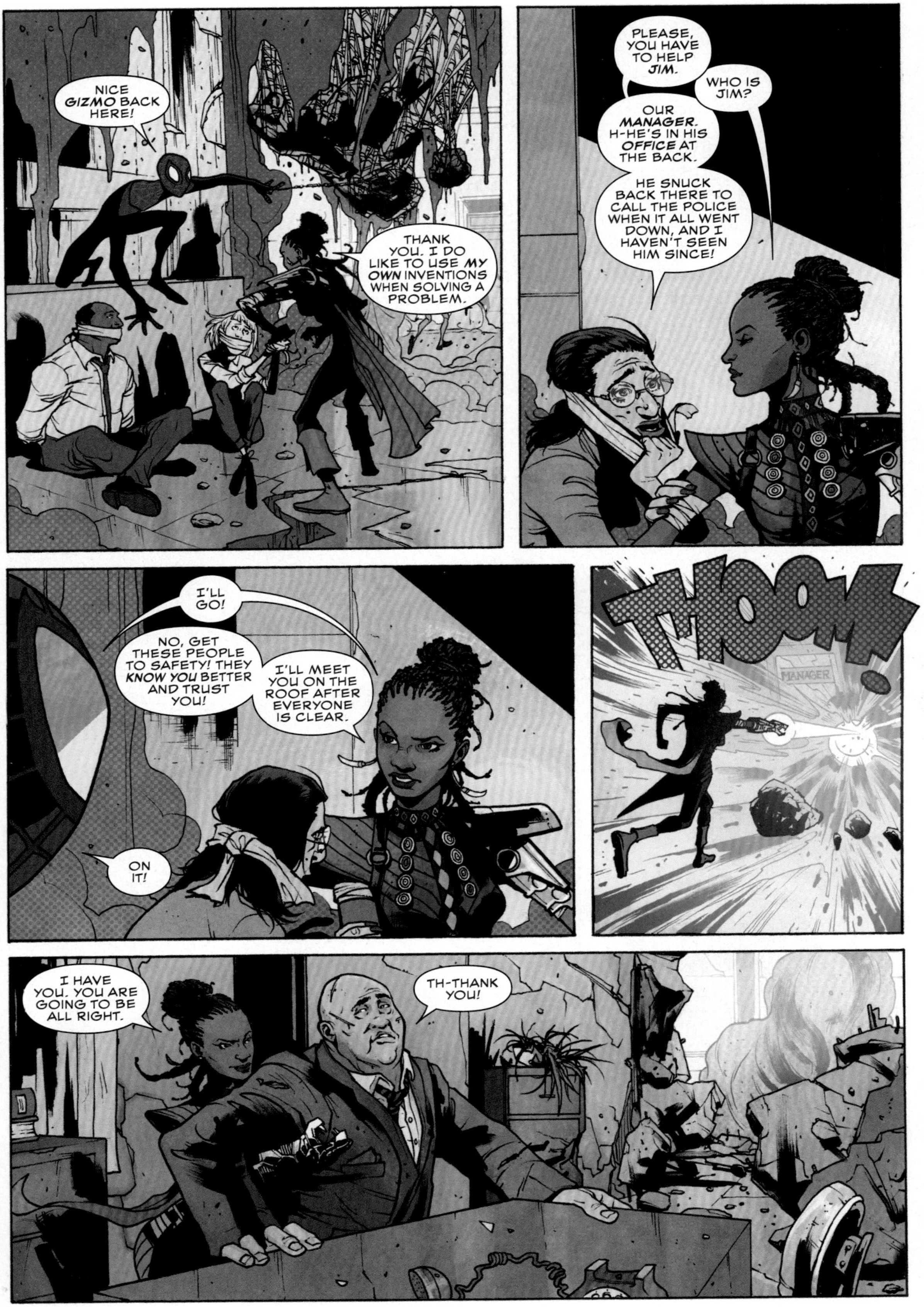
NICE GIZMO BACK HERE!
THANK YOU. I DO LIKE TO USE MY OWN INVENTIONS WHEN SOLVING A PROBLEM.
PLEASE, YOU HAVE TO HELP JIM.
WHO IS JIM?
OUR MANAGER. H-HE'S IN HIS OFFICE AT THE BACK.
HE SNUCK BACK THERE TO CALL THE POLICE WHEN IT ALL WENT DOWN, AND I HAVEN'T SEEN HIM SINCE!
I'LL GO!
NO, GET THESE PEOPLE TO SAFETY! THEY KNOW YOU BETTER AND TRUST YOU!
I'LL MEET YOU ON THE ROOF AFTER EVERYONE IS CLEAR.
ON IT!
THOOM!
MANAGER
I HAVE YOU. YOU ARE GOING TO BE ALL RIGHT.
TH-THANK YOU!

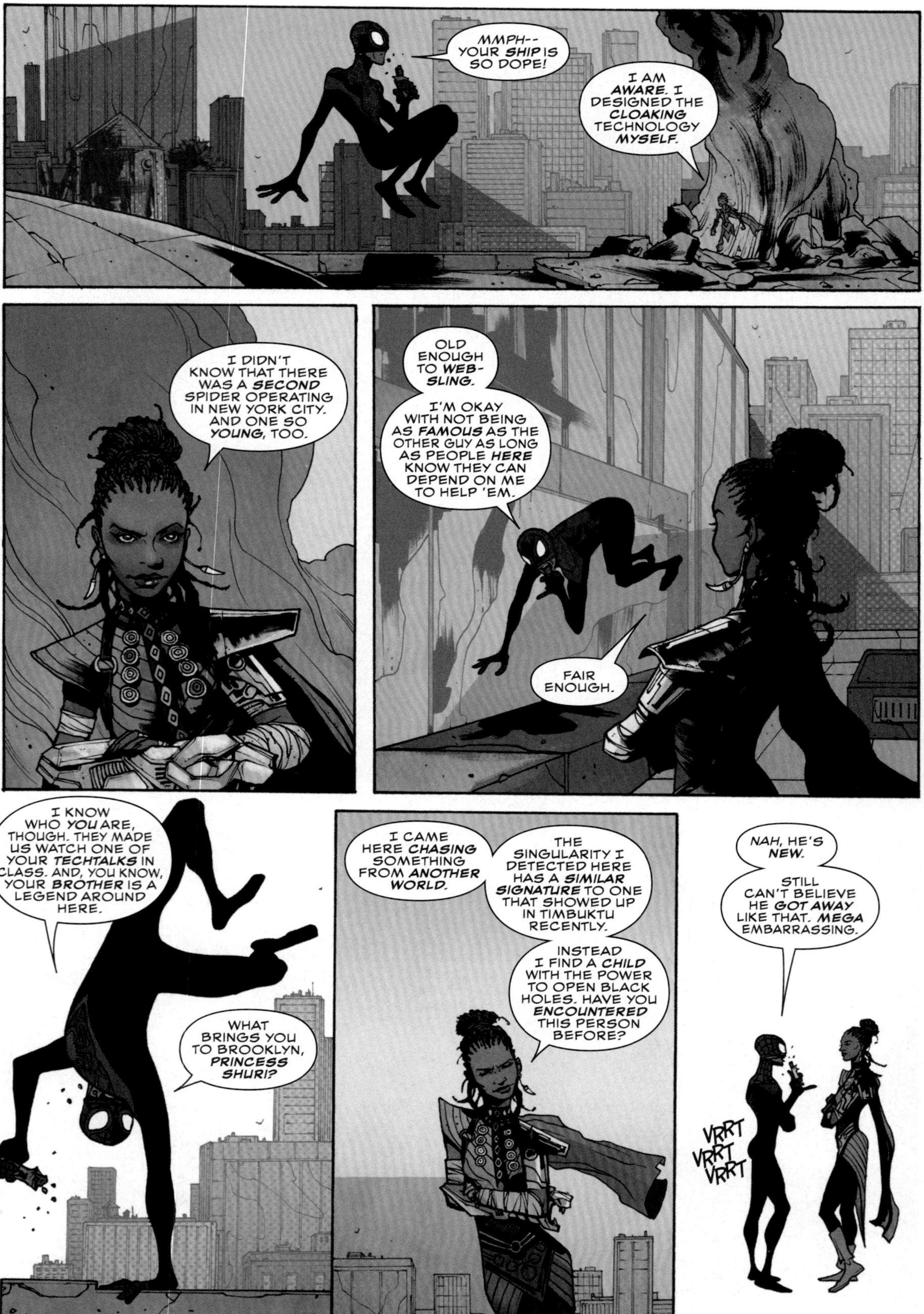
MMPH-- YOUR SHIP IS SO DOPE!
I AM AWARE. I DESIGNED THE CLOAKING TECHNOLOGY MYSELF.
I DIDN'T KNOW THAT THERE WAS A SECOND SPIDER OPERATING IN NEW YORK CITY. AND ONE SO YOUNG, TOO.
OLD ENOUGH TO WEB-SLING.
I'M OKAY WITH NOT BEING AS FAMOUS AS THE OTHER GUY AS LONG AS PEOPLE HERE KNOW THEY CAN DEPEND ON ME TO HELP 'EM.
FAIR ENOUGH.
I KNOW WHO YOU ARE, THOUGH. THEY MADE US WATCH ONE OF YOUR TECHTALKS IN CLASS. AND, YOU KNOW, YOUR BROTHER IS A LEGEND AROUND HERE.
WHAT BRINGS YOU TO BROOKLYN, PRINCESS SHURI?
I CAME HERE CHASING SOMETHING FROM ANOTHER WORLD.
THE SINGULARITY I DETECTED HERE HAS A SIMILAR SIGNATURE TO ONE THAT SHOWED UP IN TIMBUKTU RECENTLY.
INSTEAD I FIND A CHILD WITH THE POWER TO OPEN BLACK HOLES. HAVE YOU ENCOUNTERED THIS PERSON BEFORE?
NAH, HE'S NEW.
STILL CAN'T BELIEVE HE GOT AWAY LIKE THAT. MEGA EMBARRASSING.
VRRT VRRT VRRT

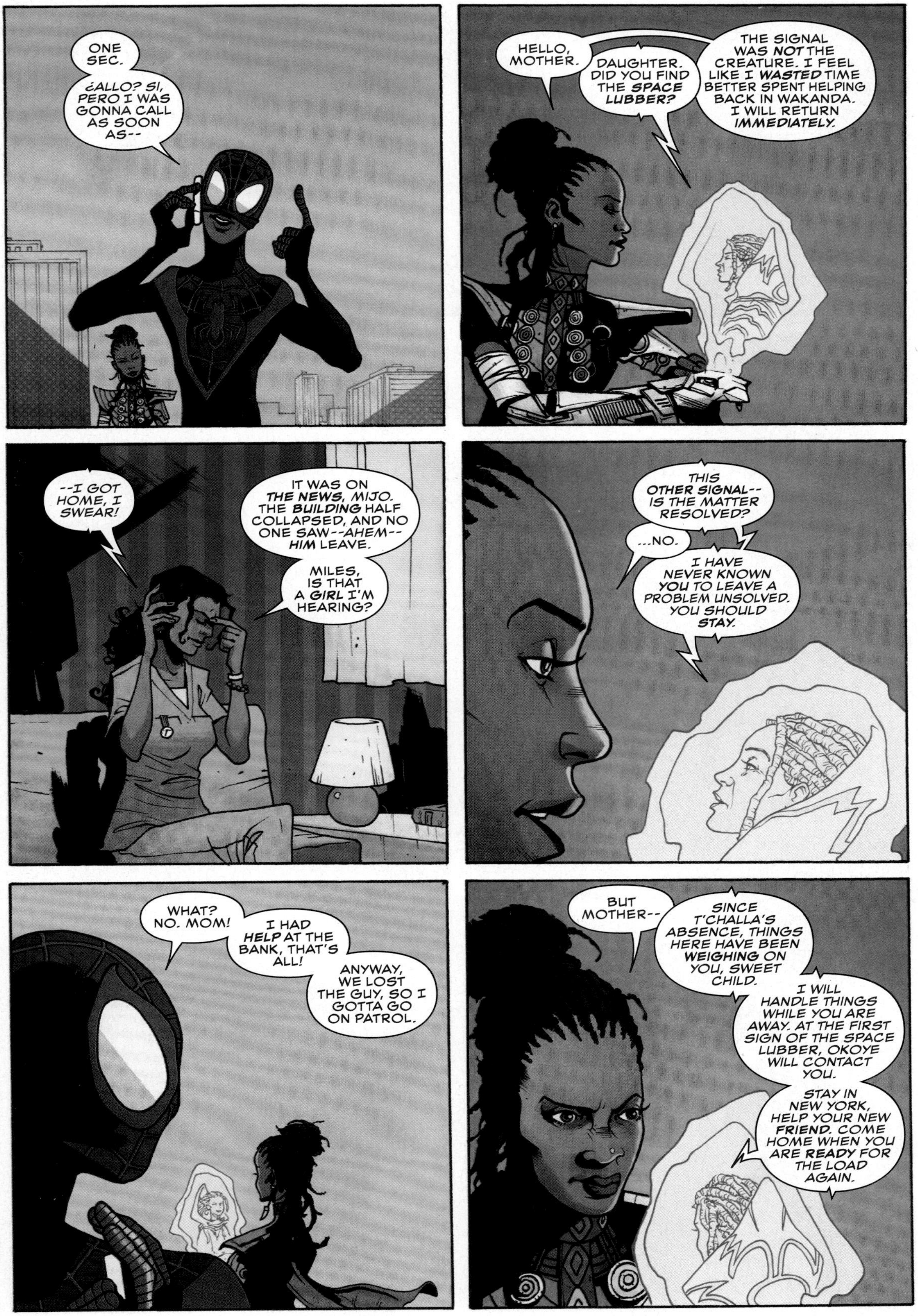
ONE SEC.
¿ALLO? SI, PERO I WAS GONNA CALL AS SOON AS--
HELLO, MOTHER.
DAUGHTER. DID YOU FIND THE SPACE LUBBER?
THE SIGNAL WAS NOT THE CREATURE. I FEEL LIKE I WASTED TIME BETTER SPENT HELPING BACK IN WAKANDA. I WILL RETURN IMMEDIATELY.
--I GOT HOME, I SWEAR!
IT WAS ON THE NEWS, MIJO. THE BUILDING HALF COLLAPSED, AND NO ONE SAW--AHEM--HIM LEAVE.
MILES, IS THAT A GIRL I'M HEARING?
THIS OTHER SIGNAL--IS THE MATTER RESOLVED?
...NO.
I HAVE NEVER KNOWN YOU TO LEAVE A PROBLEM UNSOLVED. YOU SHOULD STAY.
WHAT? NO. MOM!
I HAD HELP AT THE BANK, THAT'S ALL!
ANYWAY, WE LOST THE GUY, SO I GOTTA GO ON PATROL.
BUT MOTHER--
SINCE T'CHALLA'S ABSENCE, THINGS HERE HAVE BEEN WEIGHING ON YOU, SWEET CHILD.
I WILL HANDLE THINGS WHILE YOU ARE AWAY. AT THE FIRST SIGN OF THE SPACE LUBBER, OKOYE WILL CONTACT YOU.
STAY IN NEW YORK, HELP YOUR NEW FRIEND. COME HOME WHEN YOU ARE READY FOR THE LOAD AGAIN.

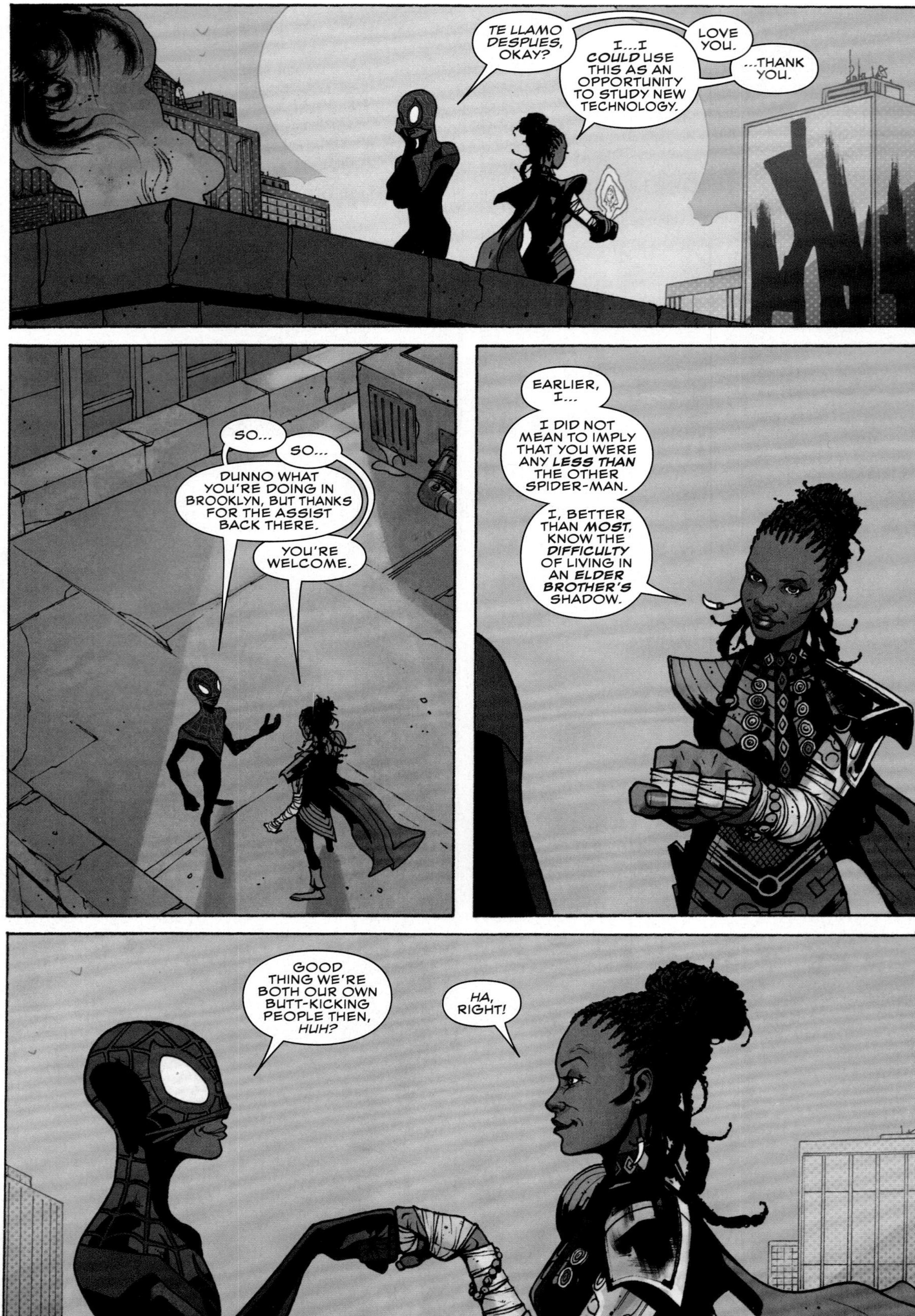
TE LLAMO DESPUES, OKAY?
LOVE YOU.
I...I COULD USE THIS AS AN OPPORTUNITY TO STUDY NEW TECHNOLOGY.
...THANK YOU.
SO...
SO...
DUNNO WHAT YOU'RE DOING IN BROOKLYN, BUT THANKS FOR THE ASSIST BACK THERE.
YOU'RE WELCOME.
EARLIER, I...
I DID NOT MEAN TO IMPLY THAT YOU WERE ANY LESS THAN THE OTHER SPIDER-MAN.
I, BETTER THAN MOST, KNOW THE DIFFICULTY OF LIVING IN AN ELDER BROTHER'S SHADOW.
GOOD THING WE'RE BOTH OUR OWN BUTT-KICKING PEOPLE THEN, HUH?
HA, RIGHT!

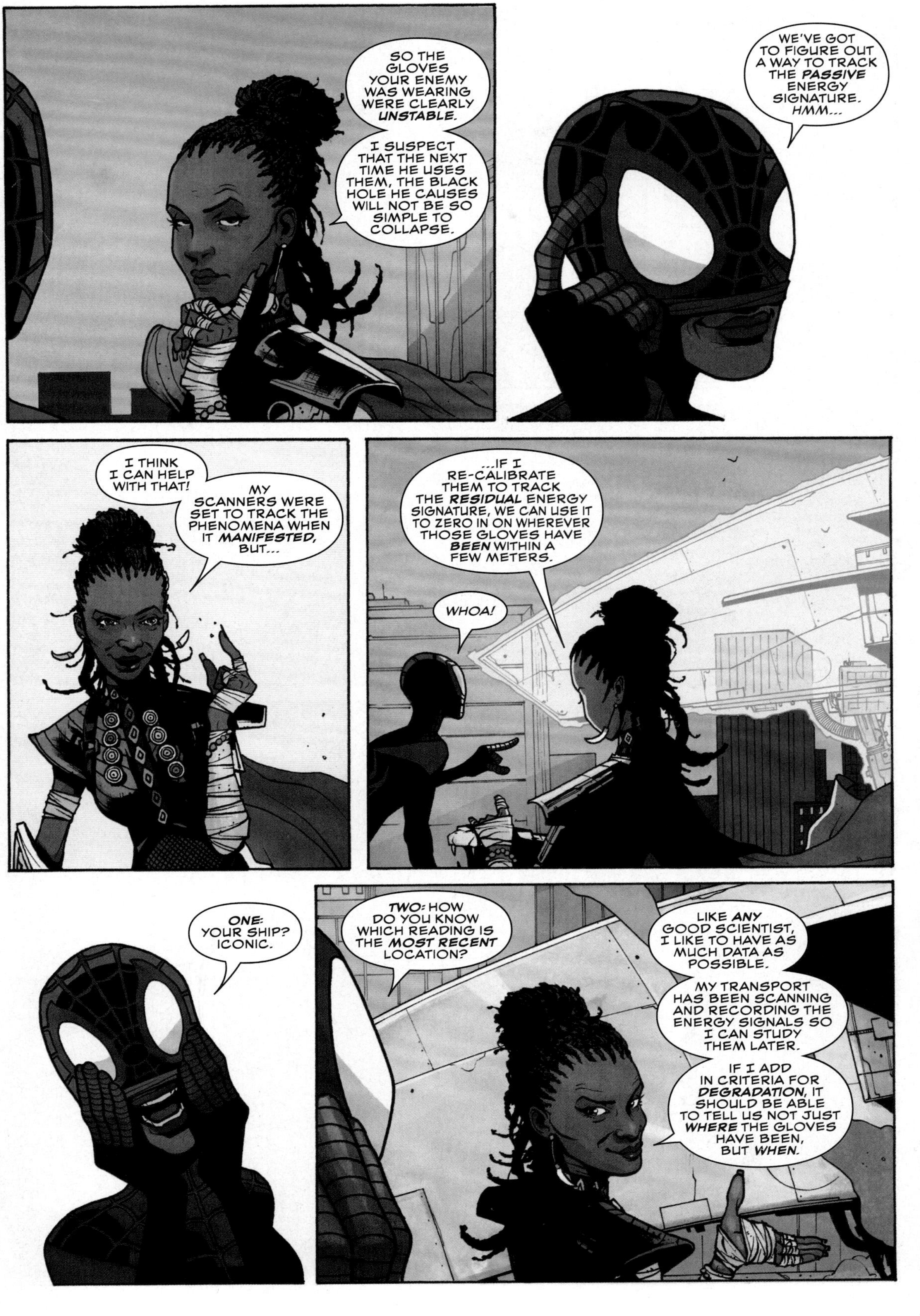
SO THE GLOVES YOUR ENEMY WAS WEARING WERE CLEARLY *UNSTABLE.*
I SUSPECT THAT THE NEXT TIME HE USES THEM, THE BLACK HOLE HE CAUSES WILL NOT BE SO SIMPLE TO COLLAPSE.
WE'VE GOT TO FIGURE OUT A WAY TO TRACK THE *PASSIVE* ENERGY SIGNATURE. HMM...
I THINK I CAN HELP WITH THAT!
MY SCANNERS WERE SET TO TRACK THE PHENOMENA WHEN IT *MANIFESTED,* BUT...
...IF I RE-CALIBRATE THEM TO TRACK THE *RESIDUAL* ENERGY SIGNATURE, WE CAN USE IT TO ZERO IN ON WHEREVER THOSE GLOVES HAVE *BEEN* WITHIN A FEW METERS.
WHOA!
ONE: YOUR SHIP? ICONIC.
TWO: HOW DO YOU KNOW WHICH READING IS THE *MOST RECENT* LOCATION?
LIKE *ANY* GOOD SCIENTIST, I LIKE TO HAVE AS MUCH DATA AS POSSIBLE.
MY TRANSPORT HAS BEEN SCANNING AND RECORDING THE ENERGY SIGNALS SO I CAN STUDY THEM LATER.
IF I ADD IN CRITERIA FOR *DEGRADATION*, IT SHOULD BE ABLE TO TELL US NOT JUST *WHERE* THE GLOVES HAVE BEEN, BUT *WHEN*.

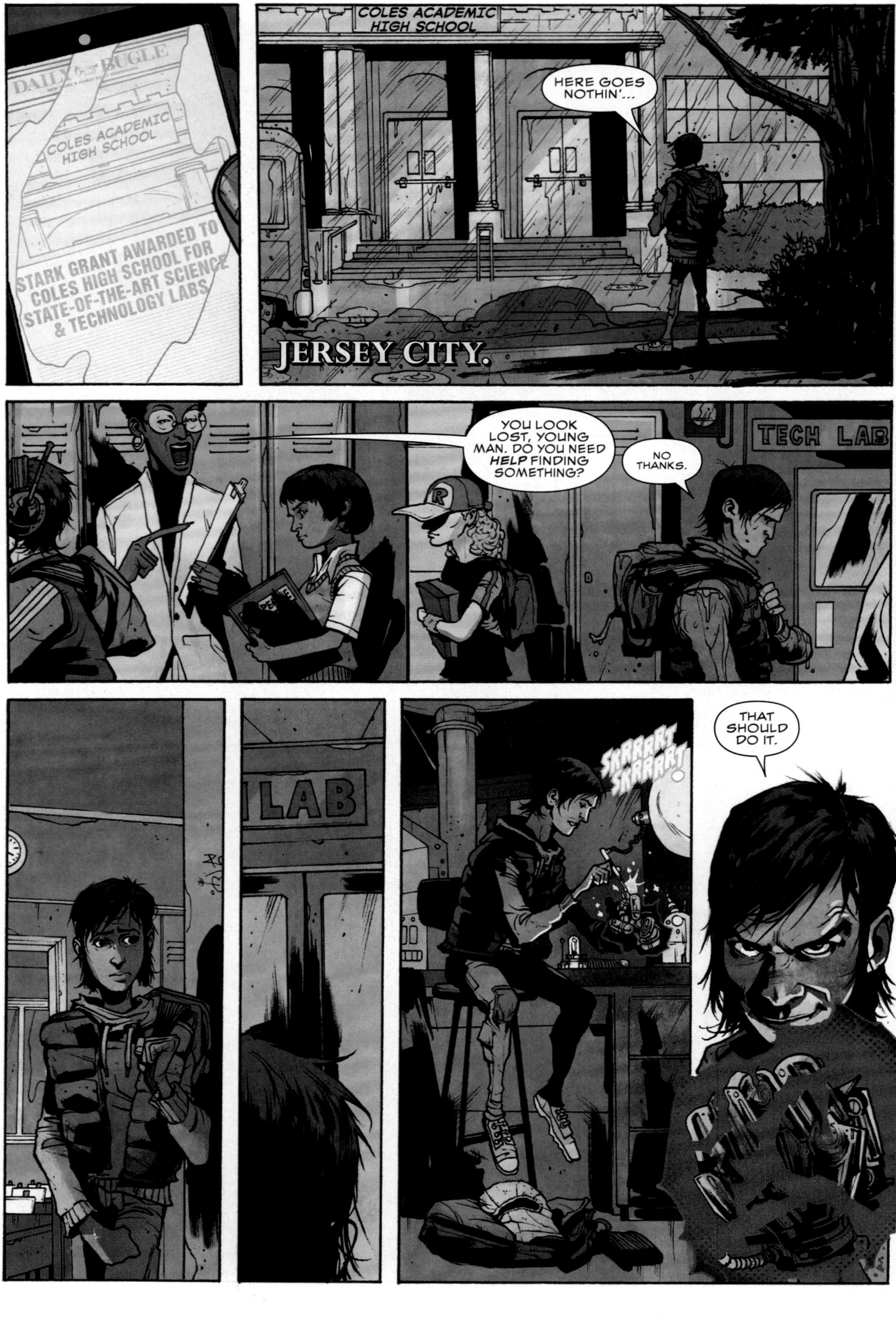
DAILY BUGLE
COLES ACADEMIC HIGH SCHOOL
STARK GRANT AWARDED TO COLES HIGH SCHOOL FOR STATE-OF-THE-ART SCIENCE & TECHNOLOGY LABS
COLES ACADEMIC HIGH SCHOOL
HERE GOES NOTHIN'...
JERSEY CITY.
TECH LAB
YOU LOOK LOST, YOUNG MAN. DO YOU NEED HELP FINDING SOMETHING?
NO THANKS.
LAB
SKRRRRT SKRRRRT!
THAT SHOULD DO IT.

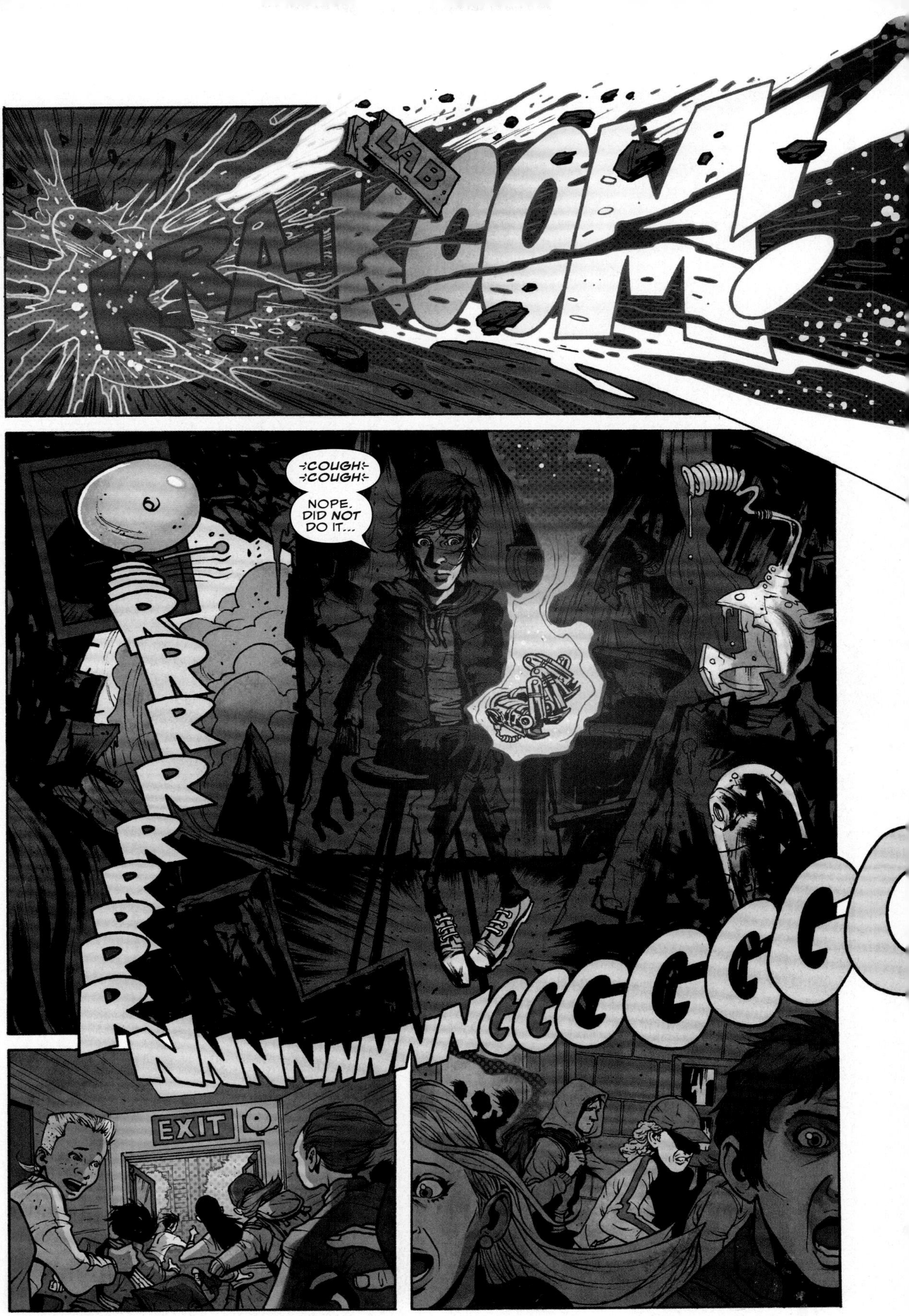
LAB
KRA-KOOM!
COUGH *COUGH*
NOPE. DID NOT DO IT...
RRRRRRRRRNNNNNNNNNGGGGGGG
EXIT

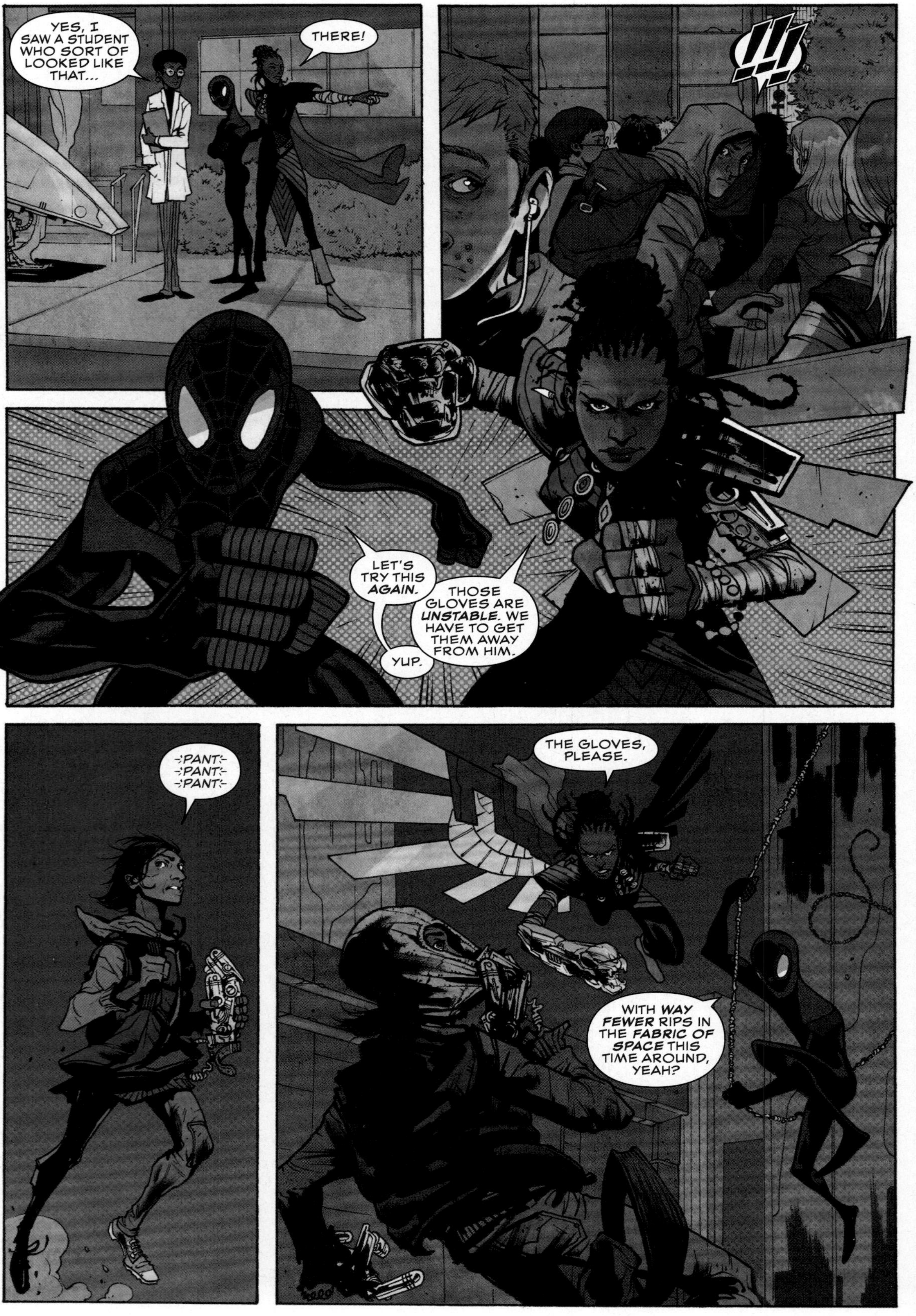
YES, I SAW A STUDENT WHO SORT OF LOOKED LIKE THAT...
THERE!
LET'S TRY THIS AGAIN.
THOSE GLOVES ARE UNSTABLE. WE HAVE TO GET THEM AWAY FROM HIM.
YUP.
PANT PANT PANT
THE GLOVES, PLEASE.
WITH WAY FEWER RIPS IN THE FABRIC OF SPACE THIS TIME AROUND, YEAH?

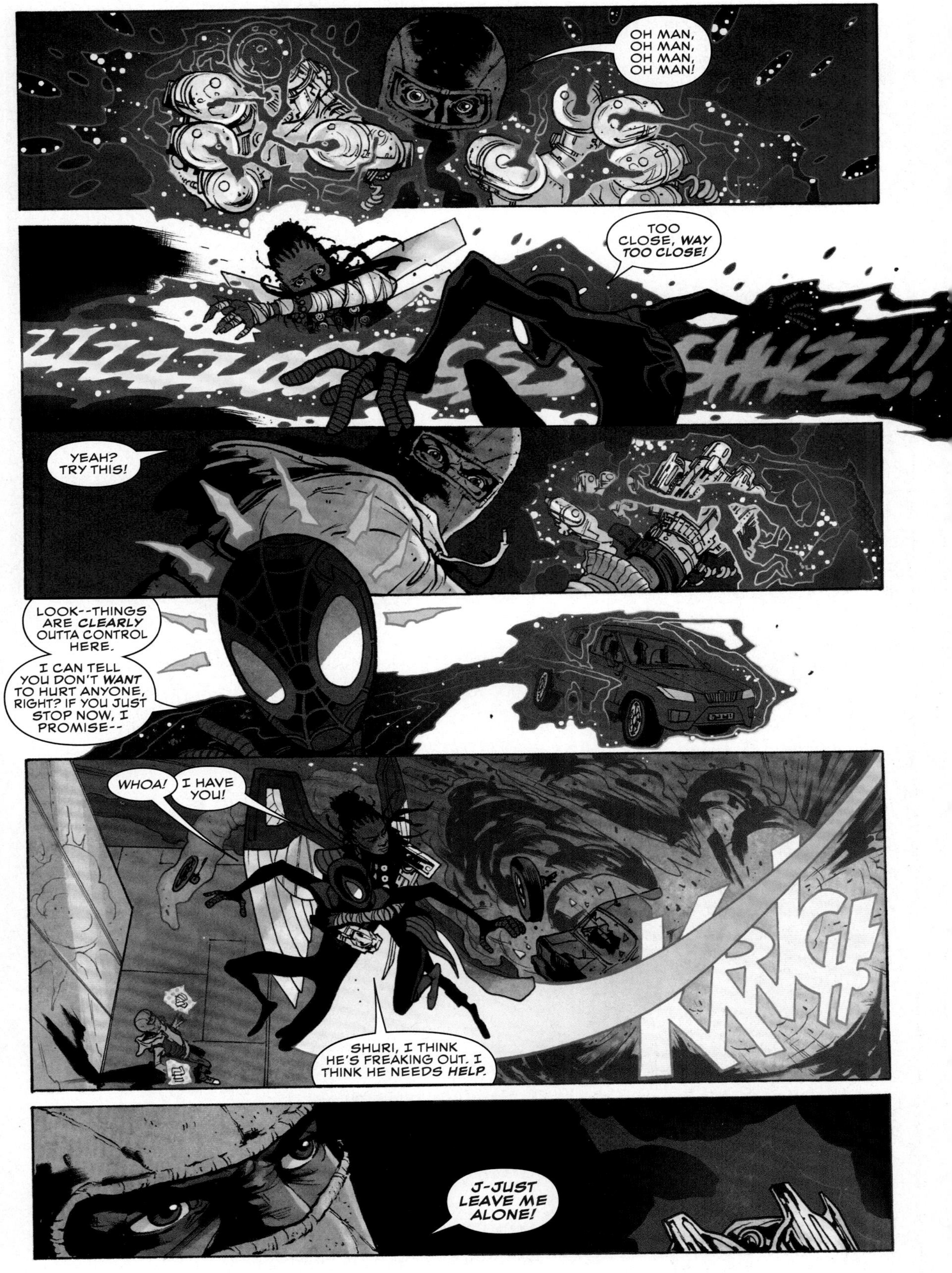
OH MAN, OH MAN, OH MAN, OH MAN!
TOO CLOSE, WAY TOO CLOSE!
ZZZZZOOMSSSSHHZZ!!
YEAH? TRY THIS!
LOOK--THINGS ARE CLEARLY OUTTA CONTROL HERE.
I CAN TELL YOU DON'T WANT TO HURT ANYONE, RIGHT? IF YOU JUST STOP NOW, I PROMISE--
WHOA!
I HAVE YOU!
KRRGH
SHURI, I THINK HE'S FREAKING OUT. I THINK HE NEEDS HELP.
J-JUST LEAVE ME ALONE!

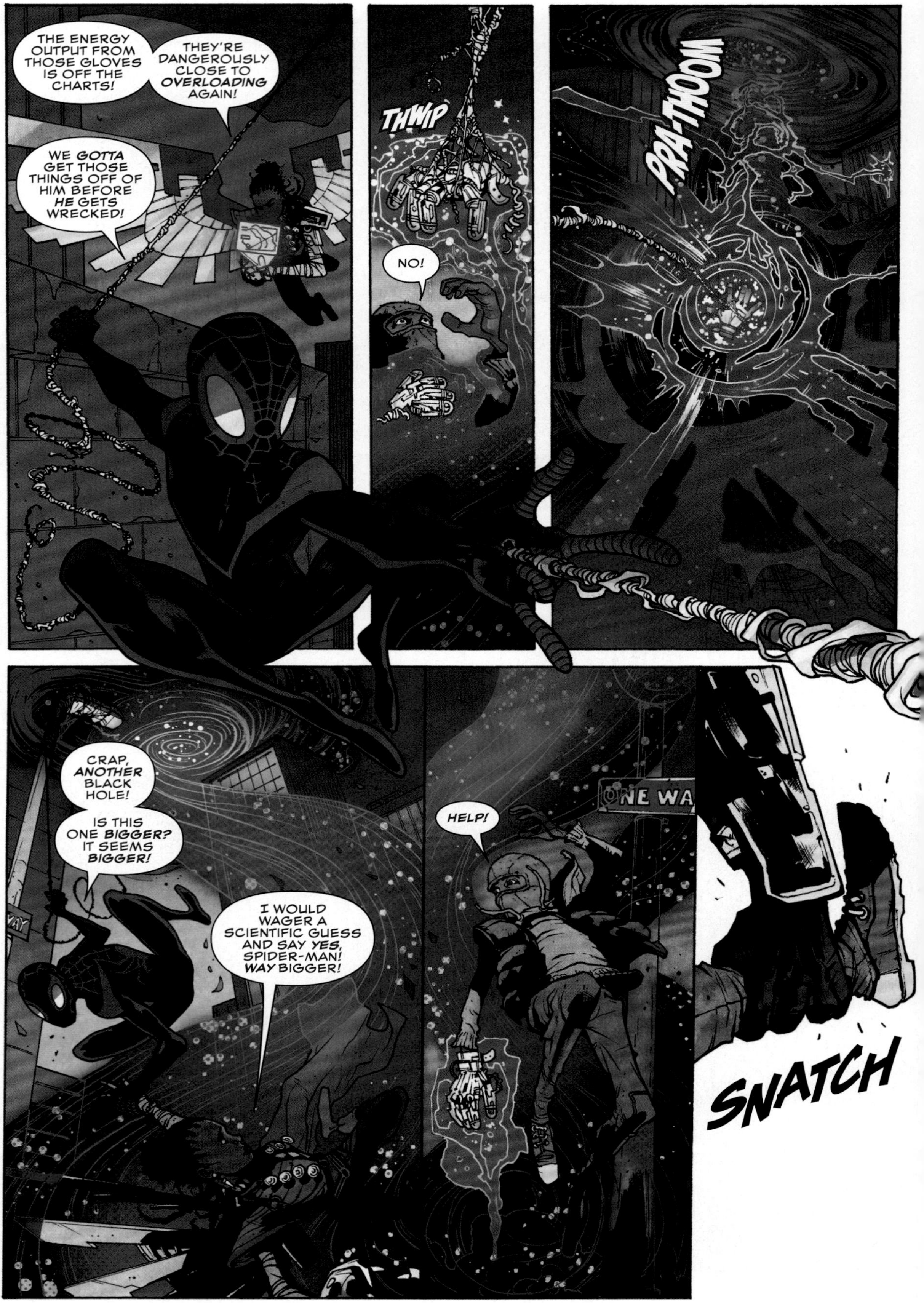
THE ENERGY OUTPUT FROM THOSE GLOVES IS OFF THE CHARTS!
THEY'RE DANGEROUSLY CLOSE TO OVERLOADING AGAIN!
WE GOTTA GET THOSE THINGS OFF OF HIM BEFORE HE GETS WRECKED!
THWIP
NO!
PRA-THOOM
CRAP, ANOTHER BLACK HOLE!
IS THIS ONE BIGGER? IT SEEMS BIGGER!
I WOULD WAGER A SCIENTIFIC GUESS AND SAY YES, SPIDER-MAN! WAY BIGGER!
ONE WA
HELP!
SNATCH

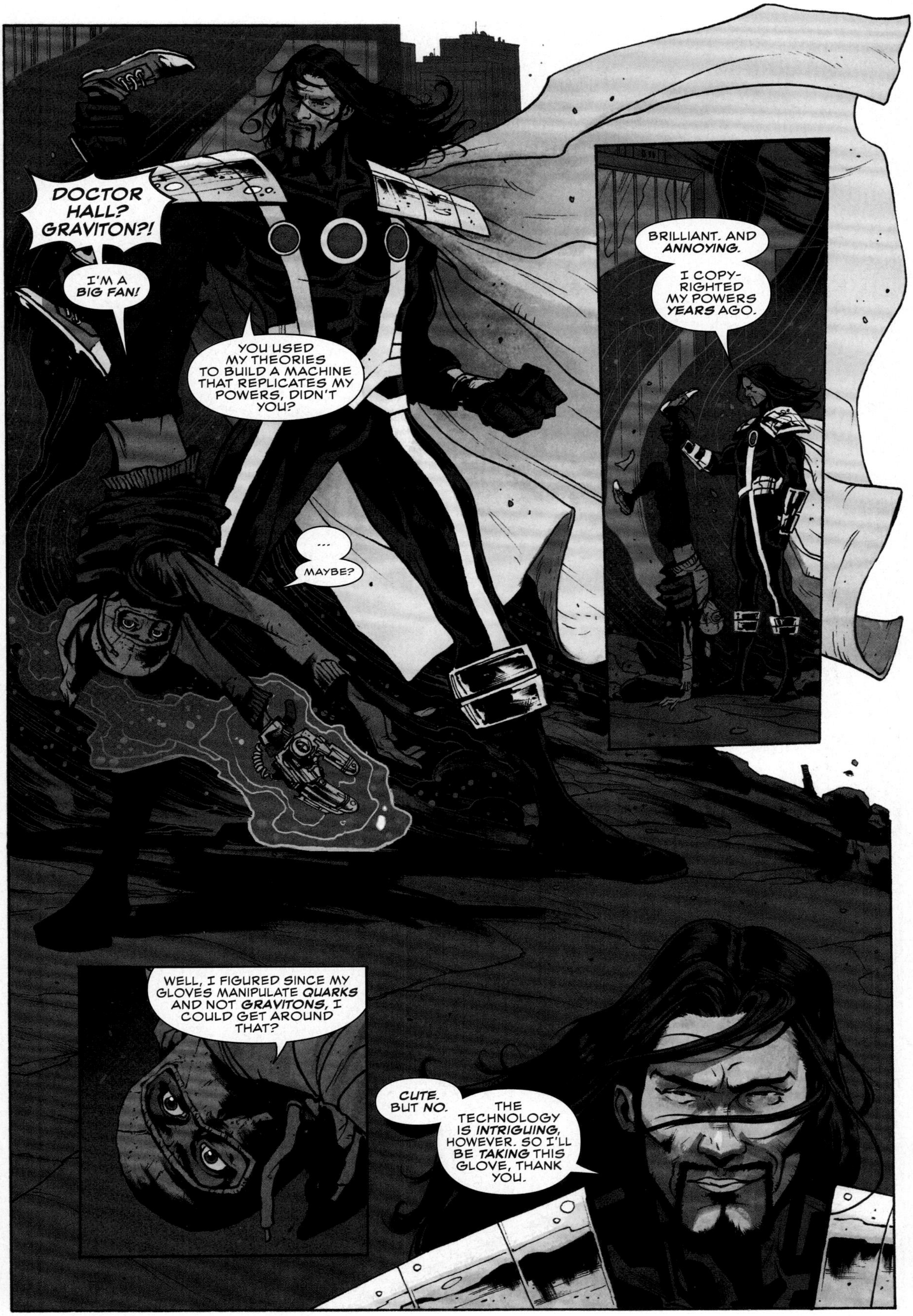
DOCTOR HALL? GRAVITON?!
I'M A BIG FAN!
YOU USED MY THEORIES TO BUILD A MACHINE THAT REPLICATES MY POWERS, DIDN'T YOU?
...
MAYBE?
BRILLIANT. AND ANNOYING.
I COPY-RIGHTED MY POWERS YEARS AGO.
WELL, I FIGURED SINCE MY GLOVES MANIPULATE QUARKS AND NOT GRAVITONS, I COULD GET AROUND THAT?
CUTE. BUT NO.
THE TECHNOLOGY IS INTRIGUING, HOWEVER. SO I'LL BE TAKING THIS GLOVE, THANK YOU.

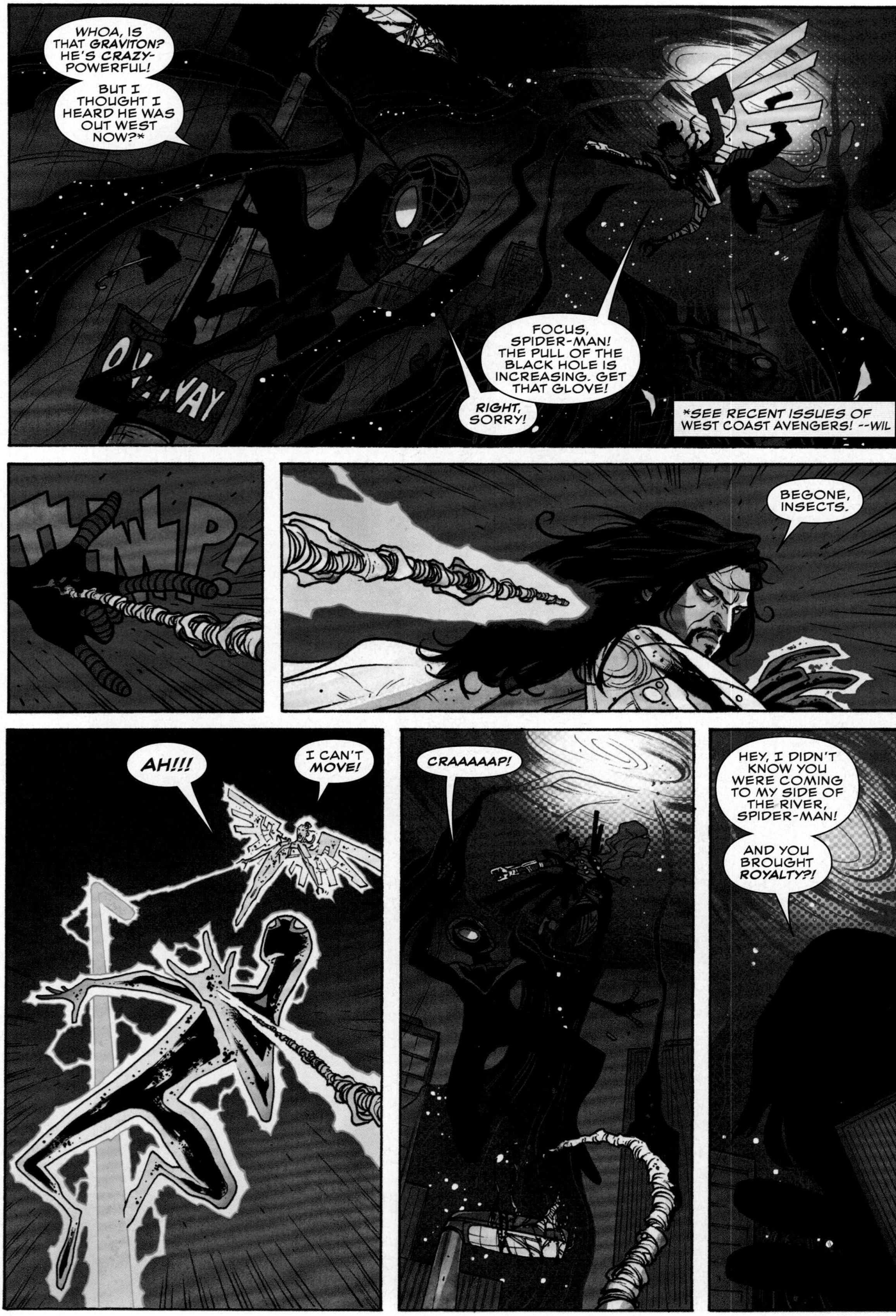
WHOA, IS THAT GRAVITON? HE'S CRAZY-POWERFUL!
BUT I THOUGHT I HEARD HE WAS OUT WEST NOW?*
FOCUS, SPIDER-MAN! THE PULL OF THE BLACK HOLE IS INCREASING. GET THAT GLOVE!
RIGHT, SORRY!
*SEE RECENT ISSUES OF WEST COAST AVENGERS! --WIL
THWP!
BEGONE, INSECTS.
AH!!!
I CAN'T MOVE!
CRAAAAAP!
HEY, I DIDN'T KNOW YOU WERE COMING TO MY SIDE OF THE RIVER, SPIDER-MAN!
AND YOU BROUGHT ROYALTY?!

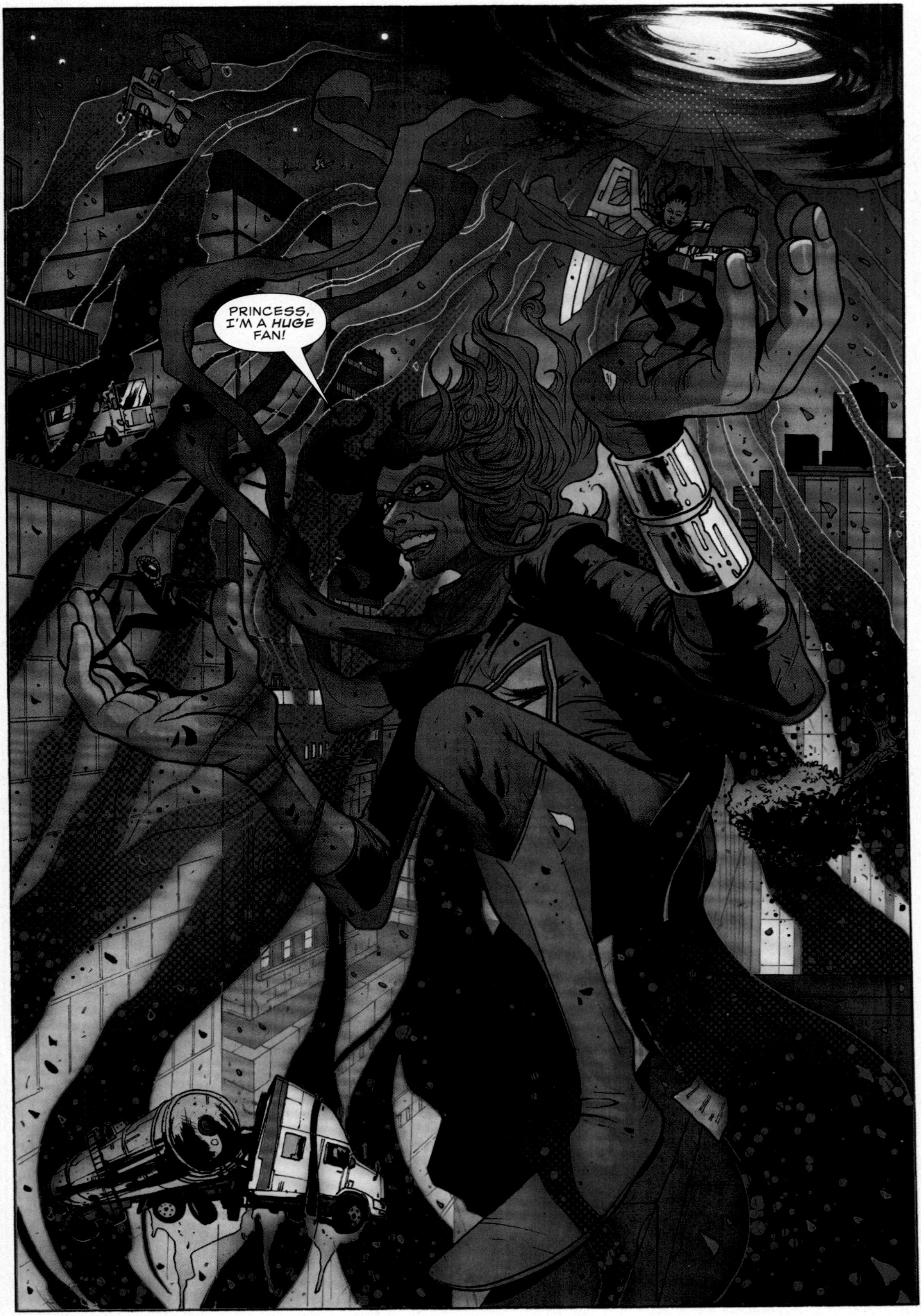
PRINCESS, I'M A HUGE FAN!

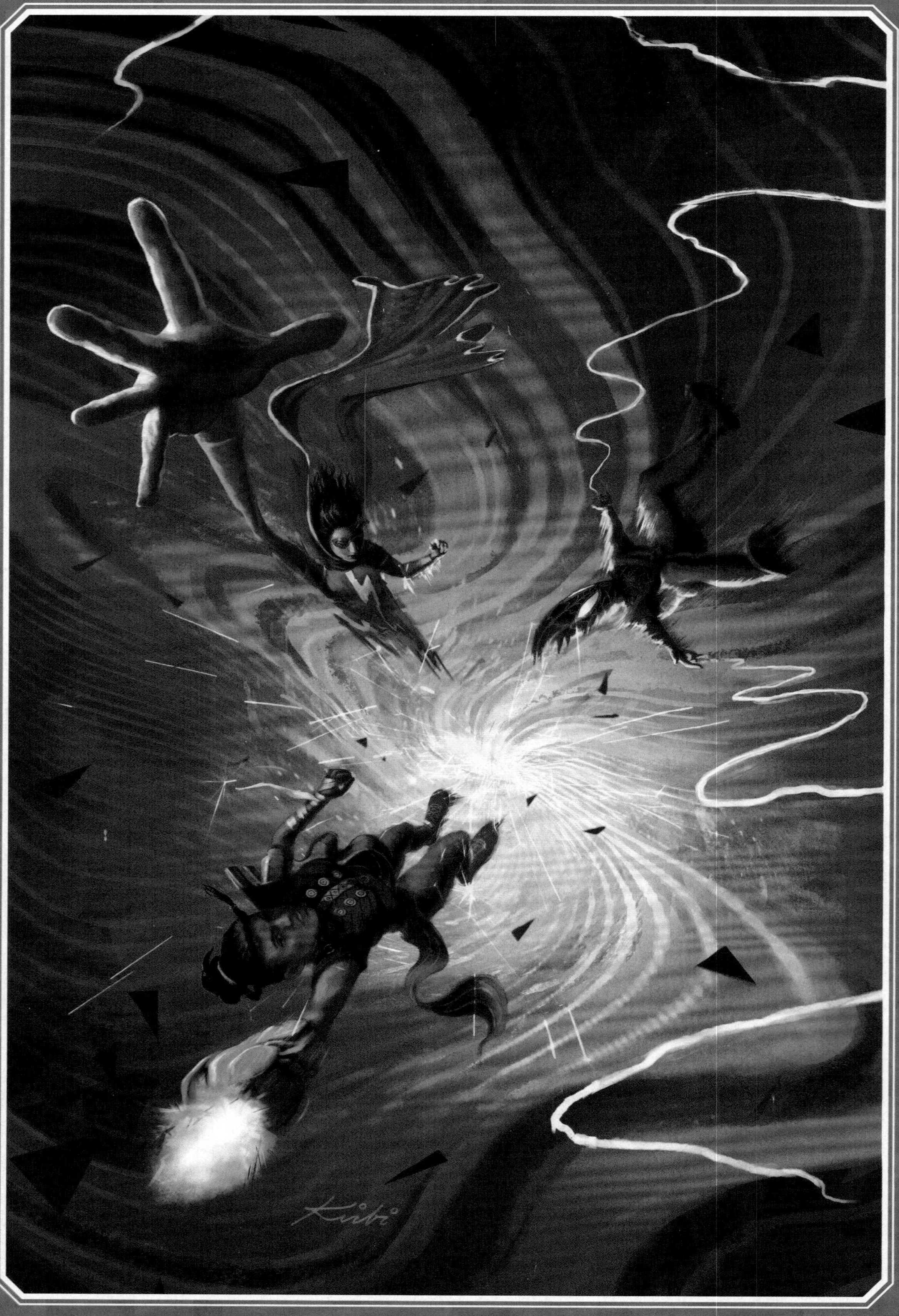

7 – A FRIEND IN NEED PART TWO

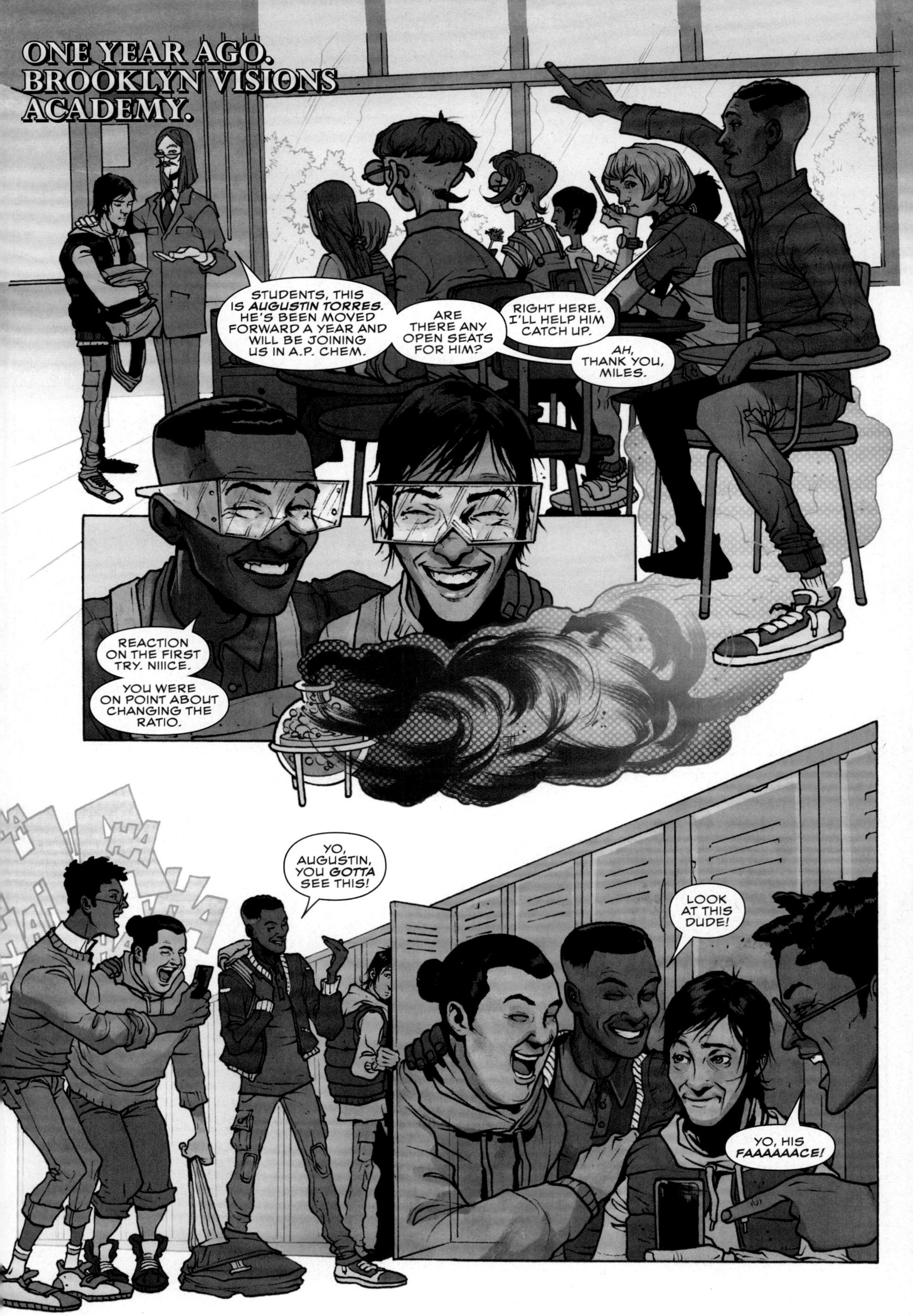
ONE YEAR AGO. BROOKLYN VISIONS ACADEMY.
STUDENTS, THIS IS AUGUSTIN TORRES. HE'S BEEN MOVED FORWARD A YEAR AND WILL BE JOINING US IN A.P. CHEM.
ARE THERE ANY OPEN SEATS FOR HIM?
RIGHT HERE. I'LL HELP HIM CATCH UP.
AH, THANK YOU, MILES.
REACTION ON THE FIRST TRY. NIIICE.
YOU WERE ON POINT ABOUT CHANGING THE RATIO.
YO, AUGUSTIN, YOU GOTTA SEE THIS!
LOOK AT THIS DUDE!
YO, HIS FAAAAAACE!

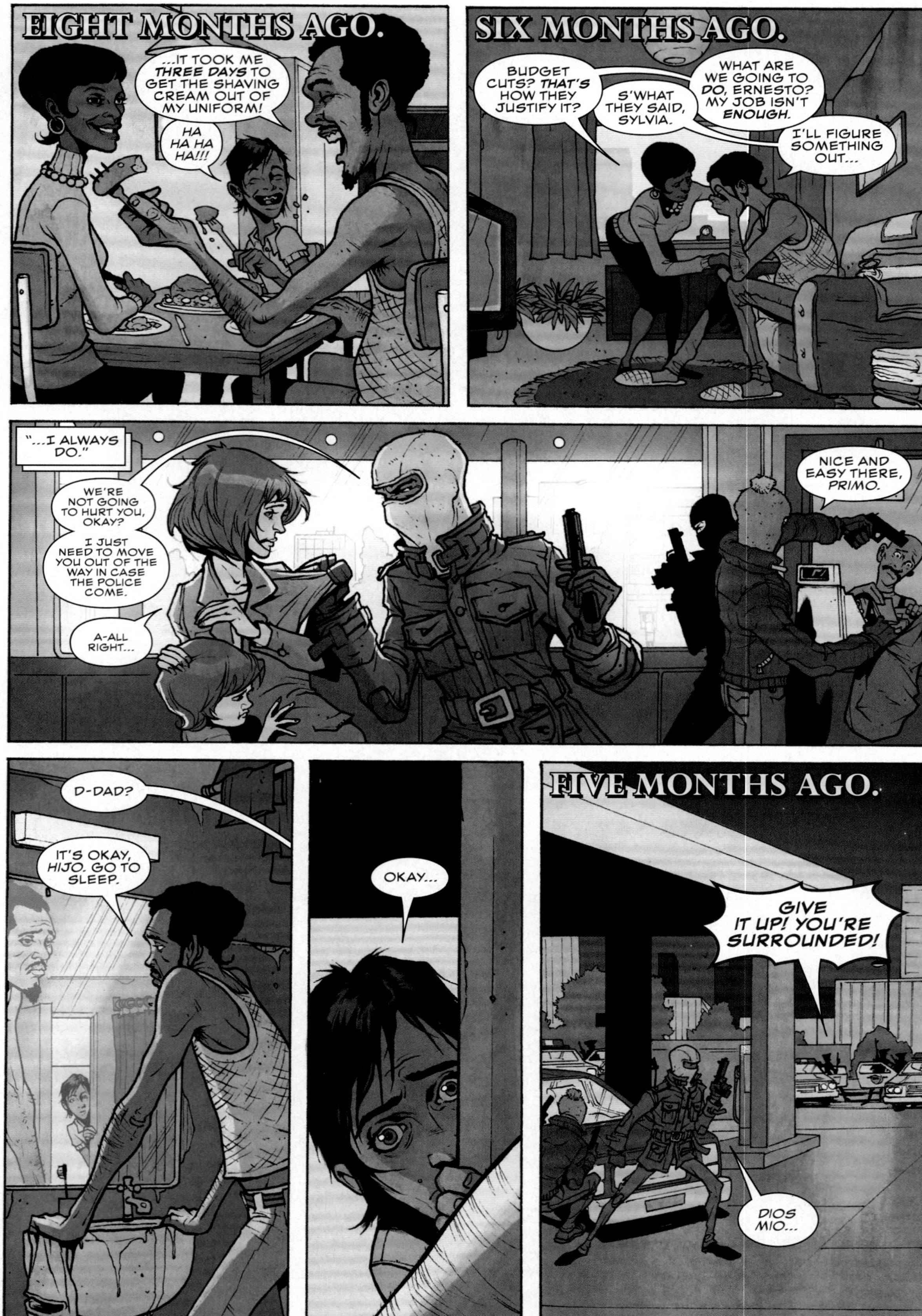
EIGHT MONTHS AGO.
...IT TOOK ME THREE DAYS TO GET THE SHAVING CREAM OUT OF MY UNIFORM!
HA HA HA HA!!!
SIX MONTHS AGO.
BUDGET CUTS? THAT'S HOW THEY JUSTIFY IT?
S'WHAT THEY SAID, SYLVIA.
WHAT ARE WE GOING TO DO, ERNESTO? MY JOB ISN'T ENOUGH.
I'LL FIGURE SOMETHING OUT...
"...I ALWAYS DO."
WE'RE NOT GOING TO HURT YOU, OKAY?
I JUST NEED TO MOVE YOU OUT OF THE WAY IN CASE THE POLICE COME.
A-ALL RIGHT...
NICE AND EASY THERE, PRIMO.
D-DAD?
IT'S OKAY, HIJO. GO TO SLEEP.
OKAY...
FIVE MONTHS AGO.
GIVE IT UP! YOU'RE SURROUNDED!
DIOS MIO...

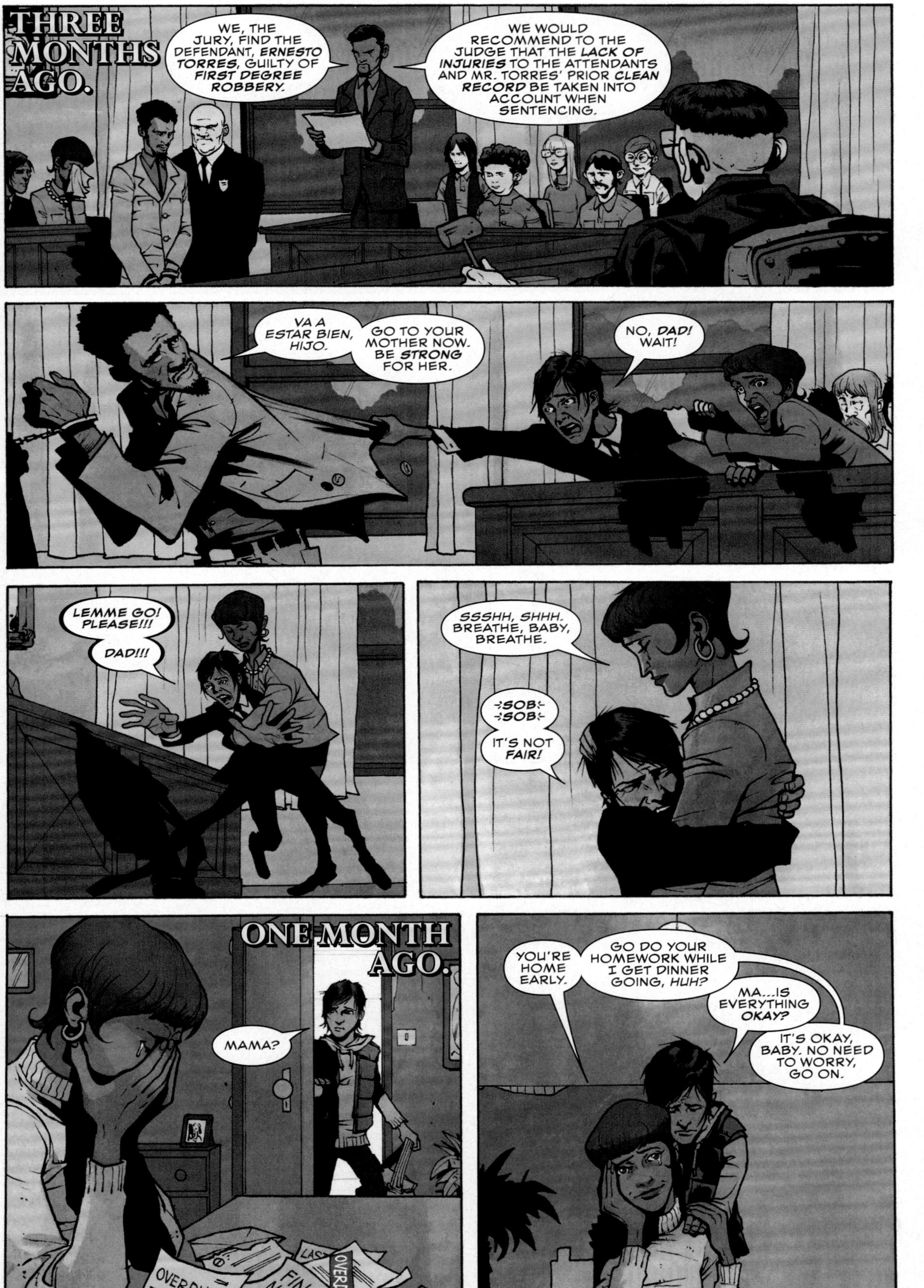
THREE MONTHS AGO.
WE, THE JURY, FIND THE DEFENDANT, ERNESTO TORRES, GUILTY OF FIRST DEGREE ROBBERY.
WE WOULD RECOMMEND TO THE JUDGE THAT THE LACK OF INJURIES TO THE ATTENDANTS AND MR. TORRES' PRIOR CLEAN RECORD BE TAKEN INTO ACCOUNT WHEN SENTENCING.
VA A ESTAR BIEN, HIJO.
GO TO YOUR MOTHER NOW. BE STRONG FOR HER.
NO, DAD! WAIT!
LEMME GO! PLEASE!!!
DAD!!!
SSSHH, SHHH. BREATHE, BABY, BREATHE.
SOB SOB
IT'S NOT FAIR!
ONE MONTH AGO.
MAMA?
OVERDUE
LAST
FINA
NOT
OVERD
YOU'RE HOME EARLY.
GO DO YOUR HOMEWORK WHILE I GET DINNER GOING, HUH?
MA...IS EVERYTHING OKAY?
IT'S OKAY, BABY. NO NEED TO WORRY, GO ON.

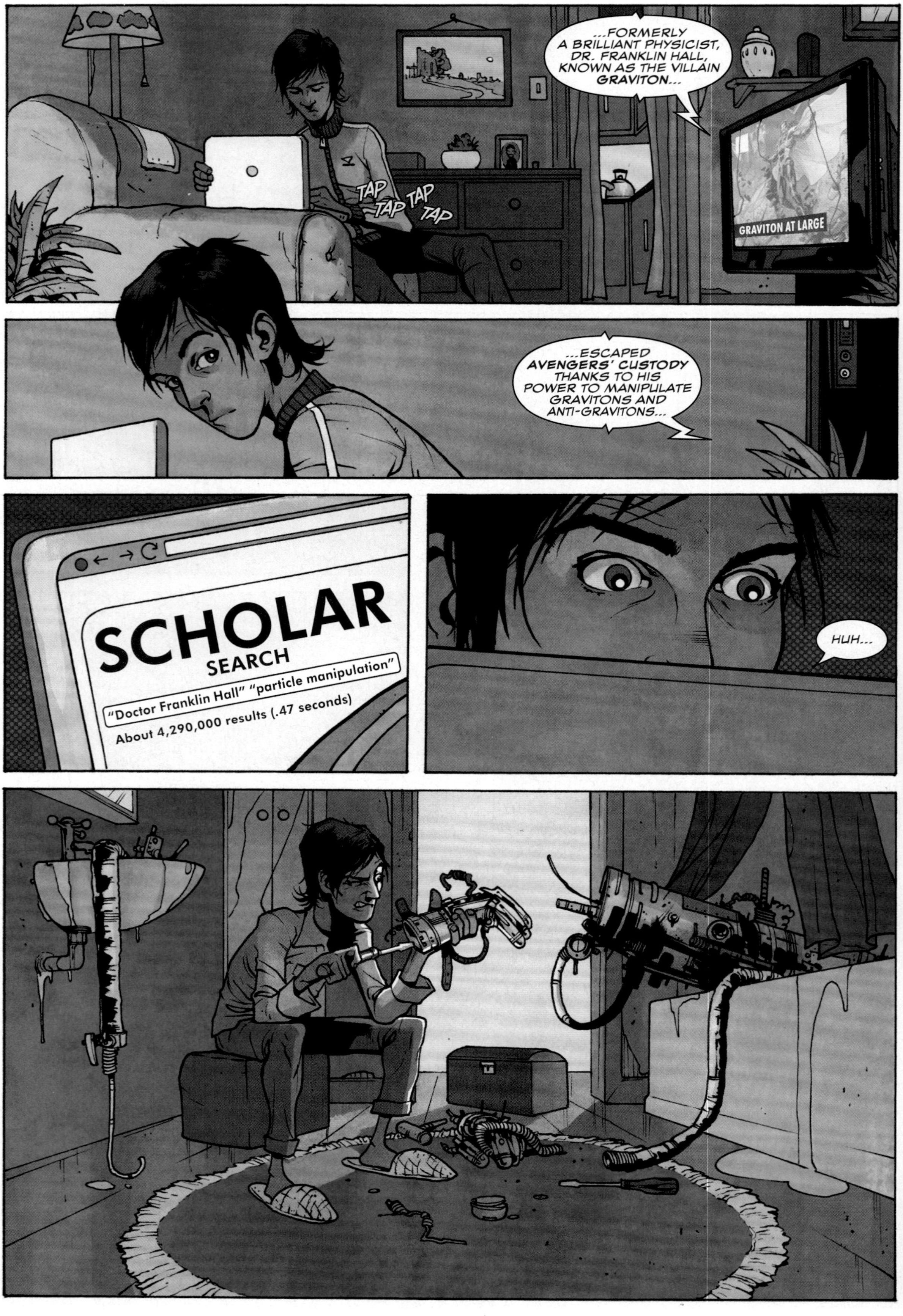
...FORMERLY A BRILLIANT PHYSICIST, DR. FRANKLIN HALL, KNOWN AS THE VILLAIN GRAVITON...
TAP TAP TAP TAP
GRAVITON AT LARGE
...ESCAPED AVENGERS' CUSTODY THANKS TO HIS POWER TO MANIPULATE GRAVITONS AND ANTI-GRAVITONS...
SCHOLAR
SEARCH
"Doctor Franklin Hall" "particle manipulation"
About 4,290,000 results (.47 seconds)
HUH...

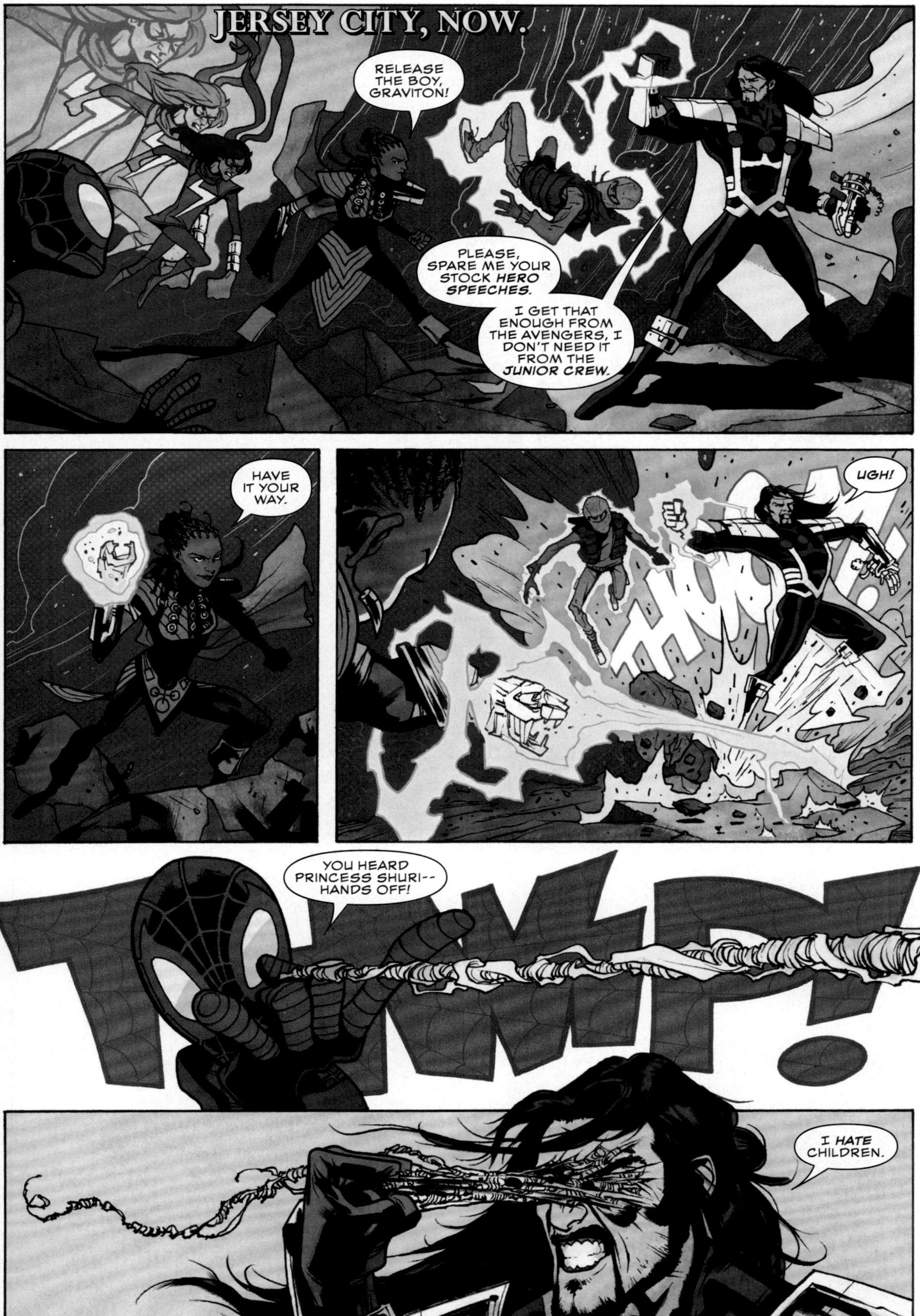
JERSEY CITY, NOW.
RELEASE THE BOY, GRAVITON!
PLEASE, SPARE ME YOUR STOCK HERO SPEECHES.
I GET THAT ENOUGH FROM THE AVENGERS, I DON'T NEED IT FROM THE JUNIOR CREW.
HAVE IT YOUR WAY.
UGH!
YOU HEARD PRINCESS SHURI-- HANDS OFF!
I HATE CHILDREN.

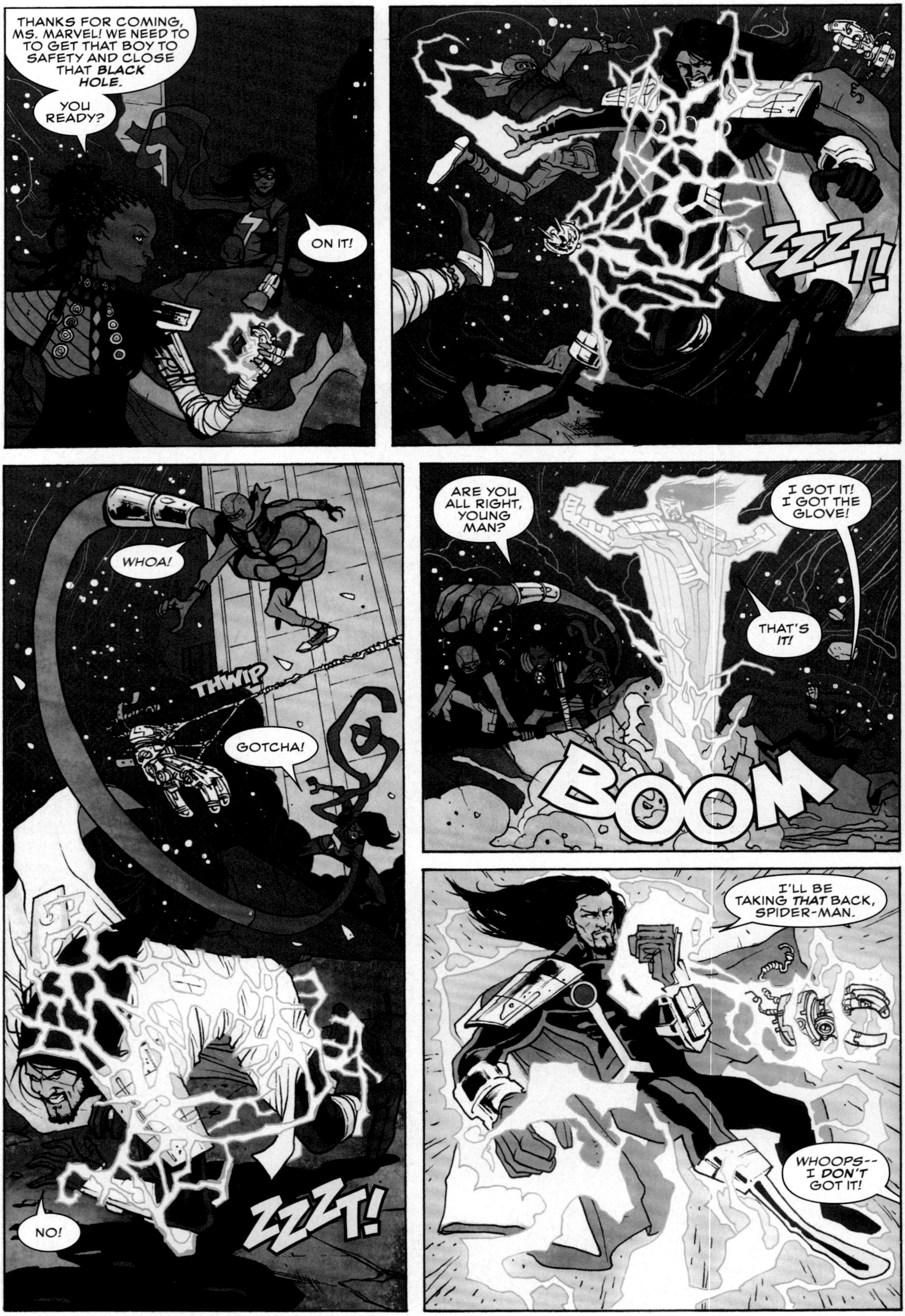
THANKS FOR COMING, MS. MARVEL! WE NEED TO TO GET THAT BOY TO SAFETY AND CLOSE THAT BLACK HOLE.
YOU READY?
ON IT!
ZZZT!
WHOA!
THWIP
GOTCHA!
NO!
ZZZT!
ARE YOU ALL RIGHT, YOUNG MAN?
I GOT IT! I GOT THE GLOVE!
THAT'S IT!
BOOM
I'LL BE TAKING THAT BACK, SPIDER-MAN.
WHOOPS-- I DON'T GOT IT!

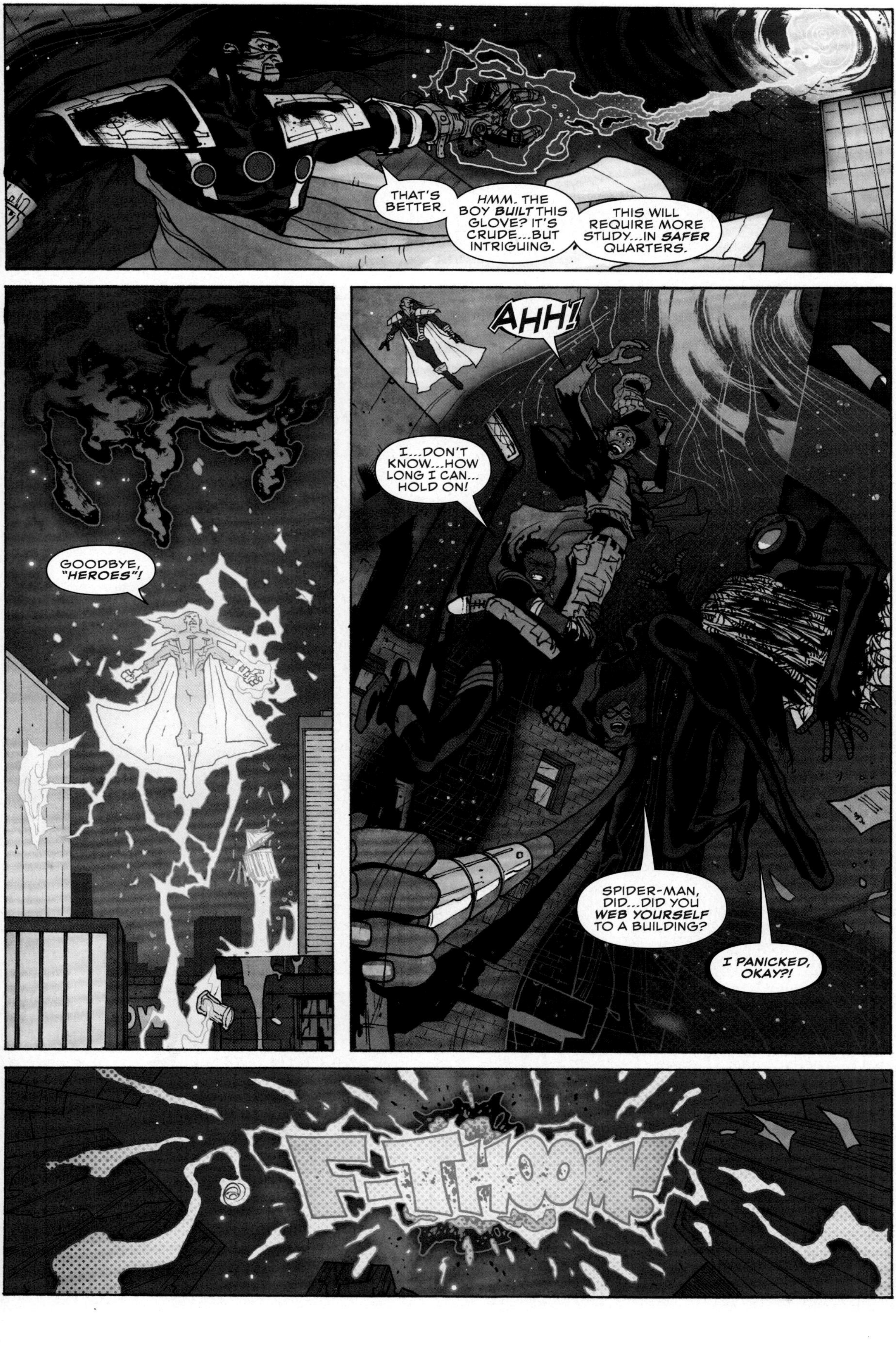
THAT'S BETTER.
HMM. THE BOY BUILT THIS GLOVE? IT'S CRUDE...BUT INTRIGUING.
THIS WILL REQUIRE MORE STUDY...IN SAFER QUARTERS.
GOODBYE, "HEROES"!
AHH!
I...DON'T KNOW...HOW LONG I CAN... HOLD ON!
SPIDER-MAN, DID...DID YOU WEB YOURSELF TO A BUILDING?
I PANICKED, OKAY?!
F-THOOM!

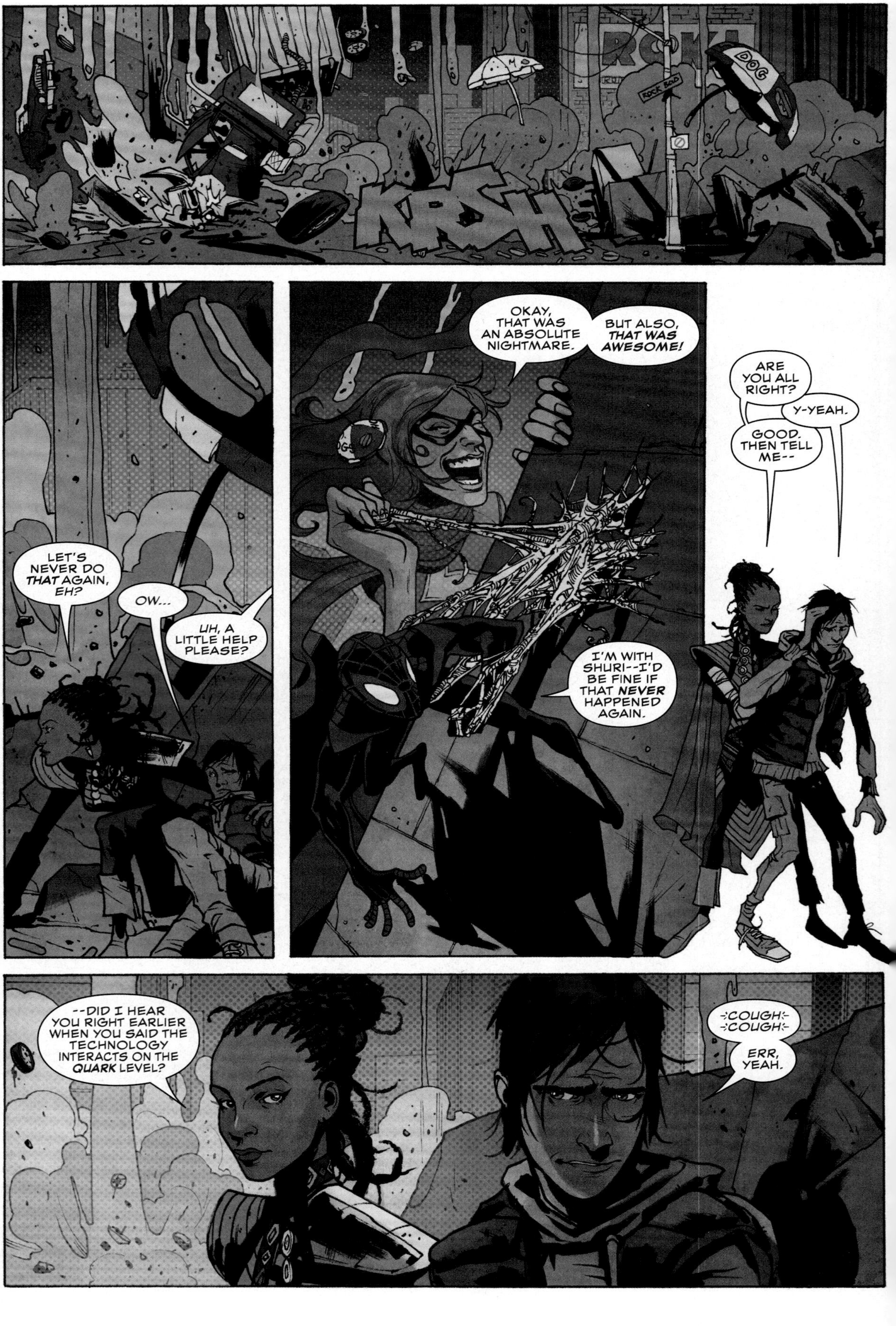
KRSH
LET'S NEVER DO THAT AGAIN, EH?
OW...
UH, A LITTLE HELP PLEASE?
OKAY, THAT WAS AN ABSOLUTE NIGHTMARE.
BUT ALSO, THAT WAS AWESOME!
I'M WITH SHURI--I'D BE FINE IF THAT NEVER HAPPENED AGAIN.
ARE YOU ALL RIGHT?
Y-YEAH.
GOOD. THEN TELL ME--
--DID I HEAR YOU RIGHT EARLIER WHEN YOU SAID THE TECHNOLOGY INTERACTS ON THE QUARK LEVEL?
-COUGH- -COUGH-
ERR, YEAH.

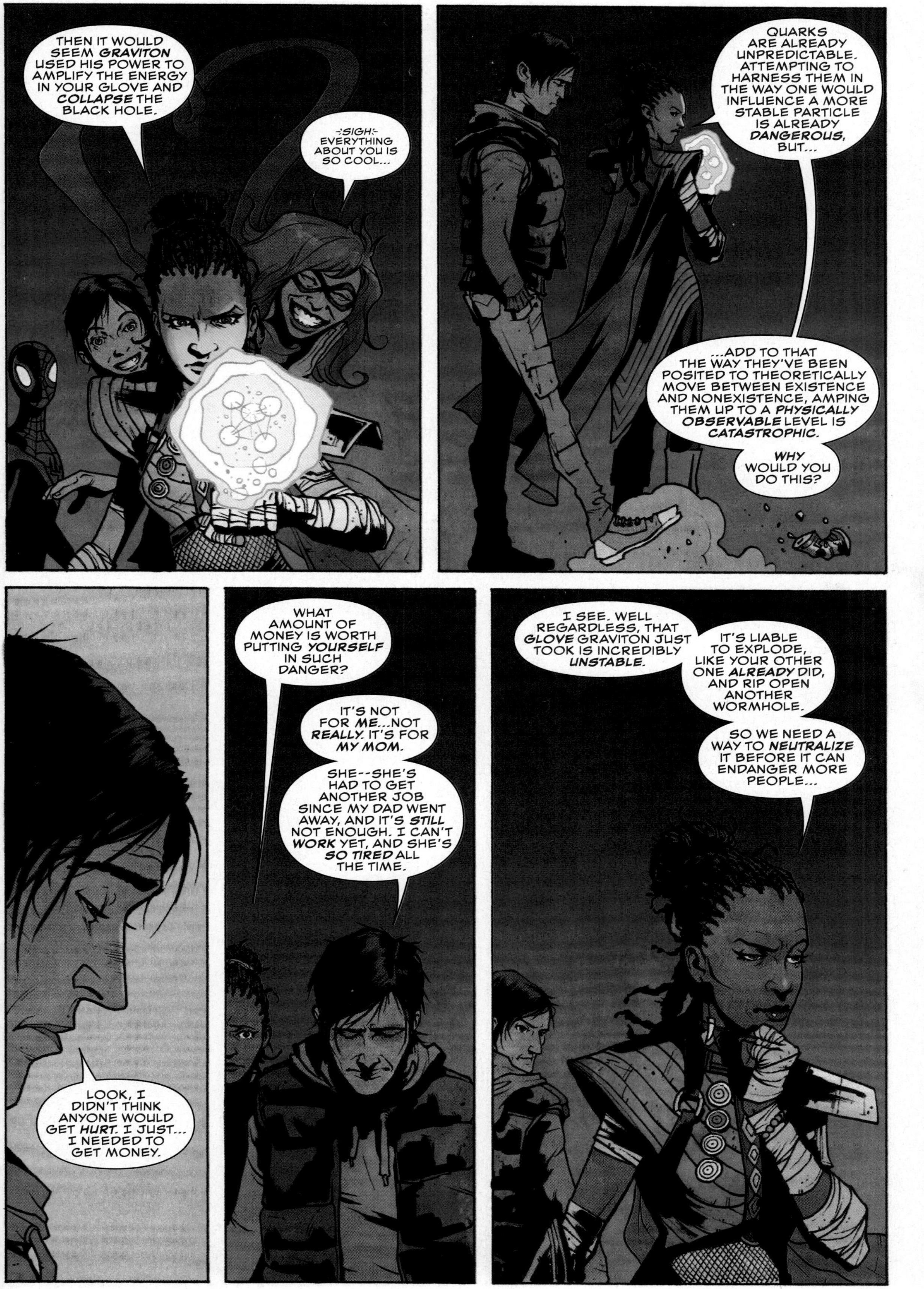

THEN IT WOULD SEEM GRAVITON USED HIS POWER TO AMPLIFY THE ENERGY IN YOUR GLOVE AND COLLAPSE THE BLACK HOLE.
-SIGH- EVERYTHING ABOUT YOU IS SO COOL...
QUARKS ARE ALREADY UNPREDICTABLE. ATTEMPTING TO HARNESS THEM IN THE WAY ONE WOULD INFLUENCE A MORE STABLE PARTICLE IS ALREADY DANGEROUS, BUT...
...ADD TO THAT THE WAY THEY'VE BEEN POSITED TO THEORETICALLY MOVE BETWEEN EXISTENCE AND NONEXISTENCE, AMPING THEM UP TO A PHYSICALLY OBSERVABLE LEVEL IS CATASTROPHIC.
WHY WOULD YOU DO THIS?
LOOK, I DIDN'T THINK ANYONE WOULD GET HURT. I JUST... I NEEDED TO GET MONEY.
WHAT AMOUNT OF MONEY IS WORTH PUTTING YOURSELF IN SUCH DANGER?
IT'S NOT FOR ME...NOT REALLY. IT'S FOR MY MOM.
SHE--SHE'S HAD TO GET ANOTHER JOB SINCE MY DAD WENT AWAY, AND IT'S STILL NOT ENOUGH. I CAN'T WORK YET, AND SHE'S SO TIRED ALL THE TIME.
I SEE. WELL REGARDLESS, THAT GLOVE GRAVITON JUST TOOK IS INCREDIBLY UNSTABLE.
IT'S LIABLE TO EXPLODE, LIKE YOUR OTHER ONE ALREADY DID, AND RIP OPEN ANOTHER WORMHOLE.
SO WE NEED A WAY TO NEUTRALIZE IT BEFORE IT CAN ENDANGER MORE PEOPLE...

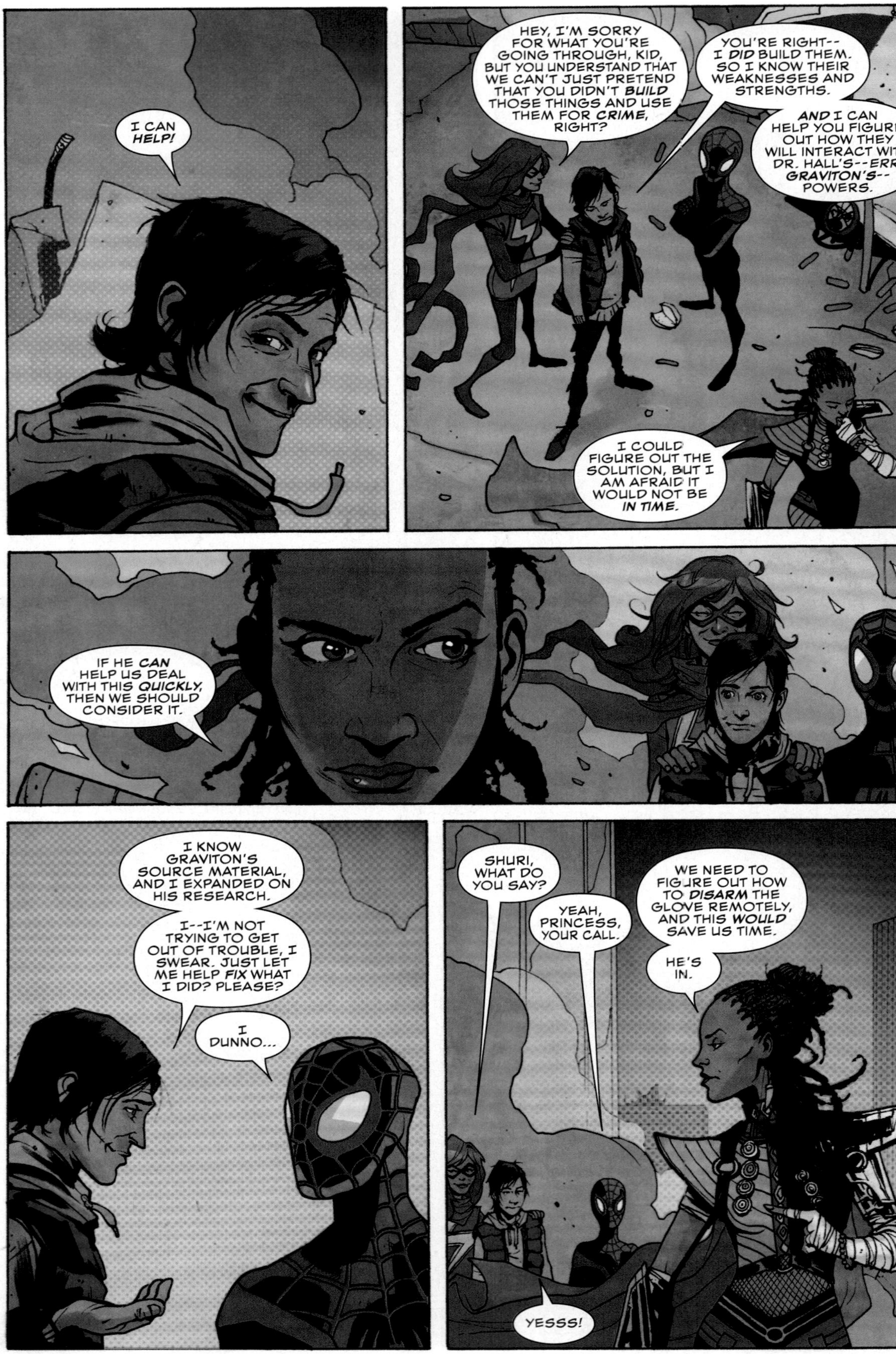
I CAN HELP!
HEY, I'M SORRY FOR WHAT YOU'RE GOING THROUGH, KID, BUT YOU UNDERSTAND THAT WE CAN'T JUST PRETEND THAT YOU DIDN'T BUILD THOSE THINGS AND USE THEM FOR CRIME, RIGHT?
YOU'RE RIGHT-- I DID BUILD THEM. SO I KNOW THEIR WEAKNESSES AND STRENGTHS.
AND I CAN HELP YOU FIGURE OUT HOW THEY WILL INTERACT WITH DR. HALL'S--ERR, GRAVITON'S-- POWERS.
I COULD FIGURE OUT THE SOLUTION, BUT I AM AFRAID IT WOULD NOT BE IN TIME.
IF HE CAN HELP US DEAL WITH THIS QUICKLY, THEN WE SHOULD CONSIDER IT.
I KNOW GRAVITON'S SOURCE MATERIAL, AND I EXPANDED ON HIS RESEARCH.
I--I'M NOT TRYING TO GET OUT OF TROUBLE, I SWEAR. JUST LET ME HELP FIX WHAT I DID? PLEASE?
I DUNNO...
SHURI, WHAT DO YOU SAY?
YEAH, PRINCESS, YOUR CALL.
WE NEED TO FIGURE OUT HOW TO DISARM THE GLOVE REMOTELY, AND THIS WOULD SAVE US TIME.
HE'S IN.
YESSS!

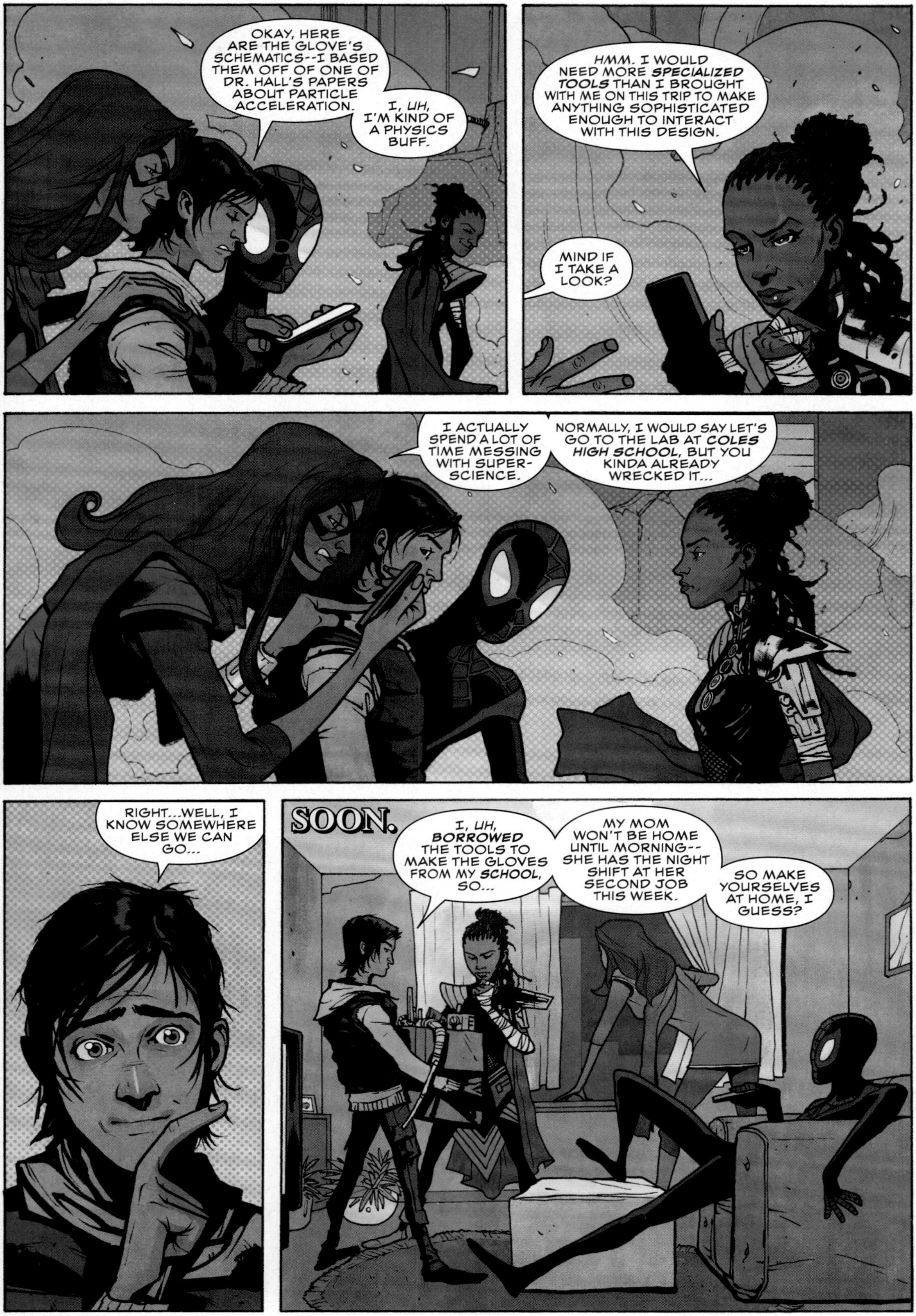
OKAY, HERE ARE THE GLOVE'S SCHEMATICS--I BASED THEM OFF OF ONE OF DR. HALL'S PAPERS ABOUT PARTICLE ACCELERATION.
I, UH, I'M KIND OF A PHYSICS BUFF.
HMM. I WOULD NEED MORE SPECIALIZED TOOLS THAN I BROUGHT WITH ME ON THIS TRIP TO MAKE ANYTHING SOPHISTICATED ENOUGH TO INTERACT WITH THIS DESIGN.
MIND IF I TAKE A LOOK?
I ACTUALLY SPEND A LOT OF TIME MESSING WITH SUPER-SCIENCE.
NORMALLY, I WOULD SAY LET'S GO TO THE LAB AT COLES HIGH SCHOOL, BUT YOU KINDA ALREADY WRECKED IT...
RIGHT...WELL, I KNOW SOMEWHERE ELSE WE CAN GO...
SOON.
I, UH, BORROWED THE TOOLS TO MAKE THE GLOVES FROM MY SCHOOL, SO...
MY MOM WON'T BE HOME UNTIL MORNING--SHE HAS THE NIGHT SHIFT AT HER SECOND JOB THIS WEEK.
SO MAKE YOURSELVES AT HOME, I GUESS?

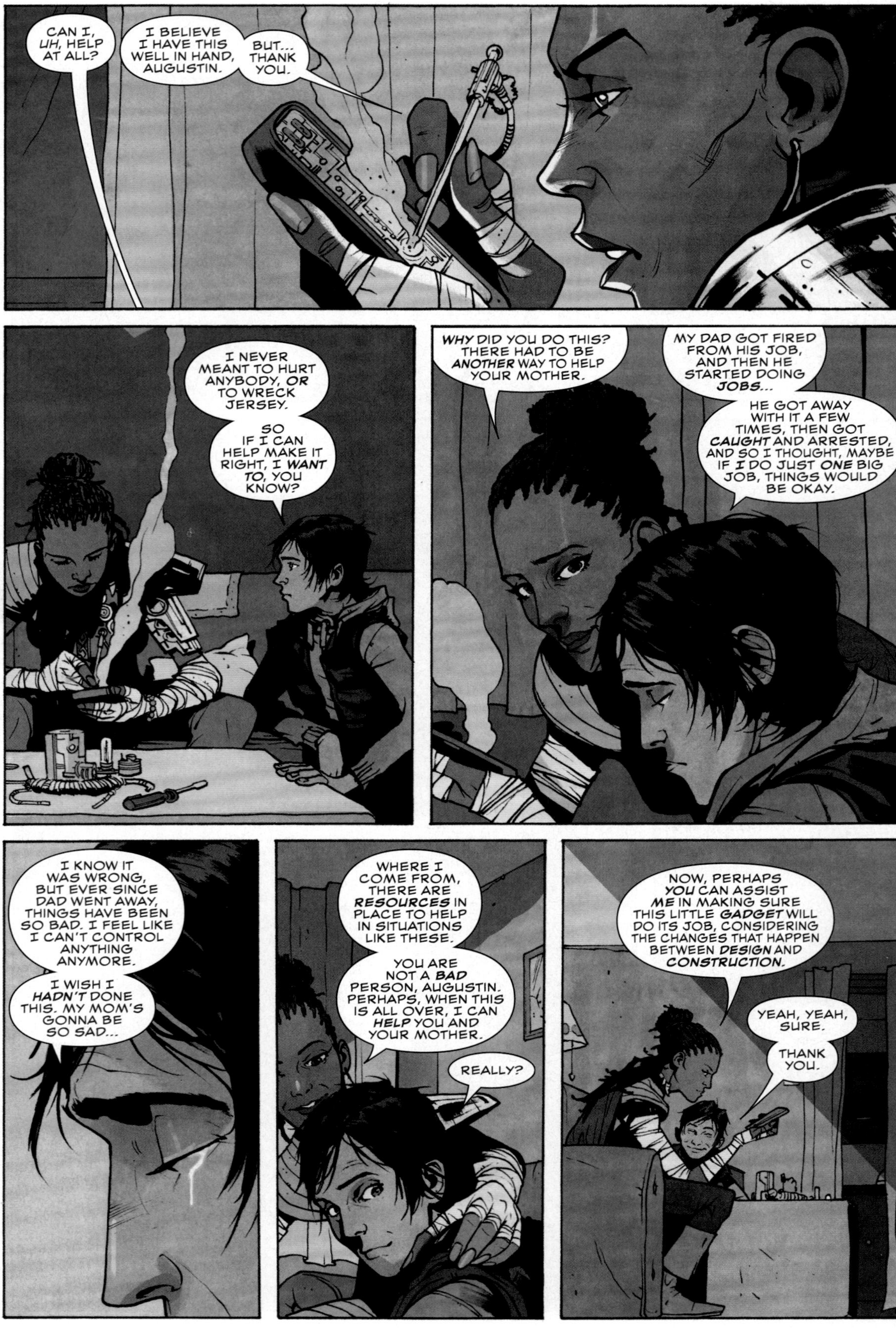

CAN I, UH, HELP AT ALL?
I BELIEVE I HAVE THIS WELL IN HAND, AUGUSTIN.
BUT... THANK YOU.
I NEVER MEANT TO HURT ANYBODY, OR TO WRECK JERSEY.
SO IF I CAN HELP MAKE IT RIGHT, I WANT TO, YOU KNOW?
WHY DID YOU DO THIS? THERE HAD TO BE ANOTHER WAY TO HELP YOUR MOTHER.
MY DAD GOT FIRED FROM HIS JOB, AND THEN HE STARTED DOING JOBS...
HE GOT AWAY WITH IT A FEW TIMES, THEN GOT CAUGHT AND ARRESTED, AND SO I THOUGHT, MAYBE IF I DO JUST ONE BIG JOB, THINGS WOULD BE OKAY.
I KNOW IT WAS WRONG, BUT EVER SINCE DAD WENT AWAY, THINGS HAVE BEEN SO BAD. I FEEL LIKE I CAN'T CONTROL ANYTHING ANYMORE.
I WISH I HADN'T DONE THIS. MY MOM'S GONNA BE SO SAD...
WHERE I COME FROM, THERE ARE RESOURCES IN PLACE TO HELP IN SITUATIONS LIKE THESE.
YOU ARE NOT A BAD PERSON, AUGUSTIN. PERHAPS, WHEN THIS IS ALL OVER, I CAN HELP YOU AND YOUR MOTHER.
REALLY?
NOW, PERHAPS YOU CAN ASSIST ME IN MAKING SURE THIS LITTLE GADGET WILL DO ITS JOB, CONSIDERING THE CHANGES THAT HAPPEN BETWEEN DESIGN AND CONSTRUCTION.
YEAH, YEAH, SURE.
THANK YOU.

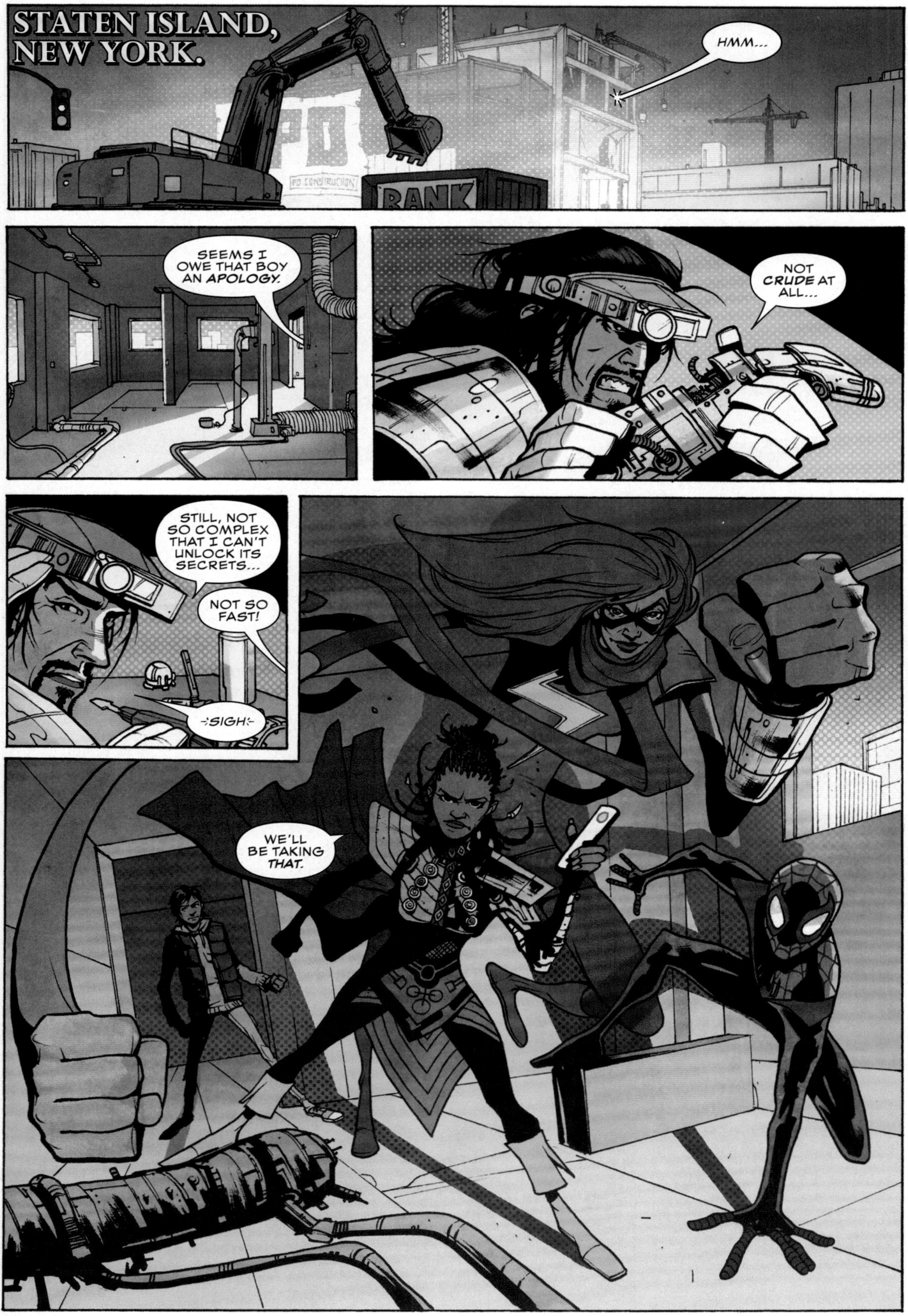
STATEN ISLAND, NEW YORK.
HMM...
SEEMS I OWE THAT BOY AN *APOLOGY.*
NOT *CRUDE* AT ALL...
STILL, NOT SO COMPLEX THAT I CAN'T UNLOCK ITS SECRETS...
NOT SO FAST!
-SIGH-
WE'LL BE TAKING *THAT.*

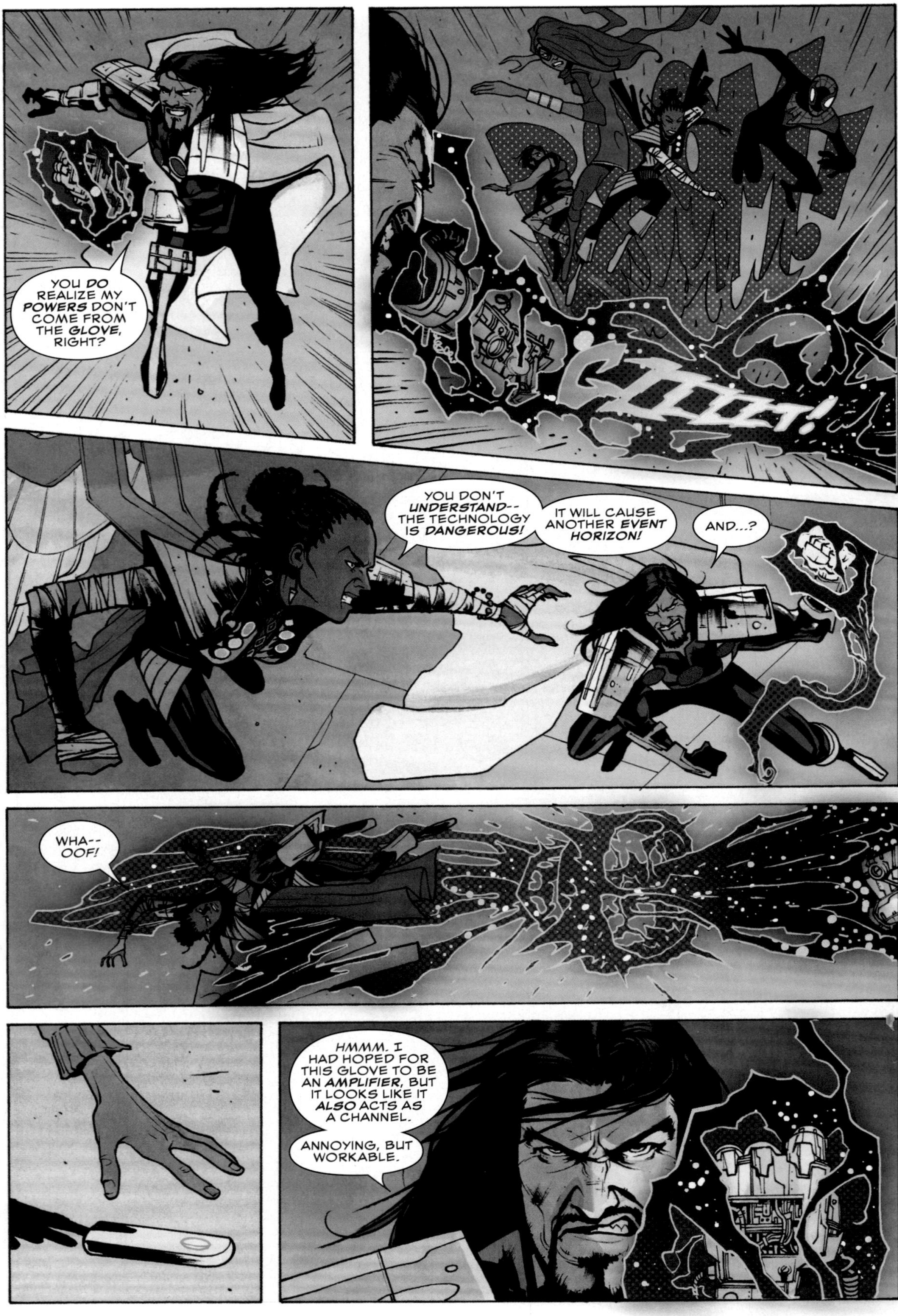
YOU DO REALIZE MY POWERS DON'T COME FROM THE GLOVE, RIGHT?
GZZZT!
YOU DON'T UNDERSTAND-- THE TECHNOLOGY IS DANGEROUS!
IT WILL CAUSE ANOTHER EVENT HORIZON!
AND...?
WHA-- OOF!
HMMM. I HAD HOPED FOR THIS GLOVE TO BE AN AMPLIFIER, BUT IT LOOKS LIKE IT ALSO ACTS AS A CHANNEL.
ANNOYING, BUT WORKABLE.

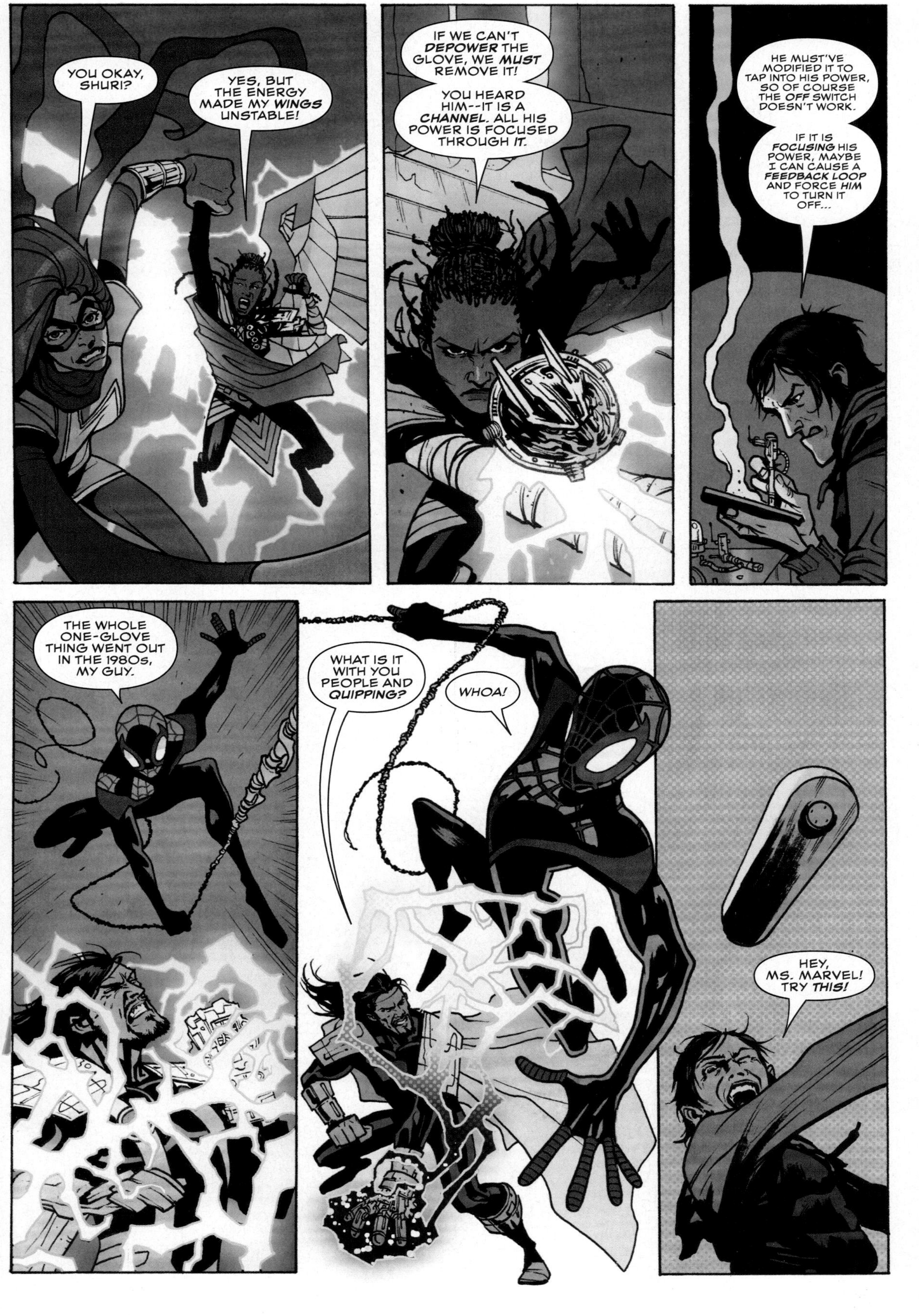
YOU OKAY, SHURI?
YES, BUT THE ENERGY MADE MY WINGS UNSTABLE!
IF WE CAN'T DEPOWER THE GLOVE, WE MUST REMOVE IT!
YOU HEARD HIM--IT IS A CHANNEL. ALL HIS POWER IS FOCUSED THROUGH IT.
HE MUST'VE MODIFIED IT TO TAP INTO HIS POWER, SO OF COURSE THE OFF SWITCH DOESN'T WORK.
IF IT IS FOCUSING HIS POWER, MAYBE I CAN CAUSE A FEEDBACK LOOP AND FORCE HIM TO TURN IT OFF...
THE WHOLE ONE-GLOVE THING WENT OUT IN THE 1980s, MY GUY.
WHAT IS IT WITH YOU PEOPLE AND QUIPPING?
WHOA!
HEY, MS. MARVEL! TRY THIS!

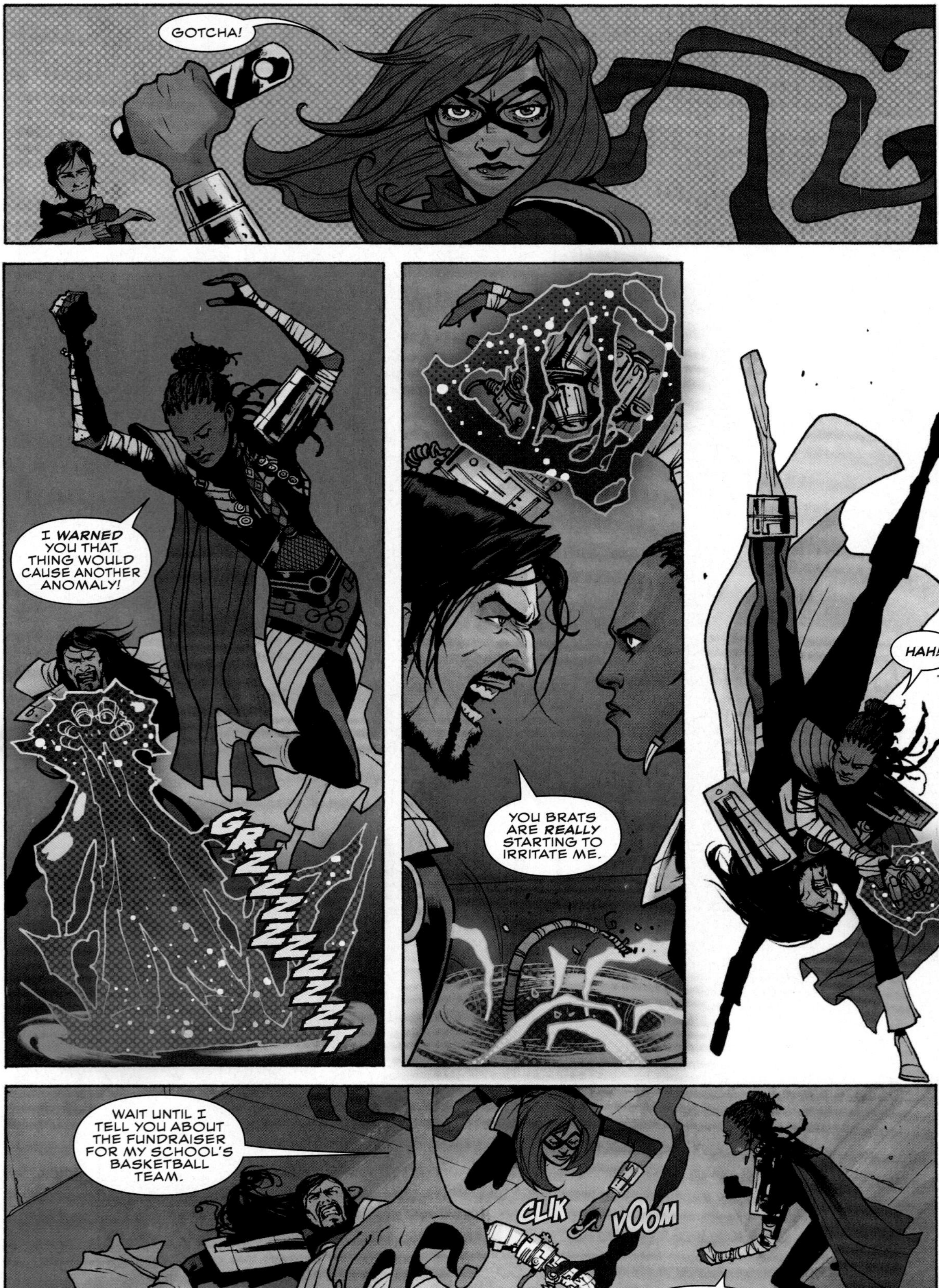
GOTCHA!
I WARNED YOU THAT THING WOULD CAUSE ANOTHER ANOMALY!
GRZZZZZZZT
YOU BRATS ARE REALLY STARTING TO IRRITATE ME.
HAH!
WAIT UNTIL I TELL YOU ABOUT THE FUNDRAISER FOR MY SCHOOL'S BASKETBALL TEAM.
CLIK
VOOM
IT'S WORKING--

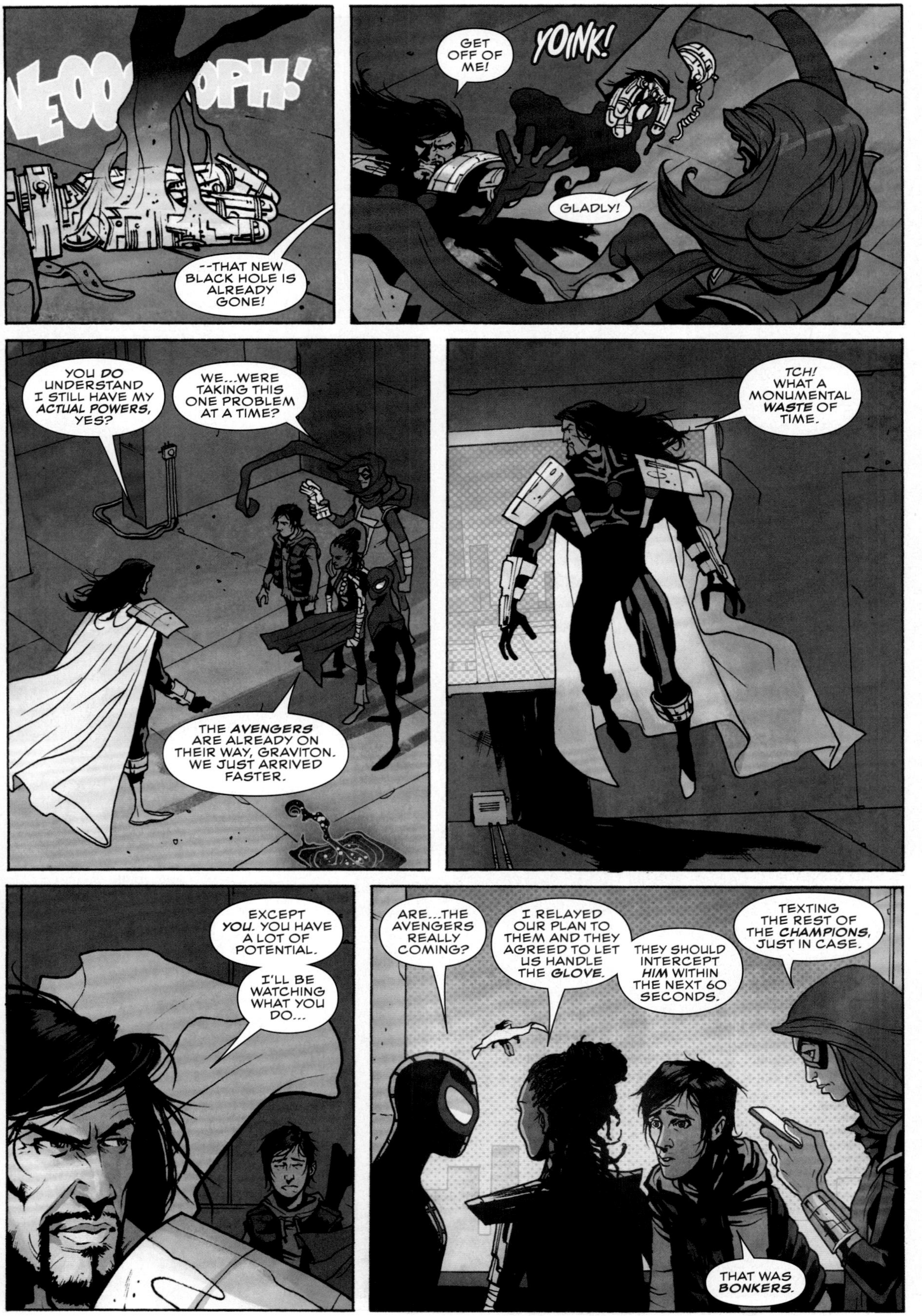

NEEOOOOOPH!
--THAT NEW BLACK HOLE IS ALREADY GONE!
GET OFF OF ME!
YOINK!
GLADLY!
YOU DO UNDERSTAND I STILL HAVE MY ACTUAL POWERS, YES?
WE...WERE TAKING THIS ONE PROBLEM AT A TIME?
THE AVENGERS ARE ALREADY ON THEIR WAY, GRAVITON. WE JUST ARRIVED FASTER.
TCH! WHAT A MONUMENTAL WASTE OF TIME.
EXCEPT YOU. YOU HAVE A LOT OF POTENTIAL.
I'LL BE WATCHING WHAT YOU DO...
ARE...THE AVENGERS REALLY COMING?
I RELAYED OUR PLAN TO THEM AND THEY AGREED TO LET US HANDLE THE GLOVE.
THEY SHOULD INTERCEPT HIM WITHIN THE NEXT 60 SECONDS.
TEXTING THE REST OF THE CHAMPIONS, JUST IN CASE.
THAT WAS BONKERS.

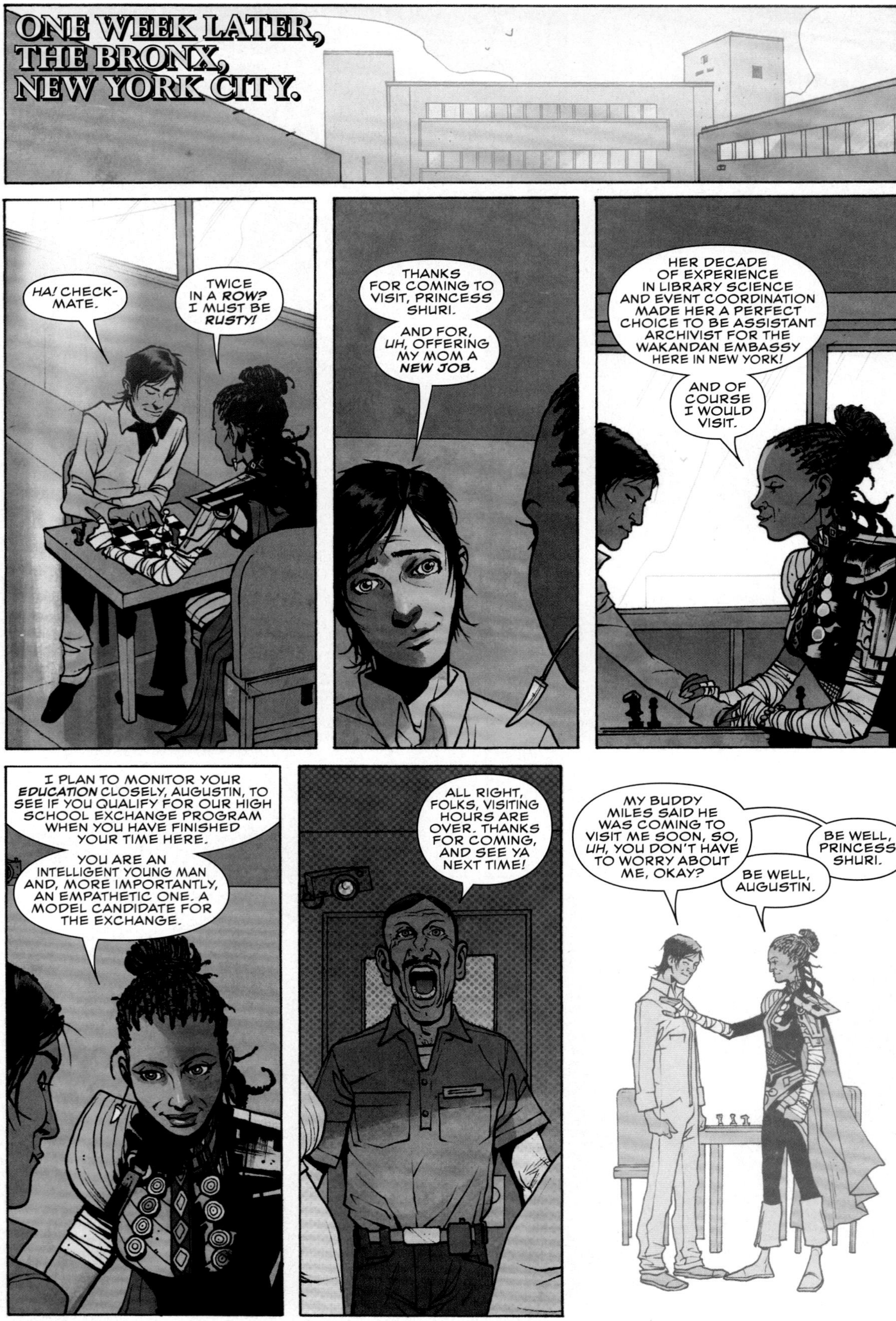
ONE WEEK LATER, THE BRONX, NEW YORK CITY.
HA! CHECK-MATE.
TWICE IN A ROW? I MUST BE RUSTY!
THANKS FOR COMING TO VISIT, PRINCESS SHURI.
AND FOR, UH, OFFERING MY MOM A NEW JOB.
HER DECADE OF EXPERIENCE IN LIBRARY SCIENCE AND EVENT COORDINATION MADE HER A PERFECT CHOICE TO BE ASSISTANT ARCHIVIST FOR THE WAKANDAN EMBASSY HERE IN NEW YORK!
AND OF COURSE I WOULD VISIT.
I PLAN TO MONITOR YOUR EDUCATION CLOSELY, AUGUSTIN, TO SEE IF YOU QUALIFY FOR OUR HIGH SCHOOL EXCHANGE PROGRAM WHEN YOU HAVE FINISHED YOUR TIME HERE.
YOU ARE AN INTELLIGENT YOUNG MAN AND, MORE IMPORTANTLY, AN EMPATHETIC ONE. A MODEL CANDIDATE FOR THE EXCHANGE.
ALL RIGHT, FOLKS, VISITING HOURS ARE OVER. THANKS FOR COMING, AND SEE YA NEXT TIME!
MY BUDDY MILES SAID HE WAS COMING TO VISIT ME SOON, SO, UH, YOU DON'T HAVE TO WORRY ABOUT ME, OKAY?
BE WELL, AUGUSTIN.
BE WELL, PRINCESS SHURI.

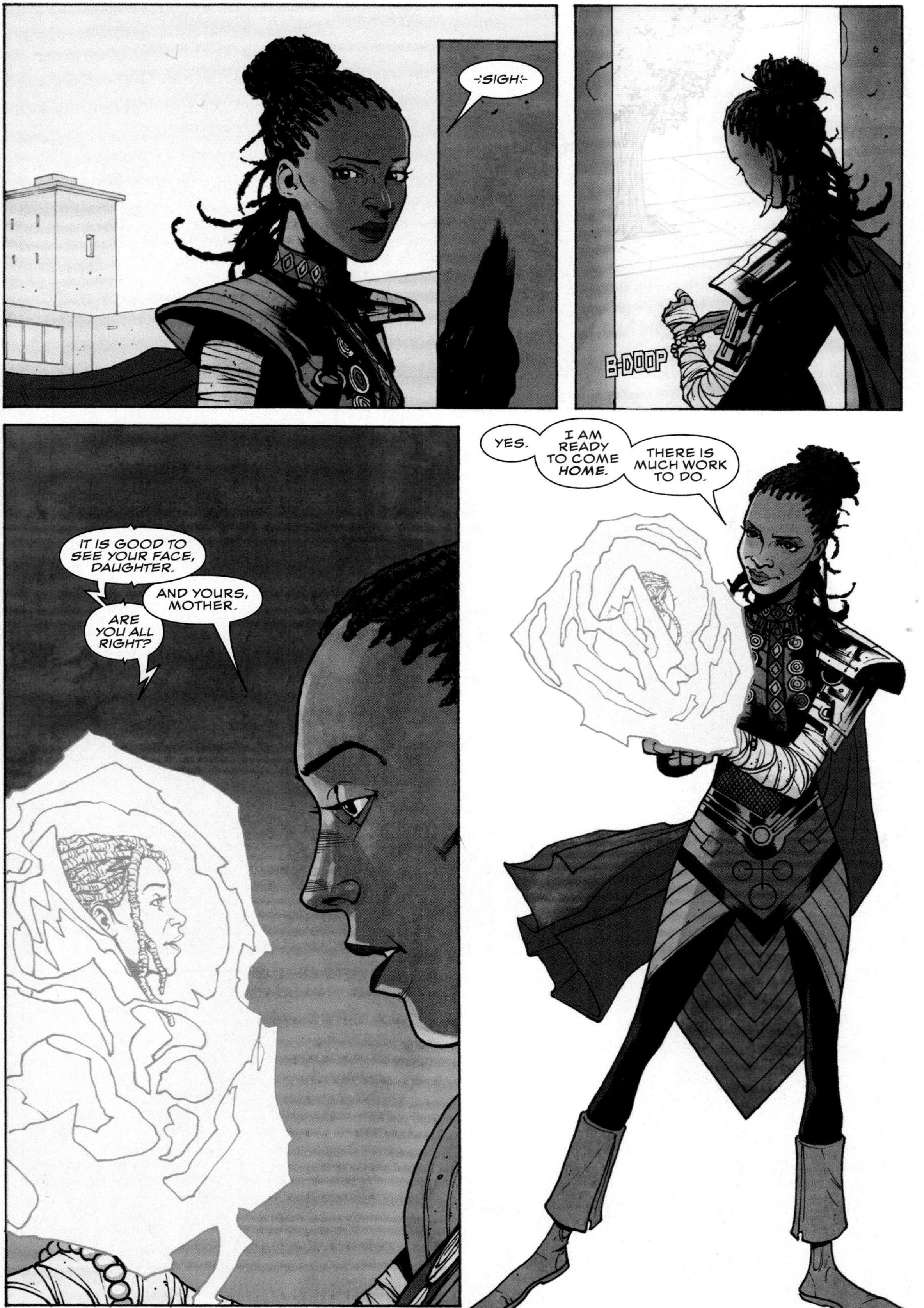
SIGH
B-DOOP
IT IS GOOD TO SEE YOUR FACE, DAUGHTER.
ARE YOU ALL RIGHT?
AND YOURS, MOTHER.
YES.
I AM READY TO COME HOME.
THERE IS MUCH WORK TO DO.

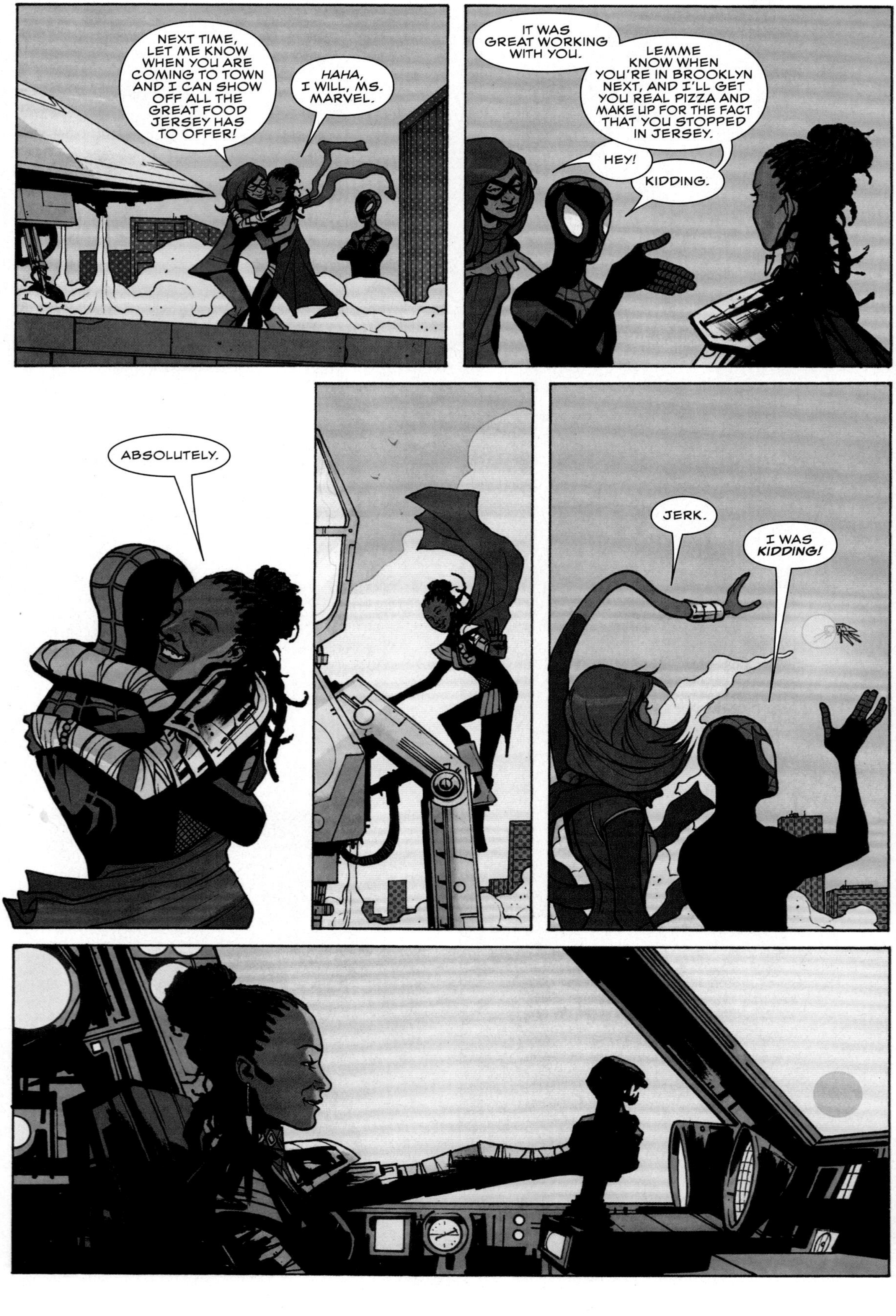

NEXT TIME, LET ME KNOW WHEN YOU ARE COMING TO TOWN AND I CAN SHOW OFF ALL THE GREAT FOOD JERSEY HAS TO OFFER!
HAHA, I WILL, MS. MARVEL.
IT WAS GREAT WORKING WITH YOU.
LEMME KNOW WHEN YOU'RE IN BROOKLYN NEXT, AND I'LL GET YOU REAL PIZZA AND MAKE UP FOR THE FACT THAT YOU STOPPED IN JERSEY.
HEY!
KIDDING.
ABSOLUTELY.
JERK.
I WAS ***KIDDING!***

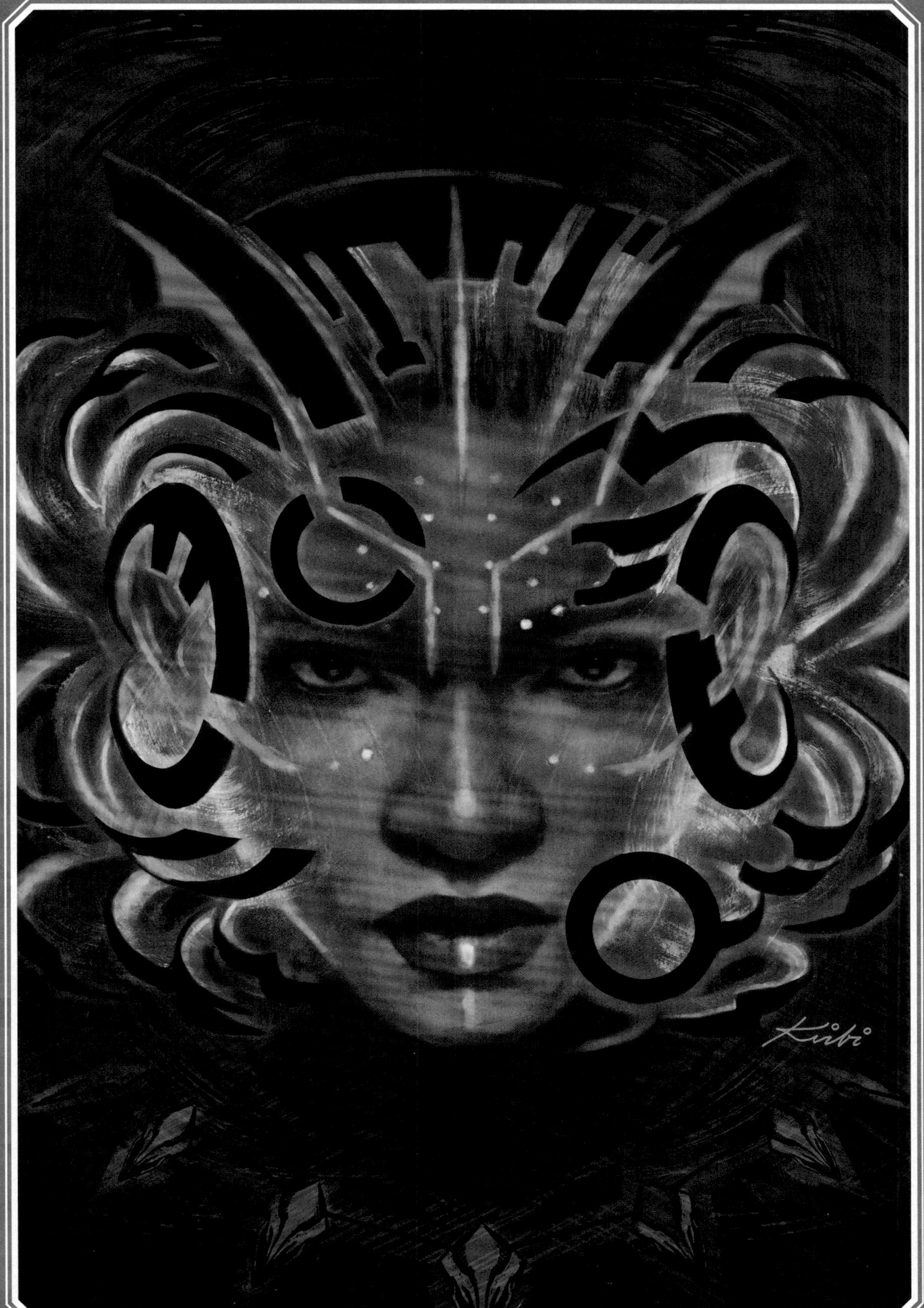
Kubi

8 – 24/7 VIBRANIUM

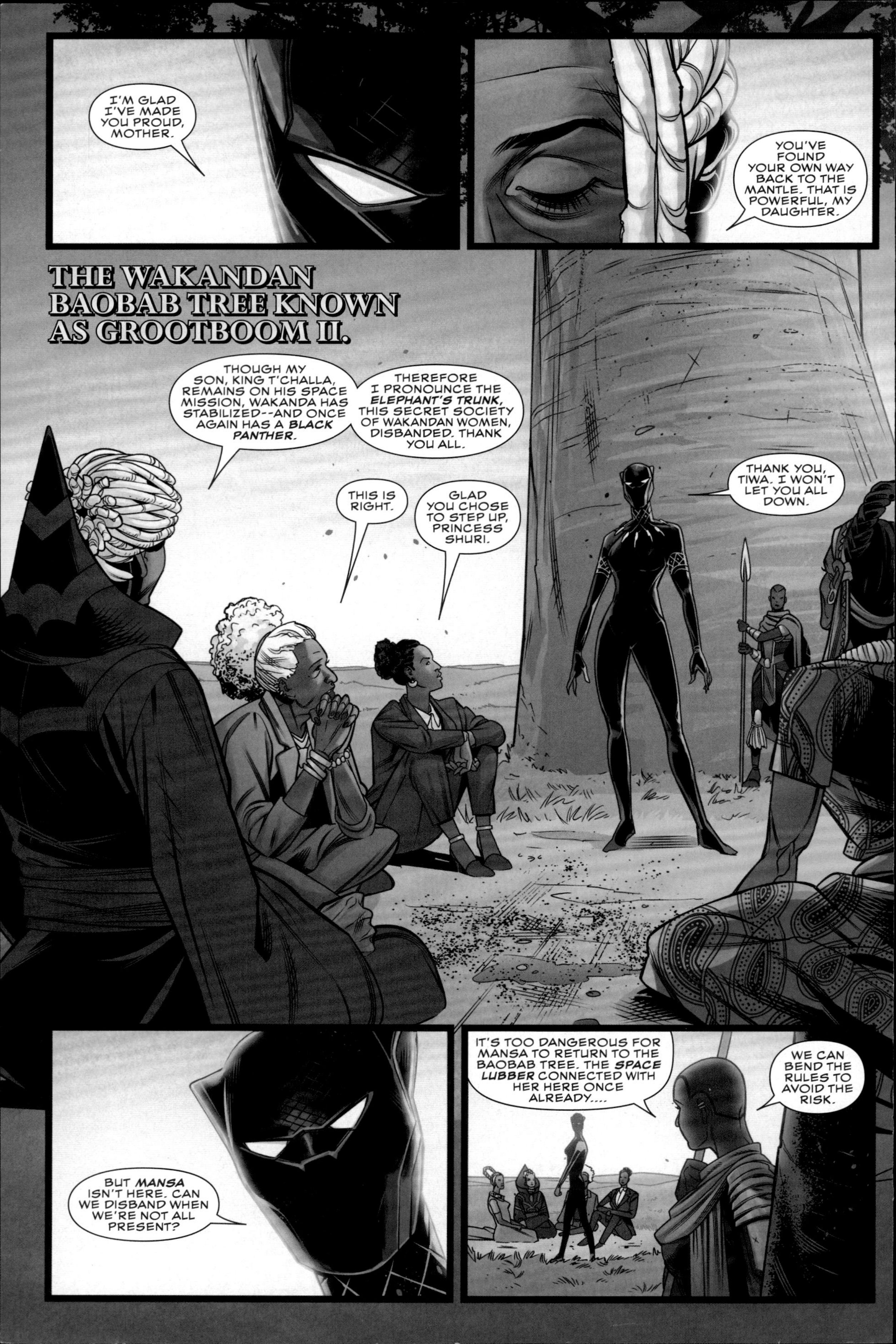
I'M GLAD I'VE MADE YOU PROUD, MOTHER.
YOU'VE FOUND YOUR OWN WAY BACK TO THE MANTLE. THAT IS POWERFUL, MY DAUGHTER.
THE WAKANDAN BAOBAB TREE KNOWN AS GROOTBOOM II.
THOUGH MY SON, KING T'CHALLA, REMAINS ON HIS SPACE MISSION, WAKANDA HAS STABILIZED--AND ONCE AGAIN HAS A BLACK PANTHER.
THEREFORE I PRONOUNCE THE ELEPHANT'S TRUNK, THIS SECRET SOCIETY OF WAKANDAN WOMEN, DISBANDED. THANK YOU ALL.
THIS IS RIGHT.
GLAD YOU CHOSE TO STEP UP, PRINCESS SHURI.
THANK YOU, TIWA. I WON'T LET YOU ALL DOWN.
BUT MANSA ISN'T HERE. CAN WE DISBAND WHEN WE'RE NOT ALL PRESENT?
IT'S TOO DANGEROUS FOR MANSA TO RETURN TO THE BAOBAB TREE. THE SPACE LUBBER CONNECTED WITH HER HERE ONCE ALREADY....
WE CAN BEND THE RULES TO AVOID THE RISK.

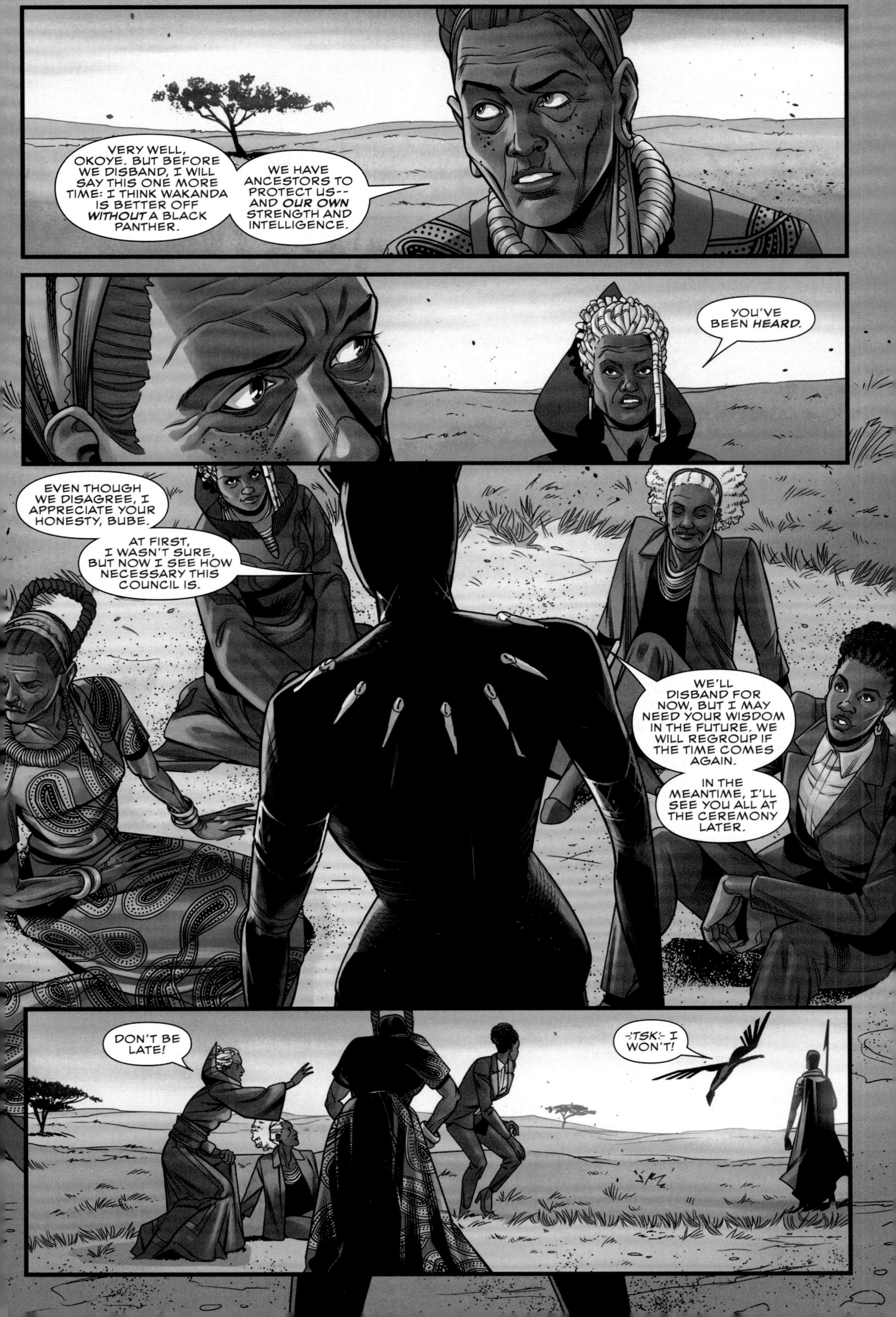
VERY WELL, OKOYE. BUT BEFORE WE DISBAND, I WILL SAY THIS ONE MORE TIME: I THINK WAKANDA IS BETTER OFF WITHOUT A BLACK PANTHER.
WE HAVE ANCESTORS TO PROTECT US-- AND OUR OWN STRENGTH AND INTELLIGENCE.
YOU'VE BEEN HEARD.
EVEN THOUGH WE DISAGREE, I APPRECIATE YOUR HONESTY, BUBE.
AT FIRST, I WASN'T SURE, BUT NOW I SEE HOW NECESSARY THIS COUNCIL IS.
WE'LL DISBAND FOR NOW, BUT I MAY NEED YOUR WISDOM IN THE FUTURE. WE WILL REGROUP IF THE TIME COMES AGAIN.
IN THE MEANTIME, I'LL SEE YOU ALL AT THE CEREMONY LATER.
DON'T BE LATE!
TSK I WON'T!

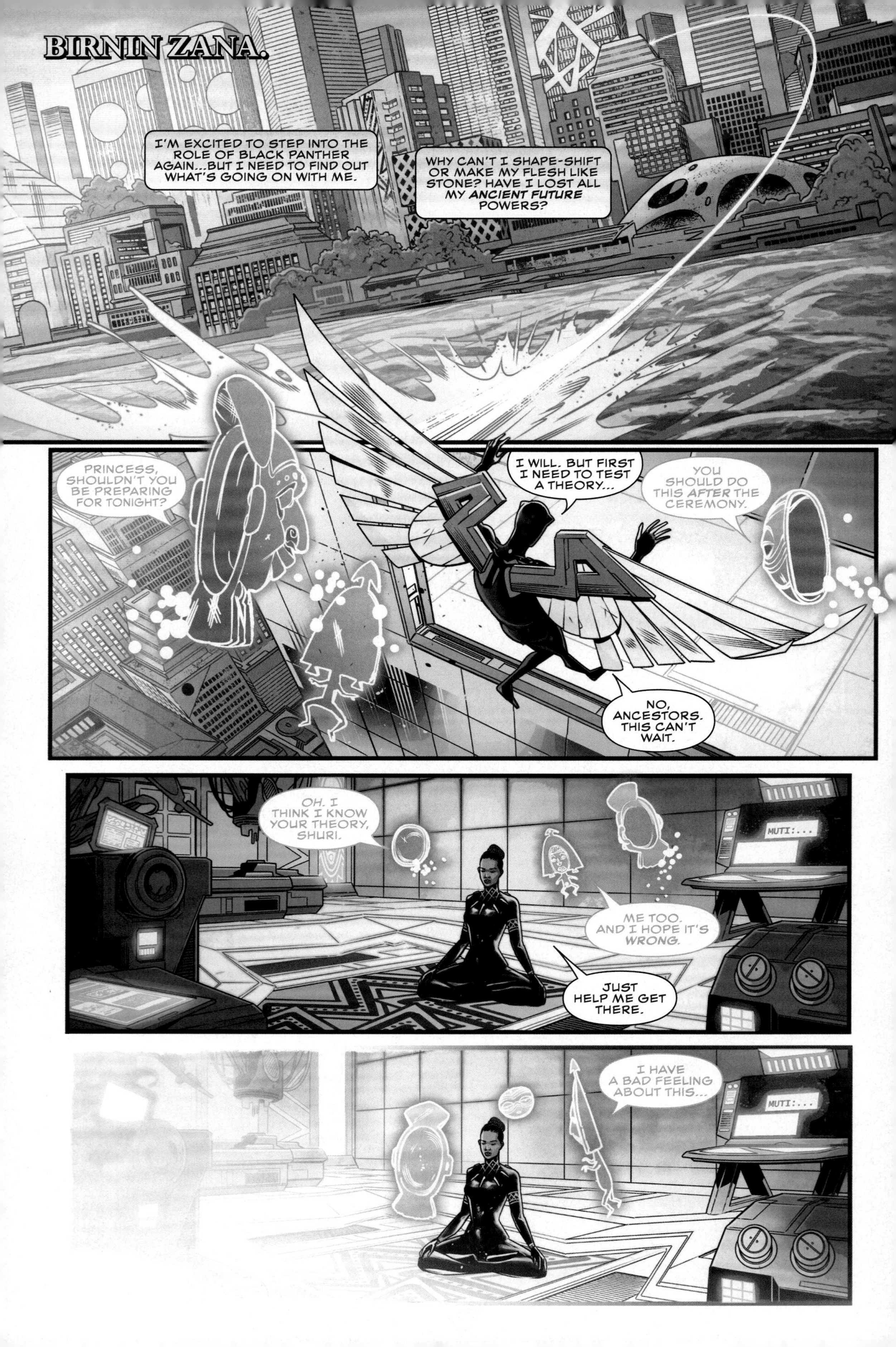
BIRNIN ZANA.
I'M EXCITED TO STEP INTO THE ROLE OF BLACK PANTHER AGAIN...BUT I NEED TO FIND OUT WHAT'S GOING ON WITH ME.
WHY CAN'T I SHAPE-SHIFT OR MAKE MY FLESH LIKE STONE? HAVE I LOST ALL MY ANCIENT FUTURE POWERS?
PRINCESS, SHOULDN'T YOU BE PREPARING FOR TONIGHT?
I WILL. BUT FIRST I NEED TO TEST A THEORY...
YOU SHOULD DO THIS AFTER THE CEREMONY.
NO, ANCESTORS. THIS CAN'T WAIT.
OH. I THINK I KNOW YOUR THEORY, SHURI.
MUTI:...
ME TOO. AND I HOPE IT'S WRONG.
JUST HELP ME GET THERE.
I HAVE A BAD FEELING ABOUT THIS...
MUTI:...

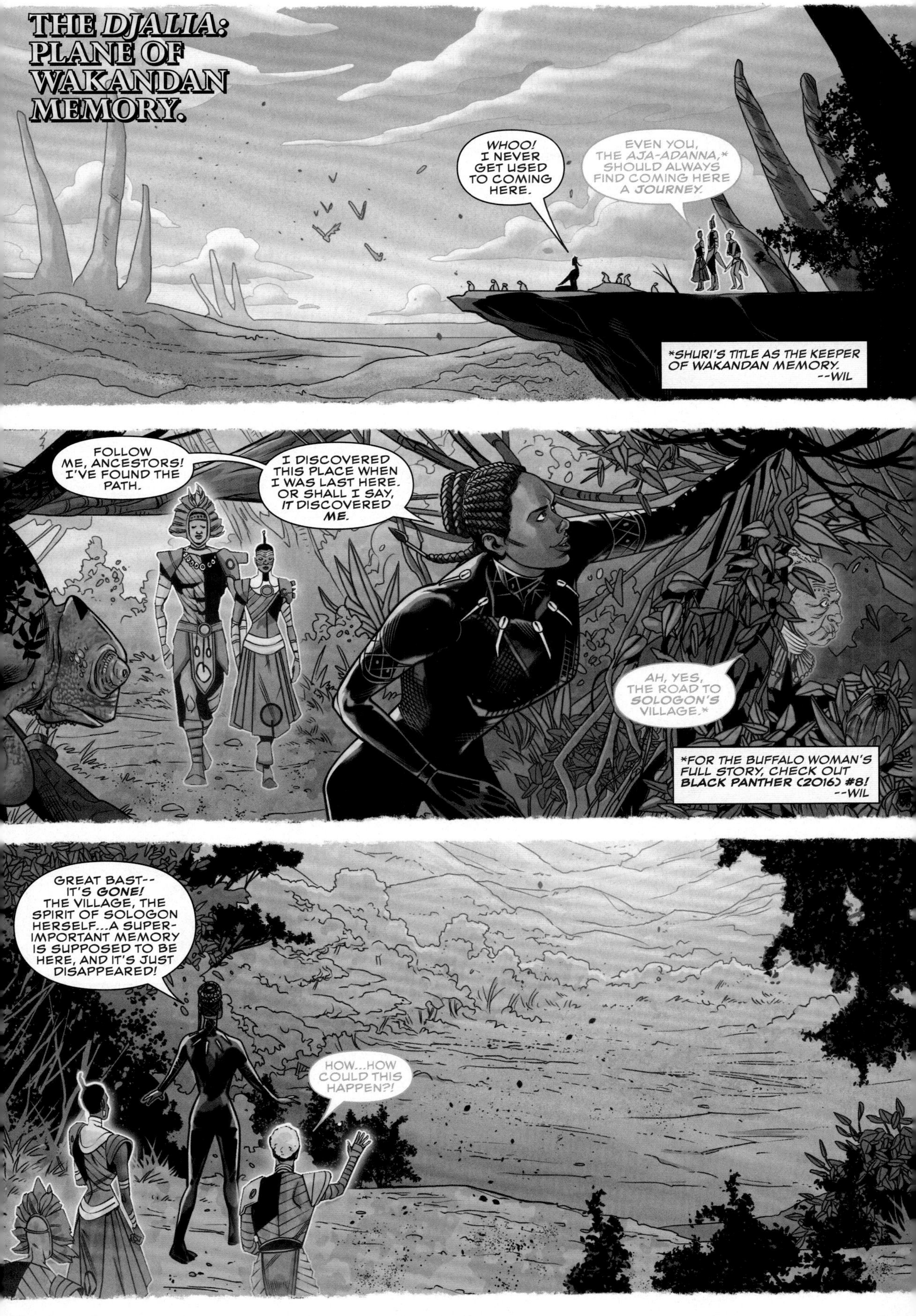
THE DJALIA: PLANE OF WAKANDAN MEMORY.
WHOO! I NEVER GET USED TO COMING HERE.
EVEN YOU, THE AJA-ADANNA,* SHOULD ALWAYS FIND COMING HERE A JOURNEY.
*SHURI'S TITLE AS THE KEEPER OF WAKANDAN MEMORY. --WIL
FOLLOW ME, ANCESTORS! I'VE FOUND THE PATH.
I DISCOVERED THIS PLACE WHEN I WAS LAST HERE. OR SHALL I SAY, IT DISCOVERED ME.
AH, YES, THE ROAD TO SOLOGON'S VILLAGE.*
*FOR THE BUFFALO WOMAN'S FULL STORY, CHECK OUT BLACK PANTHER (2016) #8! --WIL
GREAT BAST-- IT'S GONE! THE VILLAGE, THE SPIRIT OF SOLOGON HERSELF...A SUPER-IMPORTANT MEMORY IS SUPPOSED TO BE HERE, AND IT'S JUST DISAPPEARED!
HOW...HOW COULD THIS HAPPEN?!

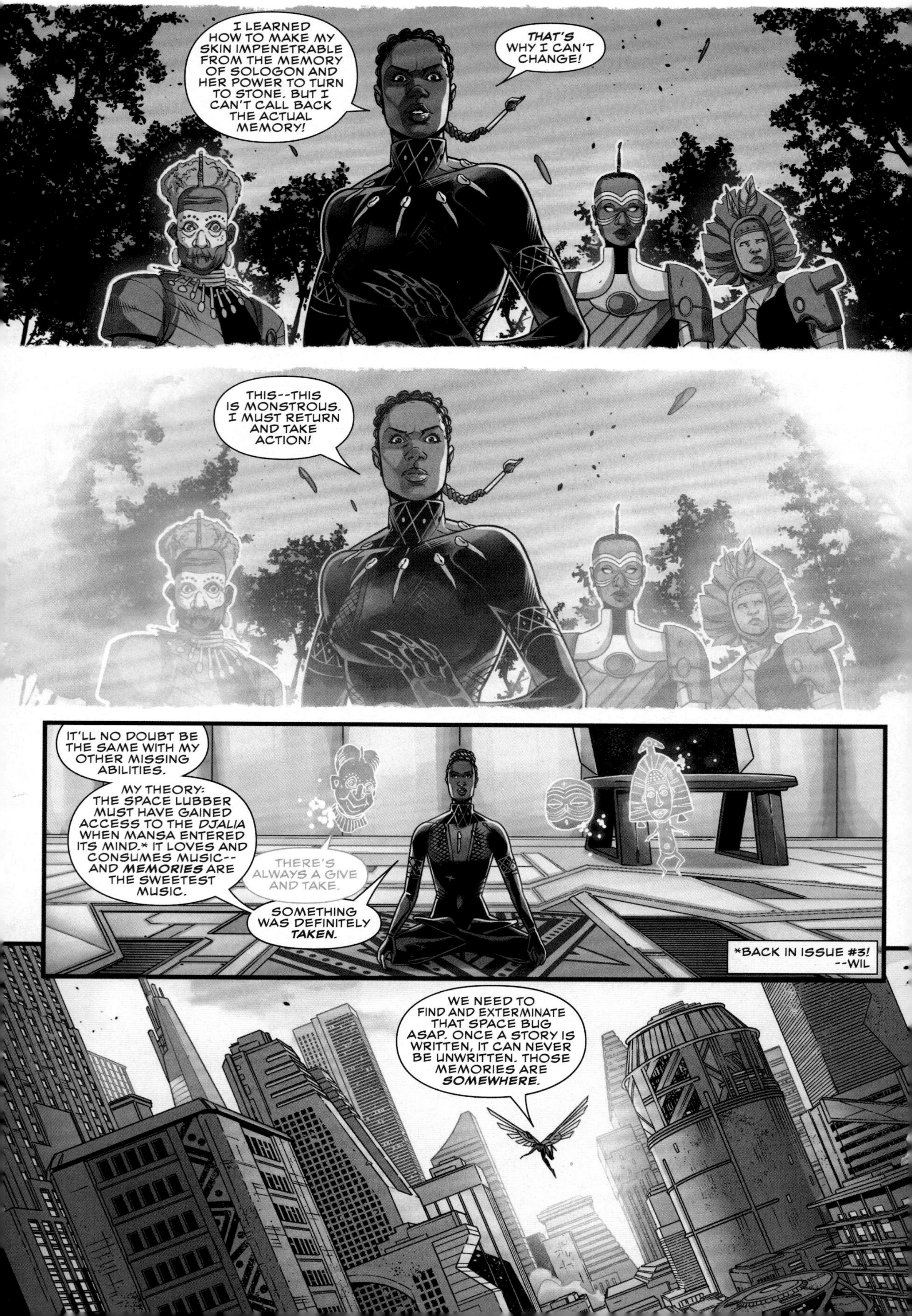
I LEARNED HOW TO MAKE MY SKIN IMPENETRABLE FROM THE MEMORY OF SOLOGON AND HER POWER TO TURN TO STONE. BUT I CAN'T CALL BACK THE ACTUAL MEMORY!
THAT'S WHY I CAN'T CHANGE!
THIS--THIS IS MONSTROUS. I MUST RETURN AND TAKE ACTION!
IT'LL NO DOUBT BE THE SAME WITH MY OTHER MISSING ABILITIES.
MY THEORY: THE SPACE LUBBER MUST HAVE GAINED ACCESS TO THE DJALIA WHEN MANSA ENTERED ITS MIND.* IT LOVES AND CONSUMES MUSIC-- AND MEMORIES ARE THE SWEETEST MUSIC.
THERE'S ALWAYS A GIVE AND TAKE.
SOMETHING WAS DEFINITELY TAKEN.
*BACK IN ISSUE #3! --WIL
WE NEED TO FIND AND EXTERMINATE THAT SPACE BUG ASAP. ONCE A STORY IS WRITTEN, IT CAN NEVER BE UNWRITTEN. THOSE MEMORIES ARE SOMEWHERE.

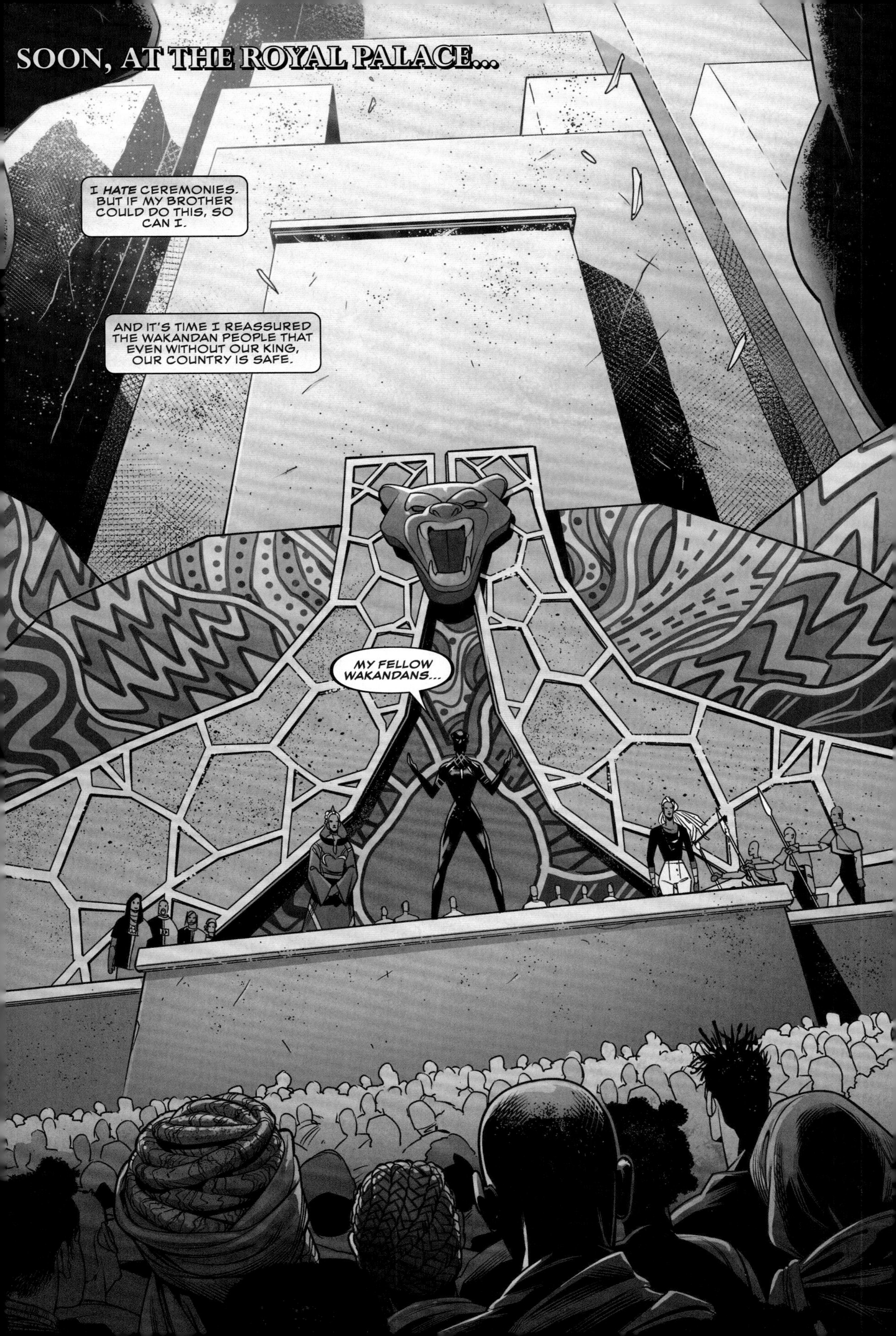
SOON, AT THE ROYAL PALACE...
I HATE CEREMONIES. BUT IF MY BROTHER COULD DO THIS, SO CAN I.
AND IT'S TIME I REASSURED THE WAKANDAN PEOPLE THAT EVEN WITHOUT OUR KING, OUR COUNTRY IS SAFE.
MY FELLOW WAKANDANS...

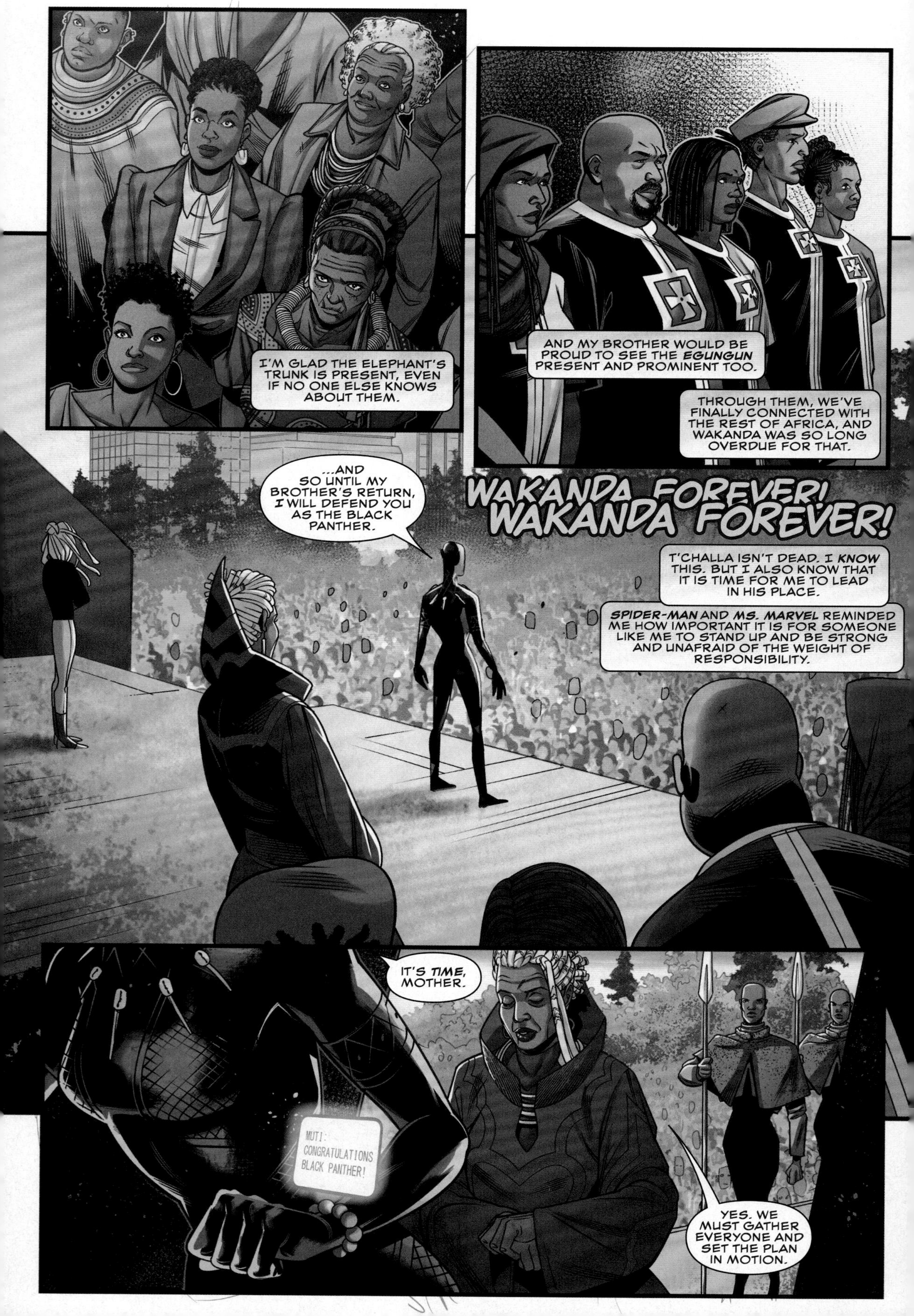
I'M GLAD THE ELEPHANT'S TRUNK IS PRESENT, EVEN IF NO ONE ELSE KNOWS ABOUT THEM.
AND MY BROTHER WOULD BE PROUD TO SEE THE EGUNGUN PRESENT AND PROMINENT TOO.
THROUGH THEM, WE'VE FINALLY CONNECTED WITH THE REST OF AFRICA, AND WAKANDA WAS SO LONG OVERDUE FOR THAT.
...AND SO UNTIL MY BROTHER'S RETURN, I WILL DEFEND YOU AS THE BLACK PANTHER.
WAKANDA FOREVER! WAKANDA FOREVER!
T'CHALLA ISN'T DEAD. I KNOW THIS. BUT I ALSO KNOW THAT IT IS TIME FOR ME TO LEAD IN HIS PLACE.
SPIDER-MAN AND MS. MARVEL REMINDED ME HOW IMPORTANT IT IS FOR SOMEONE LIKE ME TO STAND UP AND BE STRONG AND UNAFRAID OF THE WEIGHT OF RESPONSIBILITY.
IT'S TIME, MOTHER.
MUTI: CONGRATULATIONS BLACK PANTHER!
YES. WE MUST GATHER EVERYONE AND SET THE PLAN IN MOTION.

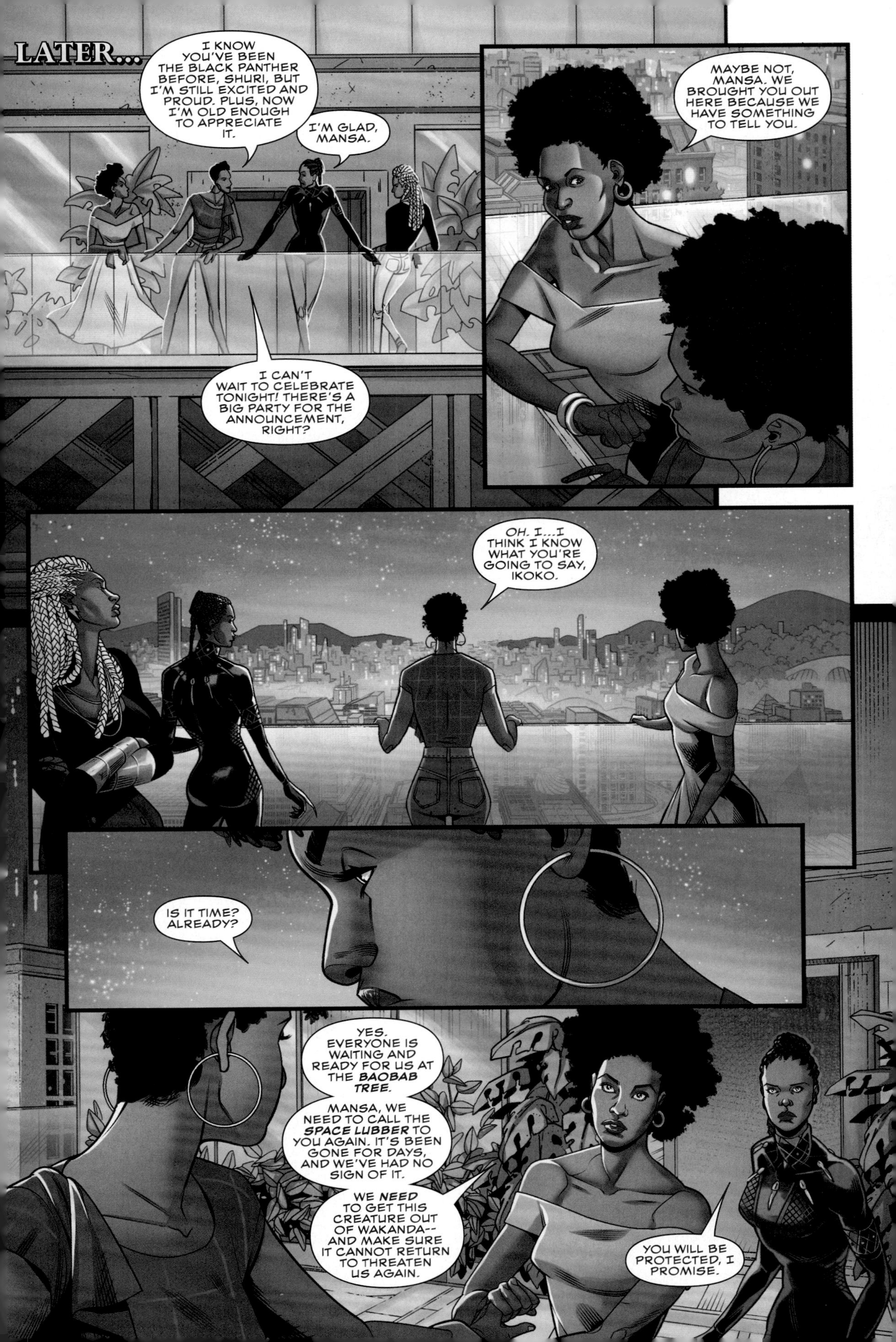
LATER...
I KNOW YOU'VE BEEN THE BLACK PANTHER BEFORE, SHURI, BUT I'M STILL EXCITED AND PROUD. PLUS, NOW I'M OLD ENOUGH TO APPRECIATE IT.
I'M GLAD, MANSA.
I CAN'T WAIT TO CELEBRATE TONIGHT! THERE'S A BIG PARTY FOR THE ANNOUNCEMENT, RIGHT?
MAYBE NOT, MANSA. WE BROUGHT YOU OUT HERE BECAUSE WE HAVE SOMETHING TO TELL YOU.
OH. I...I THINK I KNOW WHAT YOU'RE GOING TO SAY, IKOKO.
IS IT TIME? ALREADY?
YES. EVERYONE IS WAITING AND READY FOR US AT THE *BAOBAB TREE*.
MANSA, WE NEED TO CALL THE *SPACE LUBBER* TO YOU AGAIN. IT'S BEEN GONE FOR DAYS, AND WE'VE HAD NO SIGN OF IT.
WE *NEED* TO GET THIS CREATURE OUT OF WAKANDA-- AND MAKE SURE IT CANNOT RETURN TO THREATEN US AGAIN.
YOU WILL BE PROTECTED, I PROMISE.

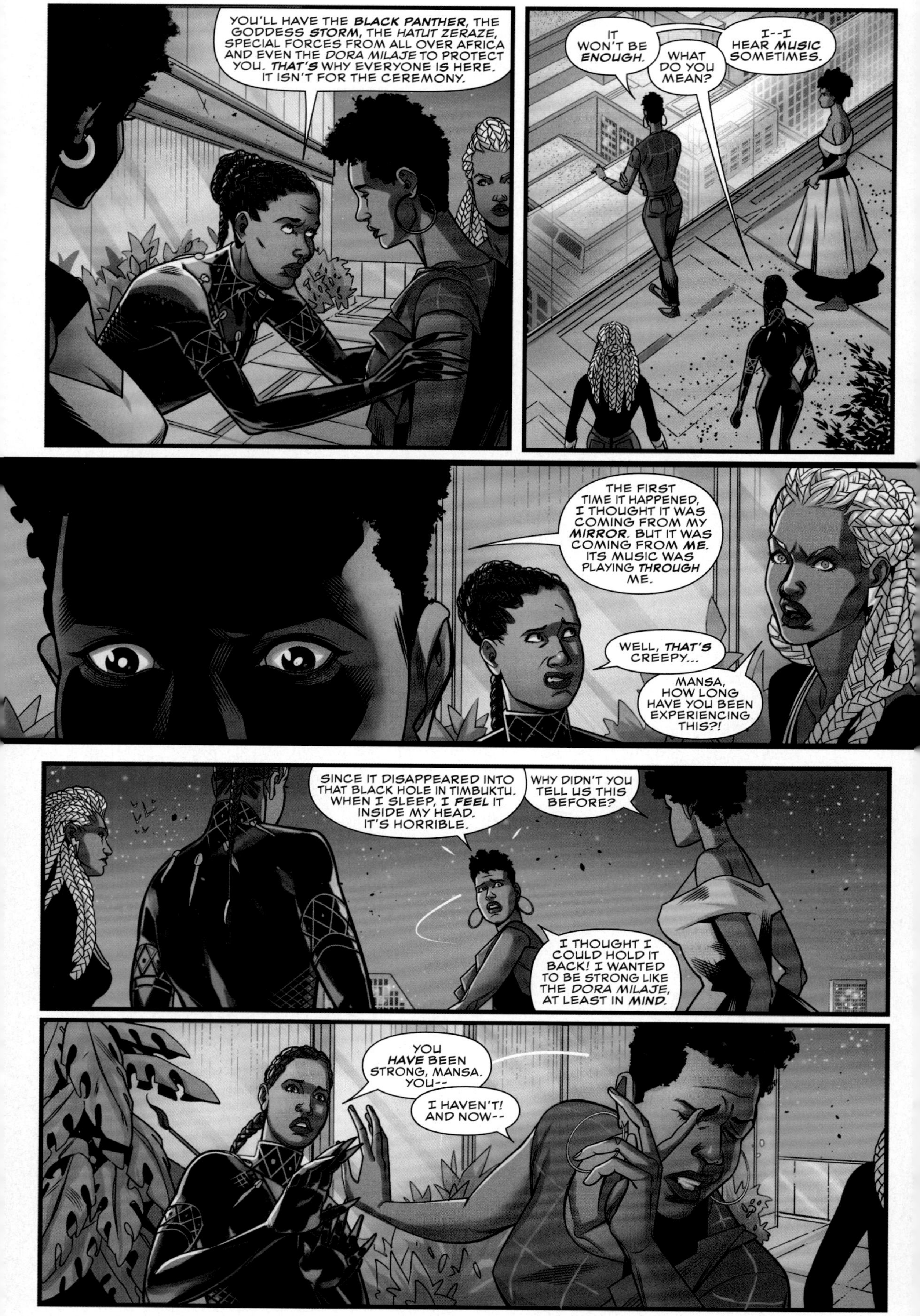
YOU'LL HAVE THE BLACK PANTHER, THE GODDESS STORM, THE HATUT ZERAZE, SPECIAL FORCES FROM ALL OVER AFRICA AND EVEN THE DORA MILAJE TO PROTECT YOU. THAT'S WHY EVERYONE IS HERE. IT ISN'T FOR THE CEREMONY.
IT WON'T BE ENOUGH.
WHAT DO YOU MEAN?
I--I HEAR MUSIC SOMETIMES.
THE FIRST TIME IT HAPPENED, I THOUGHT IT WAS COMING FROM MY MIRROR. BUT IT WAS COMING FROM ME. ITS MUSIC WAS PLAYING THROUGH ME.
WELL, THAT'S CREEPY...
MANSA, HOW LONG HAVE YOU BEEN EXPERIENCING THIS?!
SINCE IT DISAPPEARED INTO THAT BLACK HOLE IN TIMBUKTU. WHEN I SLEEP, I FEEL IT INSIDE MY HEAD. IT'S HORRIBLE.
WHY DIDN'T YOU TELL US THIS BEFORE?
I THOUGHT I COULD HOLD IT BACK! I WANTED TO BE STRONG LIKE THE DORA MILAJE, AT LEAST IN MIND.
YOU HAVE BEEN STRONG, MANSA. YOU--
I HAVEN'T! AND NOW--

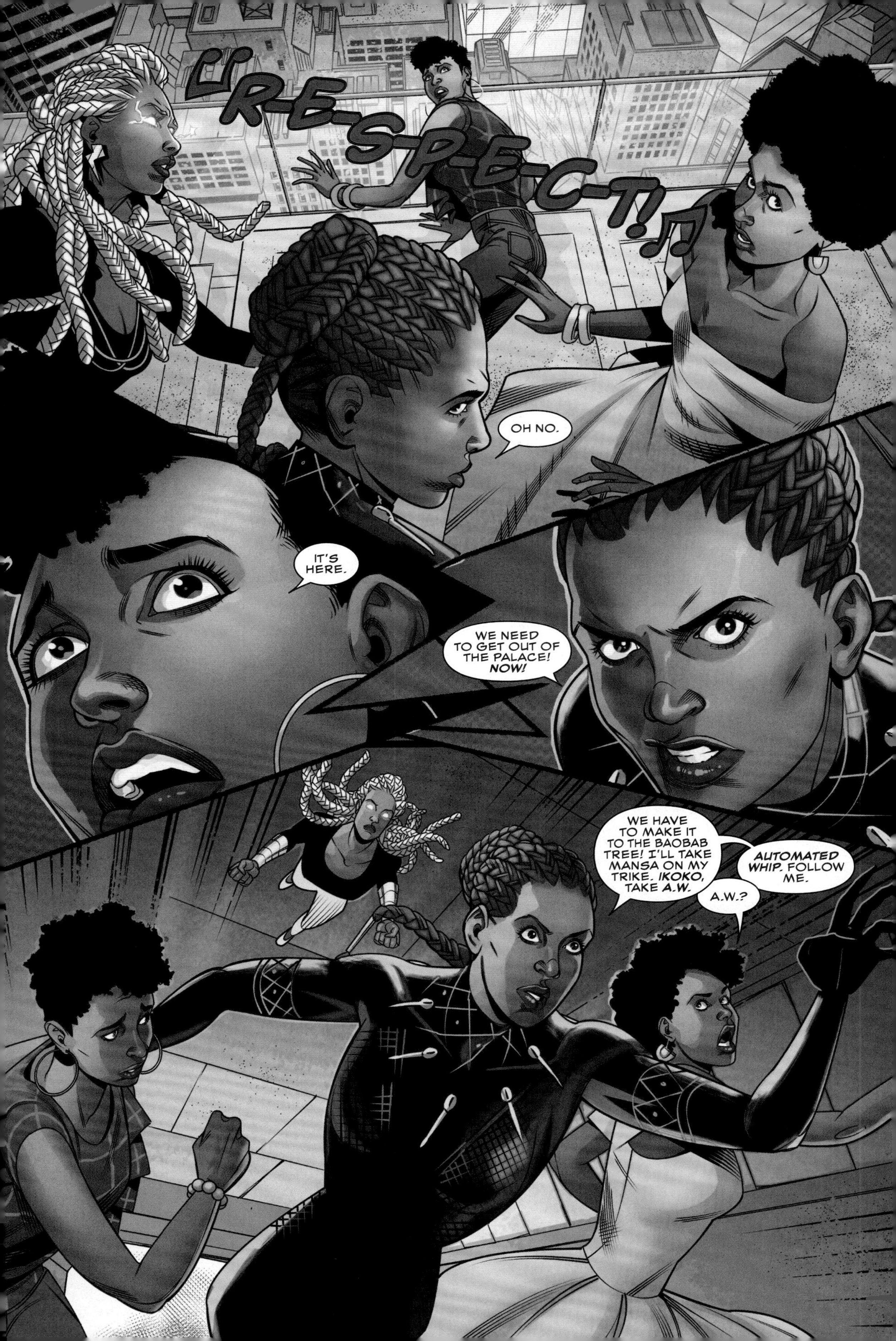
R-E-S-P-E-C-T!
OH NO.
IT'S HERE.
WE NEED TO GET OUT OF THE PALACE! *NOW!*
WE HAVE TO MAKE IT TO THE BAOBAB TREE! I'LL TAKE MANSA ON MY TRIKE. *IKOKO,* TAKE A.W.
A.W.?
AUTOMATED WHIP. FOLLOW ME.

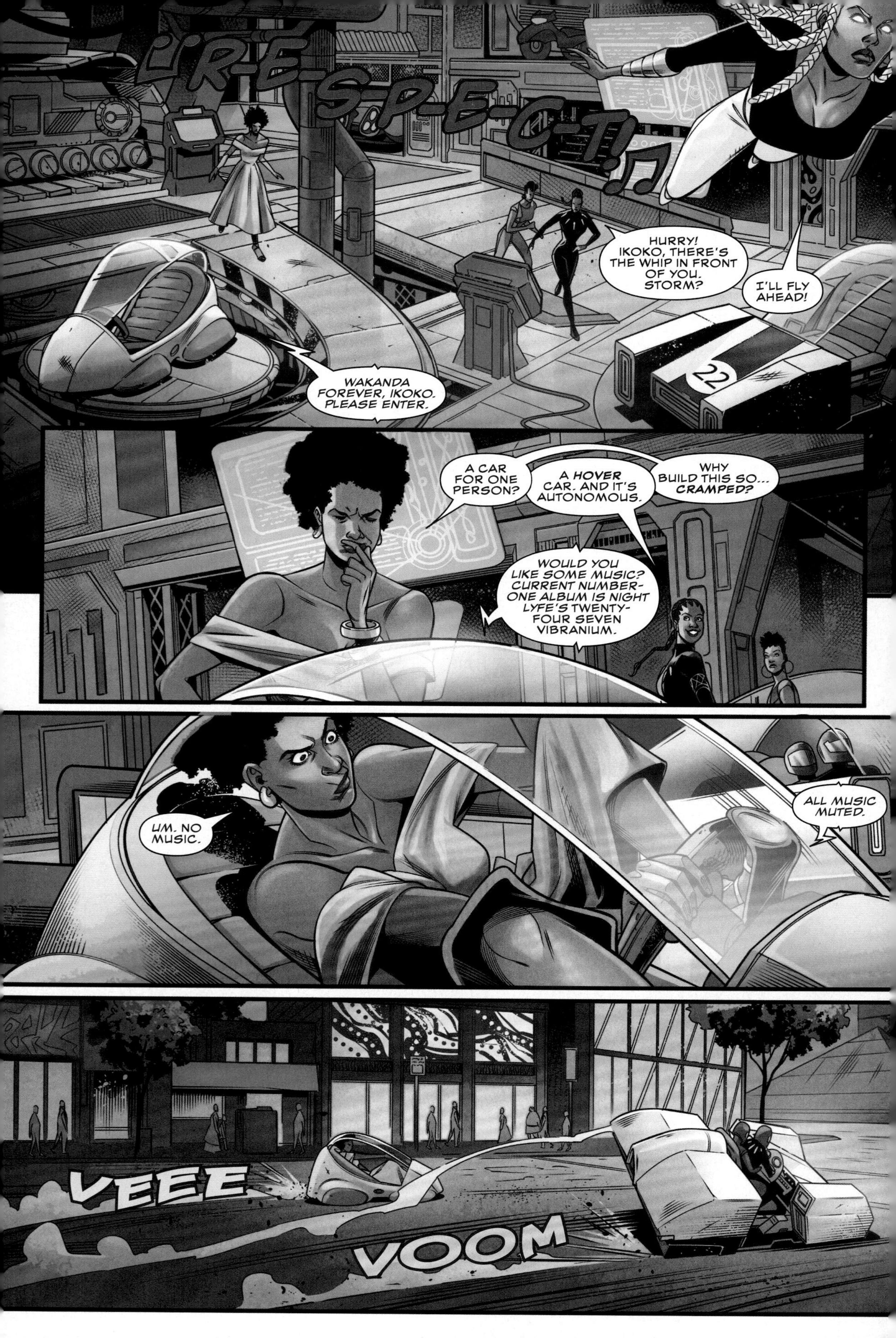
R-E-S-P-E-C-T!
HURRY! IKOKO, THERE'S THE WHIP IN FRONT OF YOU. STORM?
I'LL FLY AHEAD!
WAKANDA FOREVER, IKOKO. PLEASE ENTER.
22
A CAR FOR ONE PERSON?
A *HOVER* CAR. AND IT'S AUTONOMOUS.
WHY BUILD THIS SO... *CRAMPED?*
WOULD YOU LIKE SOME MUSIC? CURRENT NUMBER-ONE ALBUM IS NIGHT LYFE'S TWENTY-FOUR SEVEN VIBRANIUM.
UM. NO MUSIC.
ALL MUSIC MUTED.
VEEE
VOOM

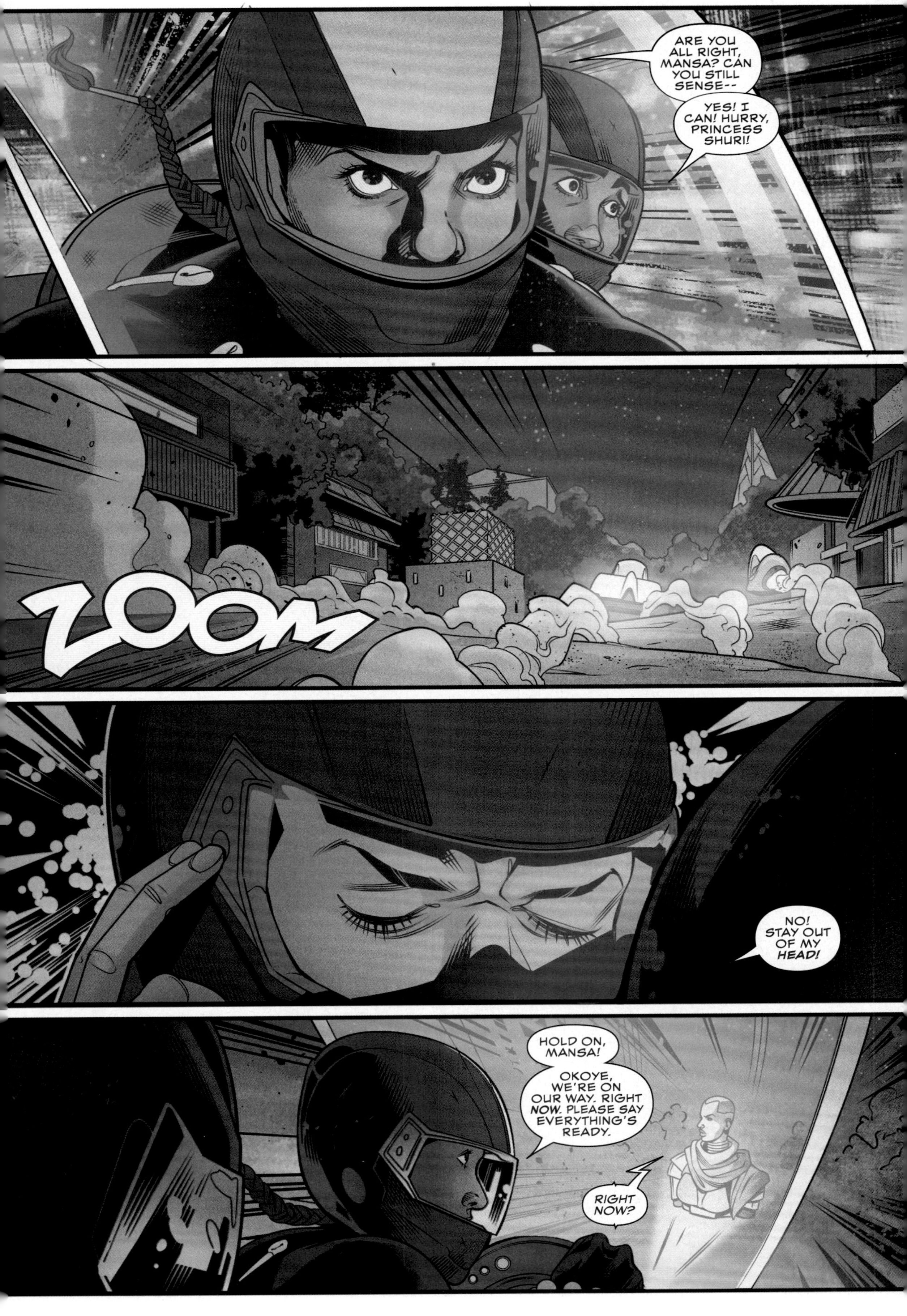
ARE YOU ALL RIGHT, MANSA? CAN YOU STILL SENSE--
YES! I CAN! HURRY, PRINCESS SHURI!
ZOOM
NO! STAY OUT OF MY HEAD!
HOLD ON, MANSA!
OKOYE, WE'RE ON OUR WAY. RIGHT NOW. PLEASE SAY EVERYTHING'S READY.
RIGHT NOW?

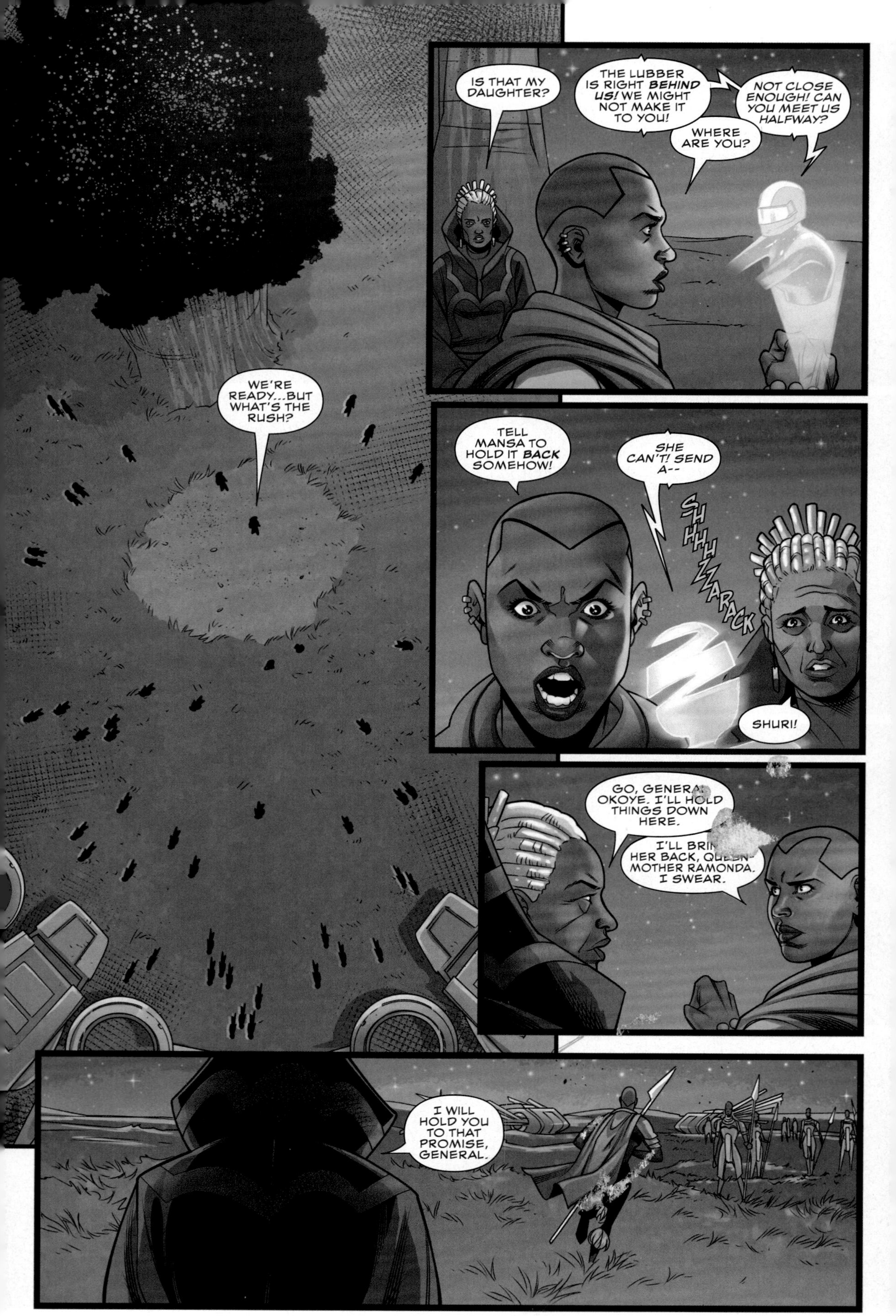

WE'RE READY...BUT WHAT'S THE RUSH?
IS THAT MY DAUGHTER?
THE LUBBER IS RIGHT BEHIND US! WE MIGHT NOT MAKE IT TO YOU!
WHERE ARE YOU?
NOT CLOSE ENOUGH! CAN YOU MEET US HALFWAY?
TELL MANSA TO HOLD IT BACK SOMEHOW!
SHE CAN'T! SEND A--
SHHHZZARACK
SHURI!
GO, GENERA OKOYE. I'LL HOLD THINGS DOWN HERE.
I'LL BRIN HER BACK, QUEEN-MOTHER RAMONDA. I SWEAR.
I WILL HOLD YOU TO THAT PROMISE, GENERAL.

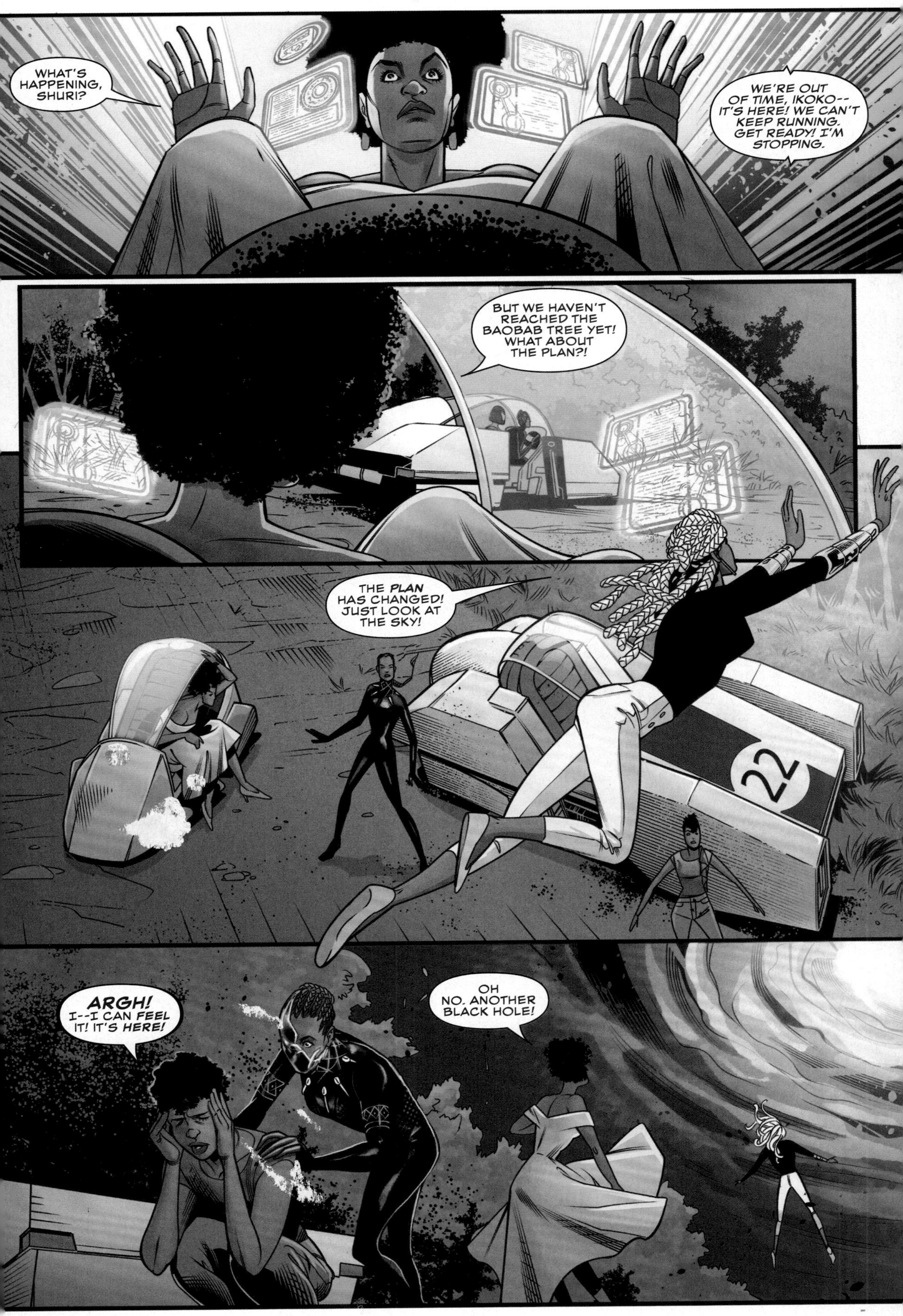
WHAT'S HAPPENING, SHURI!?
WE'RE OUT OF TIME, IKOKO-- IT'S HERE! WE CAN'T KEEP RUNNING. GET READY! I'M STOPPING.
BUT WE HAVEN'T REACHED THE BAOBAB TREE YET! WHAT ABOUT THE PLAN?!
THE PLAN HAS CHANGED! JUST LOOK AT THE SKY!
22
ARGH! I--I CAN FEEL IT! IT'S HERE!
OH NO. ANOTHER BLACK HOLE!

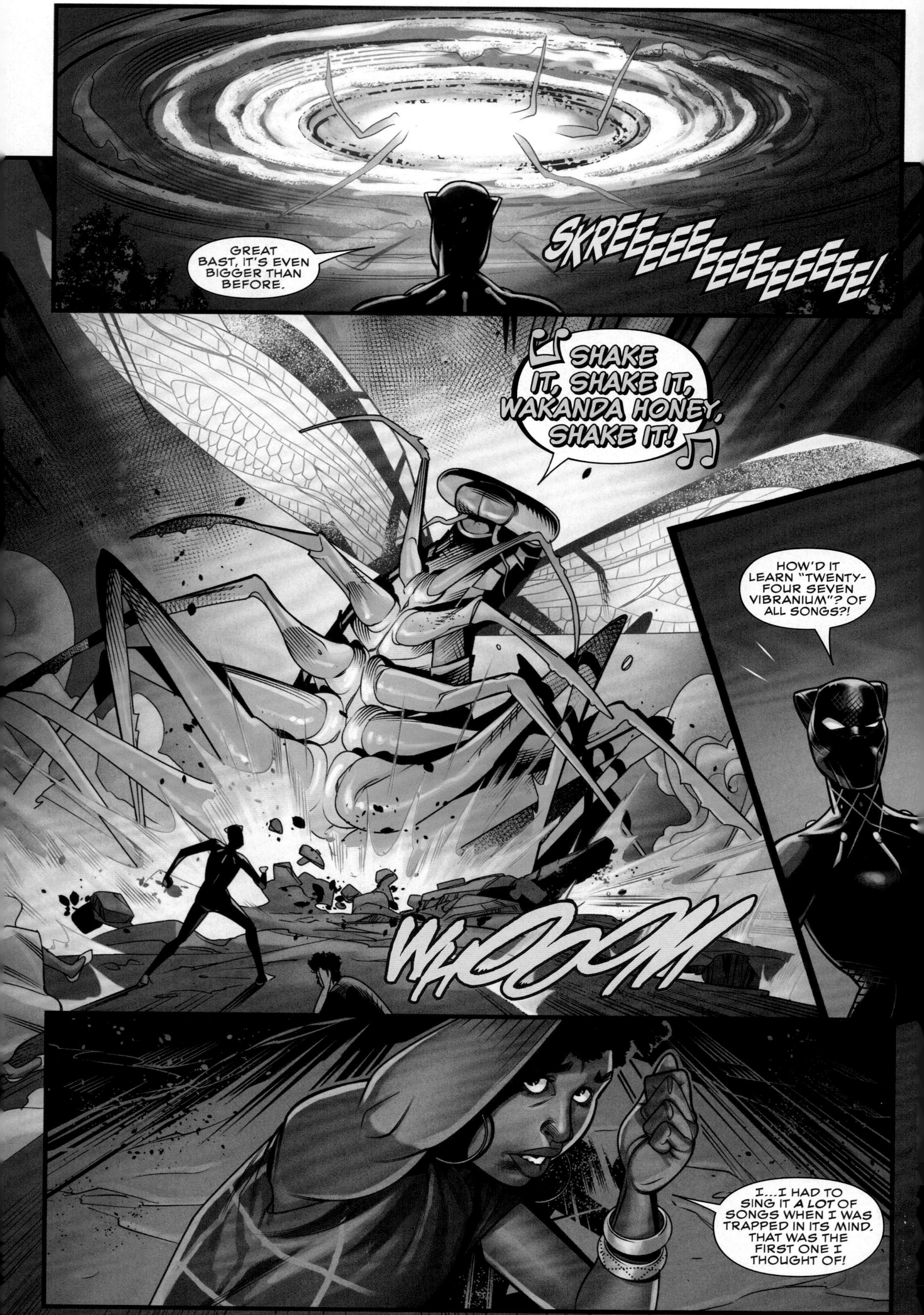
GREAT BAST, IT'S EVEN BIGGER THAN BEFORE.
SKREEEEEEEEEEEEEEEE!
SHAKE IT, SHAKE IT, WAKANDA HONEY, SHAKE IT!
HOW'D IT LEARN "TWENTY-FOUR SEVEN VIBRANIUM"? OF ALL SONGS?!
WHOOOM
I...I HAD TO SING IT A LOT OF SONGS WHEN I WAS TRAPPED IN ITS MIND. THAT WAS THE FIRST ONE I THOUGHT OF!

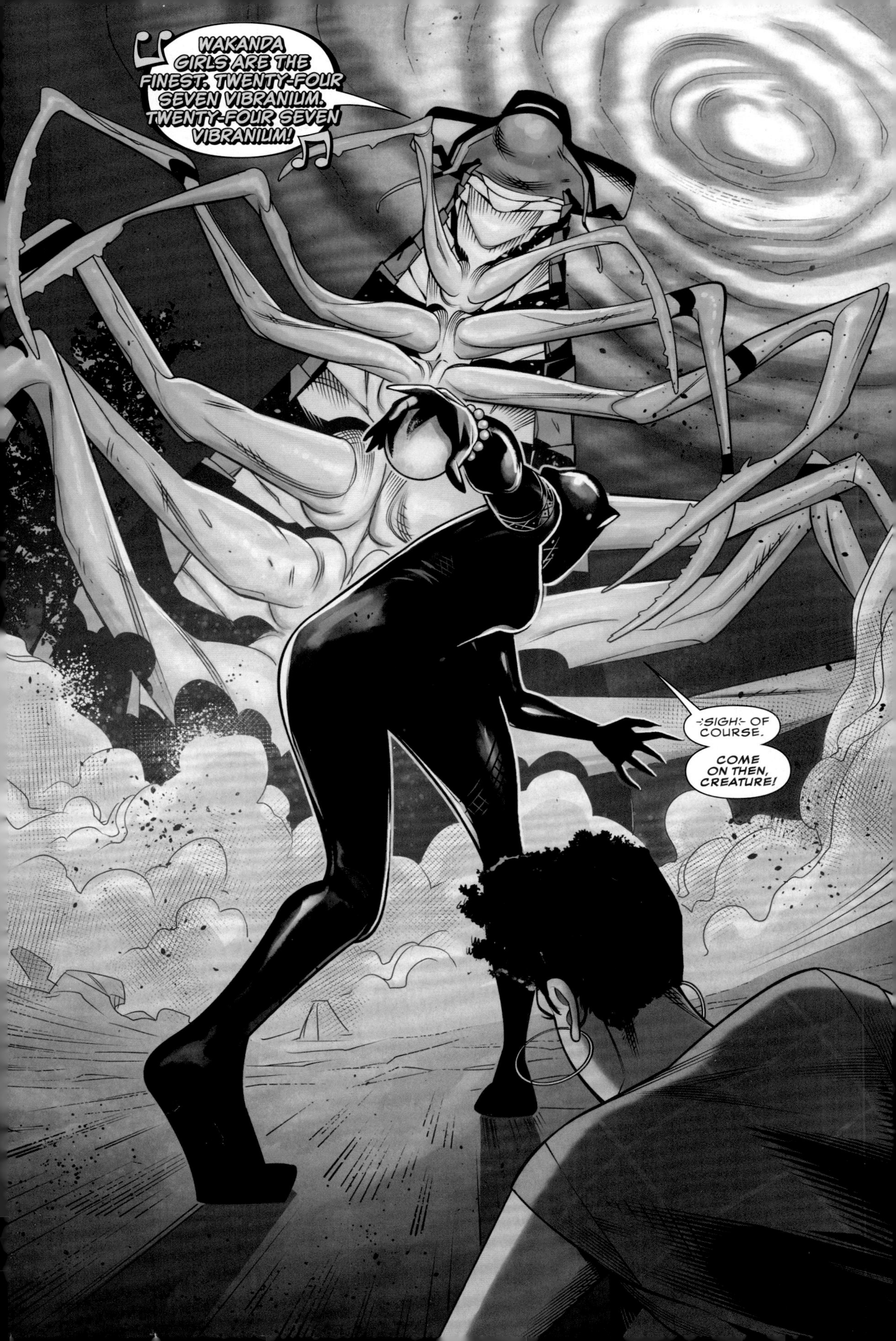
WAKANDA GIRLS ARE THE FINEST. TWENTY-FOUR SEVEN VIBRANIUM. TWENTY-FOUR SEVEN VIBRANIUM!
-SIGH- OF COURSE.
COME ON THEN, CREATURE!

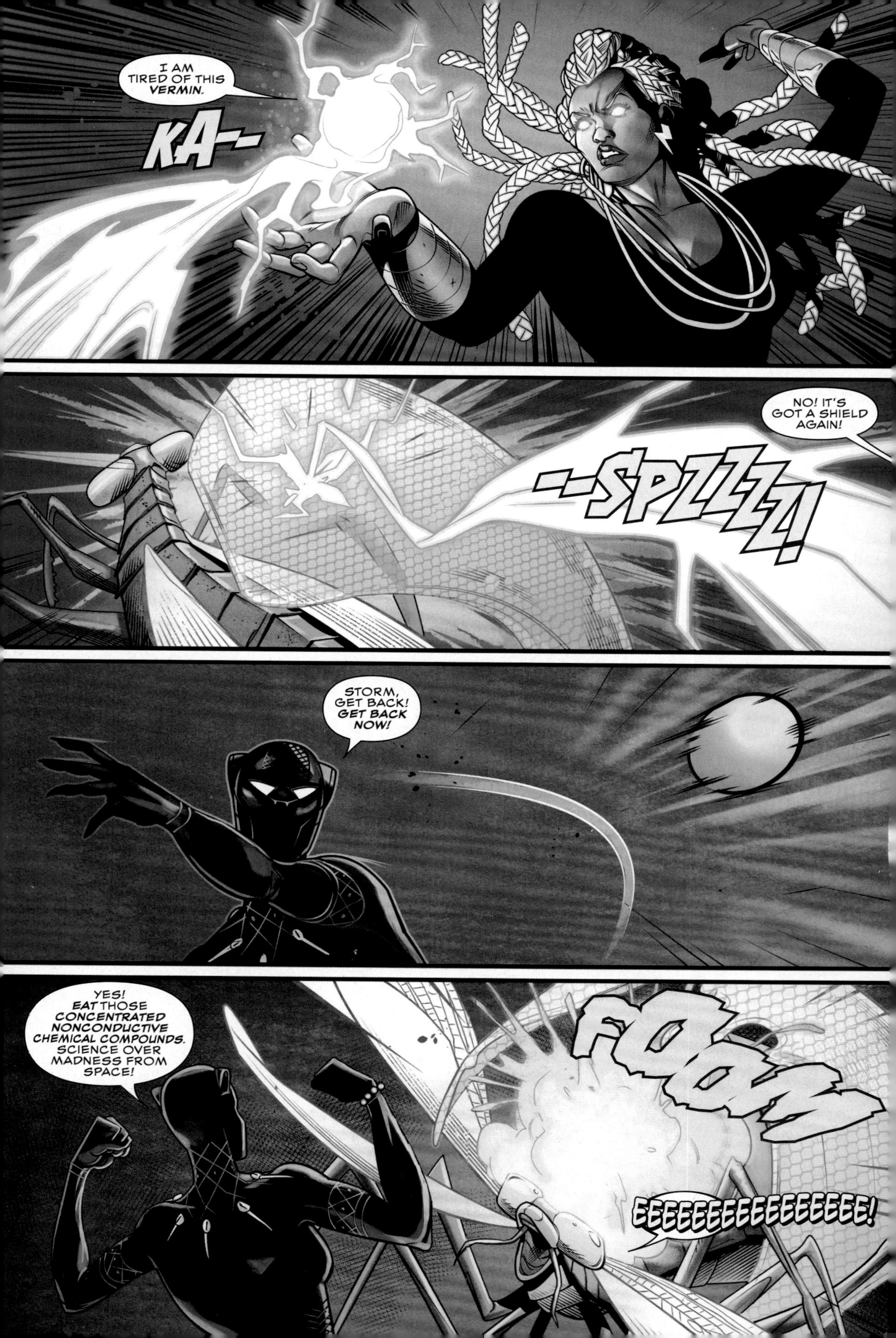

I AM TIRED OF THIS VERMIN.
KA--
NO! IT'S GOT A SHIELD AGAIN!
--SPZZZZ!
STORM, GET BACK! GET BACK NOW!
YES! EAT THOSE CONCENTRATED NONCONDUCTIVE CHEMICAL COMPOUNDS. SCIENCE OVER MADNESS FROM SPACE!
FOOM
EEEEEEEEEEEEEEEEE!

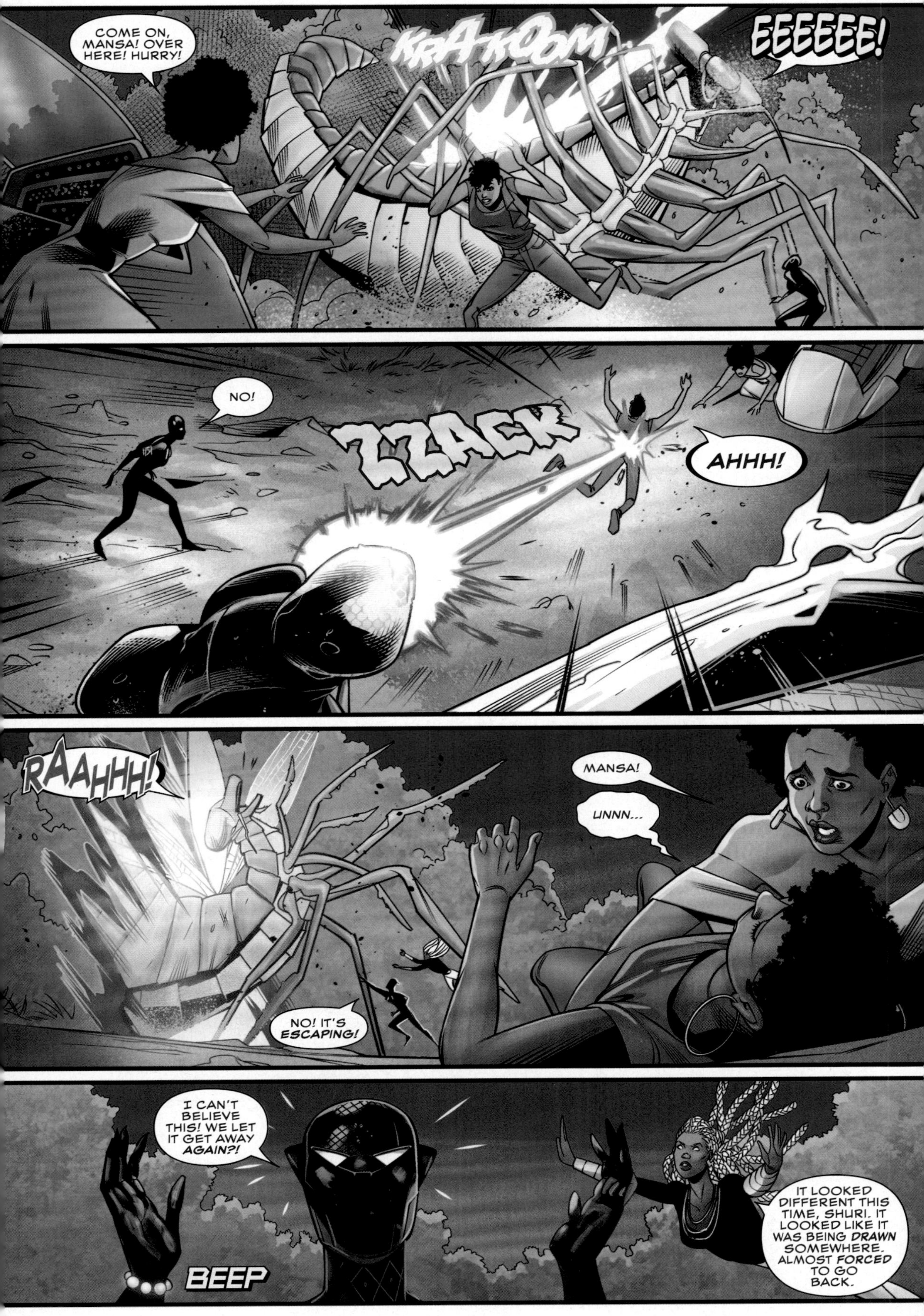
COME ON, MANSA! OVER HERE! HURRY!
KRAKOOM
EEEEEEE!
NO!
ZZACK
AHHH!
RAAHHH!
MANSA!
UNNN...
NO! IT'S ESCAPING!
I CAN'T BELIEVE THIS! WE LET IT GET AWAY AGAIN?!
BEEP
IT LOOKED DIFFERENT THIS TIME, SHURI. IT LOOKED LIKE IT WAS BEING DRAWN SOMEWHERE. ALMOST FORCED TO GO BACK.

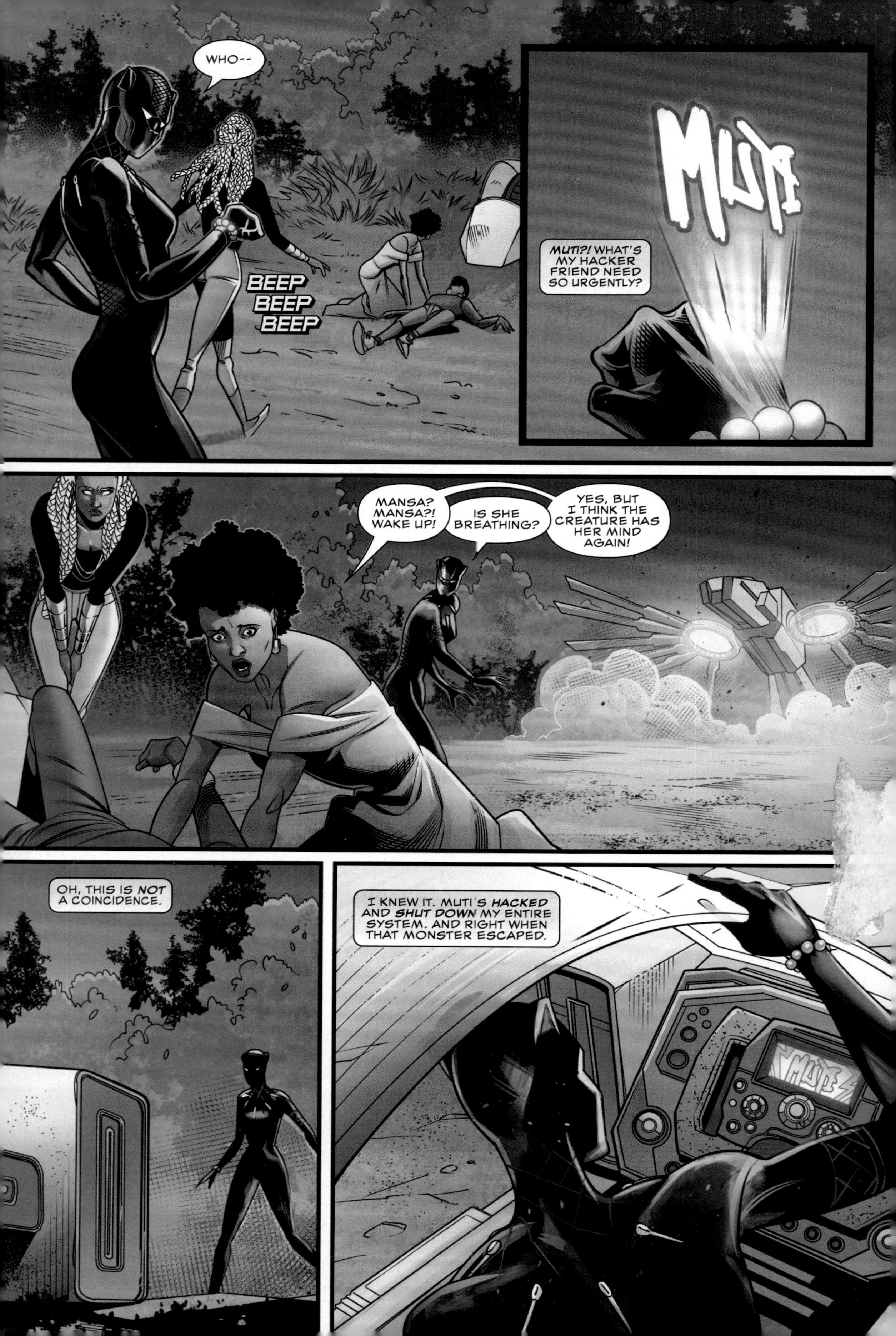
WHO--
BEEP BEEP BEEP
MUTI
MUTI?! WHAT'S MY HACKER FRIEND NEED SO URGENTLY?
MANSA? MANSA?! WAKE UP!
IS SHE BREATHING?
YES, BUT I THINK THE CREATURE HAS HER MIND AGAIN!
OH, THIS IS NOT A COINCIDENCE.
I KNEW IT. MUTI'S HACKED AND SHUT DOWN MY ENTIRE SYSTEM. AND RIGHT WHEN THAT MONSTER ESCAPED.
MUTI

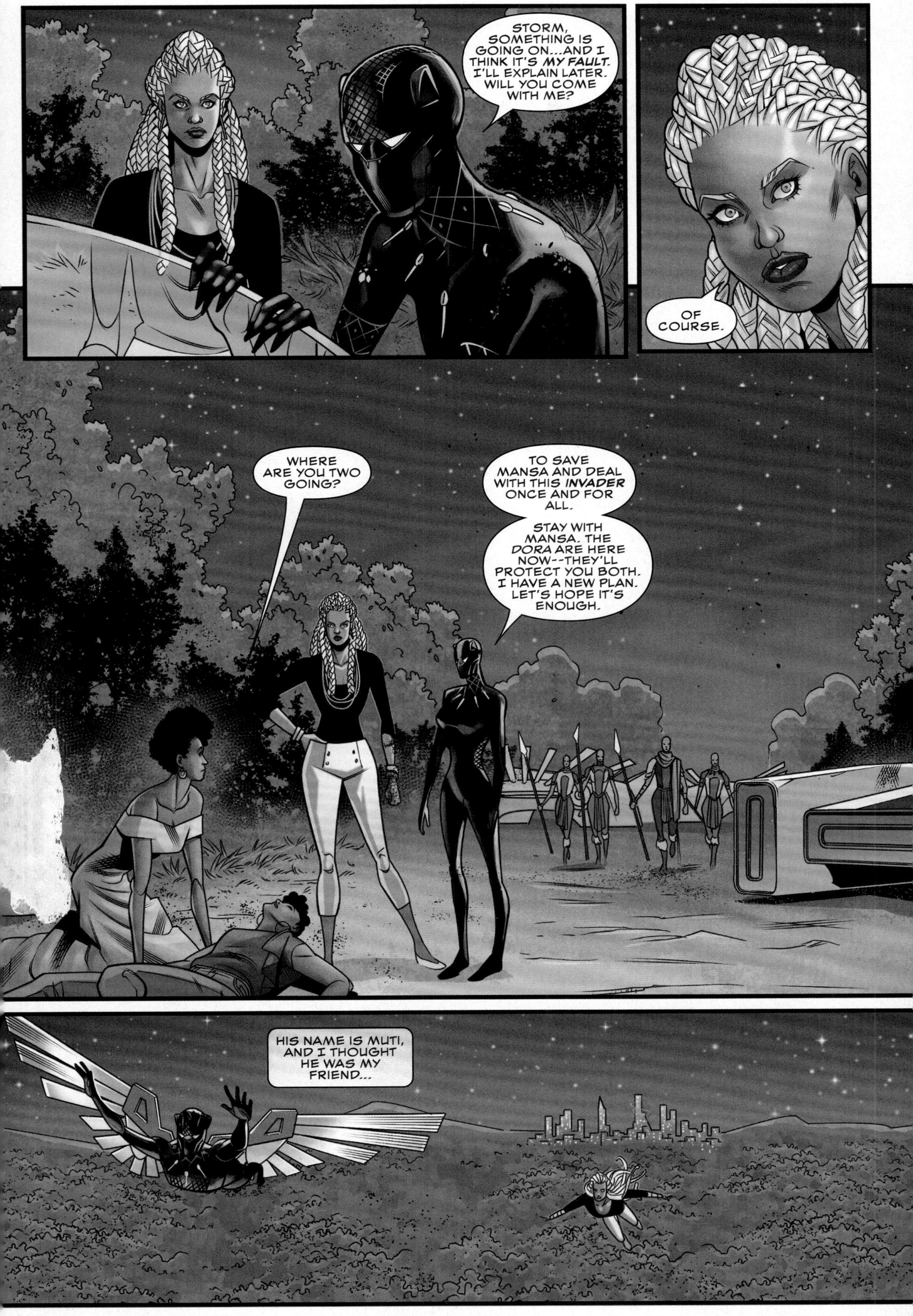
STORM, SOMETHING IS GOING ON...AND I THINK IT'S MY FAULT. I'LL EXPLAIN LATER. WILL YOU COME WITH ME?
OF COURSE.
WHERE ARE YOU TWO GOING?
TO SAVE MANSA AND DEAL WITH THIS INVADER ONCE AND FOR ALL.
STAY WITH MANSA. THE DORA ARE HERE NOW--THEY'LL PROTECT YOU BOTH. I HAVE A NEW PLAN. LET'S HOPE IT'S ENOUGH.
HIS NAME IS MUTI, AND I THOUGHT HE WAS MY FRIEND...

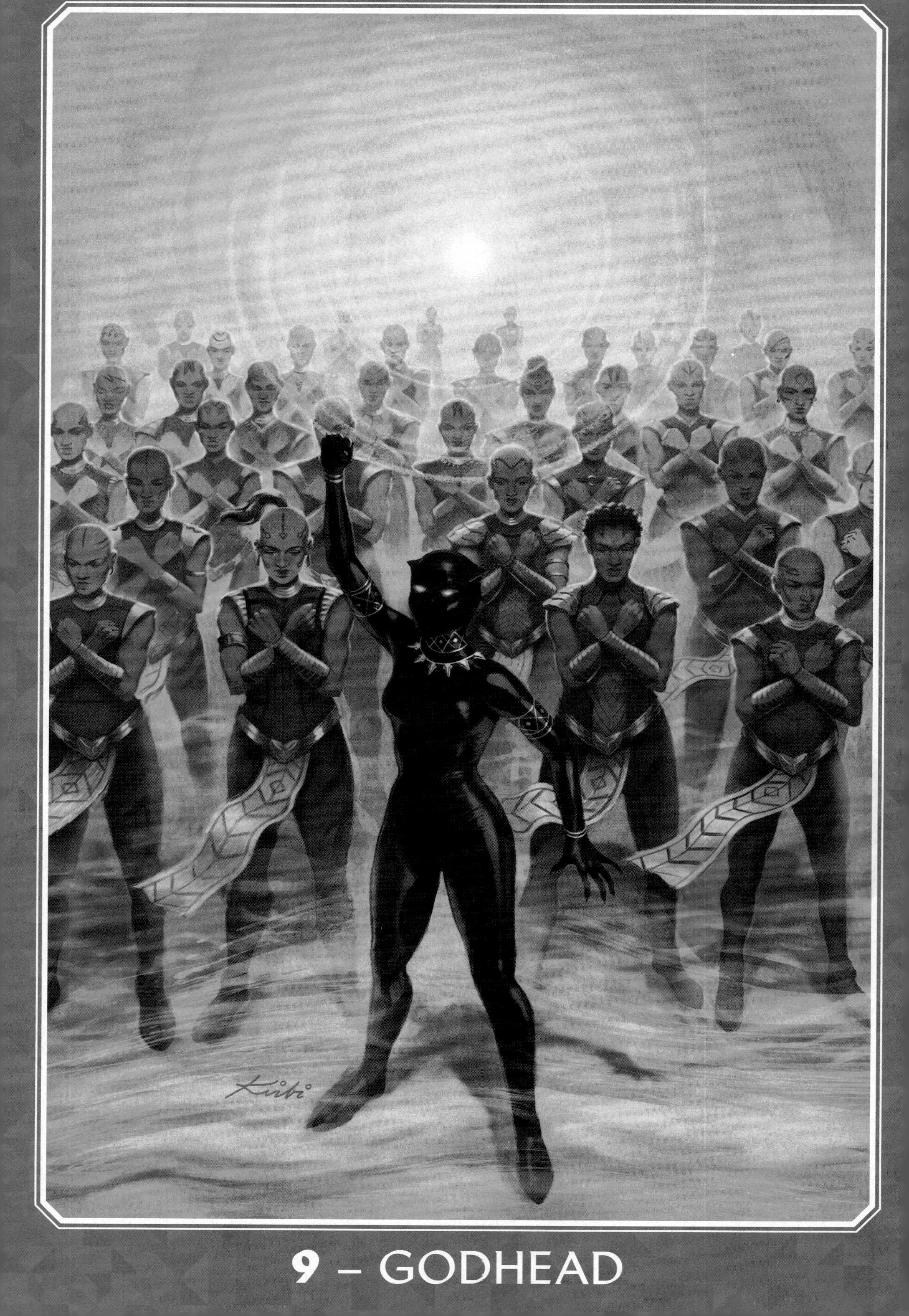

9 – GODHEAD

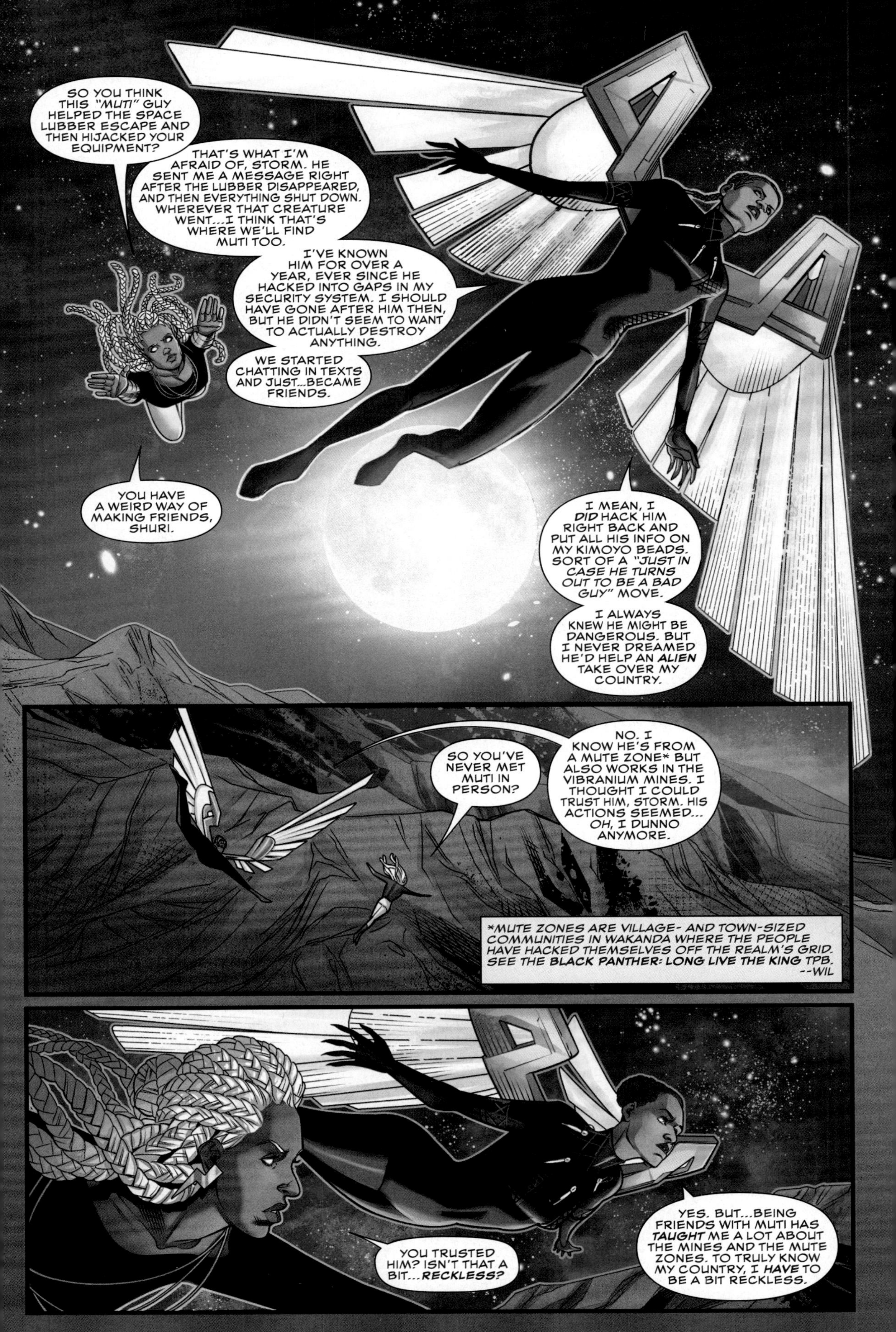
SO YOU THINK THIS "MUTI" GUY HELPED THE SPACE LUBBER ESCAPE AND THEN HIJACKED YOUR EQUIPMENT?
THAT'S WHAT I'M AFRAID OF, STORM. HE SENT ME A MESSAGE RIGHT AFTER THE LUBBER DISAPPEARED, AND THEN EVERYTHING SHUT DOWN. WHEREVER THAT CREATURE WENT... I THINK THAT'S WHERE WE'LL FIND MUTI TOO.
I'VE KNOWN HIM FOR OVER A YEAR, EVER SINCE HE HACKED INTO GAPS IN MY SECURITY SYSTEM. I SHOULD HAVE GONE AFTER HIM THEN, BUT HE DIDN'T SEEM TO WANT TO ACTUALLY DESTROY ANYTHING.
WE STARTED CHATTING IN TEXTS AND JUST...BECAME FRIENDS.
YOU HAVE A WEIRD WAY OF MAKING FRIENDS, SHURI.
I MEAN, I DID HACK HIM RIGHT BACK AND PUT ALL HIS INFO ON MY KIMOYO BEADS. SORT OF A "JUST IN CASE HE TURNS OUT TO BE A BAD GUY" MOVE.
I ALWAYS KNEW HE MIGHT BE DANGEROUS. BUT I NEVER DREAMED HE'D HELP AN ALIEN TAKE OVER MY COUNTRY.
SO YOU'VE NEVER MET MUTI IN PERSON?
NO. I KNOW HE'S FROM A MUTE ZONE* BUT ALSO WORKS IN THE VIBRANIUM MINES. I THOUGHT I COULD TRUST HIM, STORM. HIS ACTIONS SEEMED... OH, I DUNNO ANYMORE.
*MUTE ZONES ARE VILLAGE- AND TOWN-SIZED COMMUNITIES IN WAKANDA WHERE THE PEOPLE HAVE HACKED THEMSELVES OFF THE REALM'S GRID. SEE THE BLACK PANTHER: LONG LIVE THE KING TPB. --WIL
YOU TRUSTED HIM? ISN'T THAT A BIT...RECKLESS?
YES. BUT...BEING FRIENDS WITH MUTI HAS TAUGHT ME A LOT ABOUT THE MINES AND THE MUTE ZONES. TO TRULY KNOW MY COUNTRY, I HAVE TO BE A BIT RECKLESS.

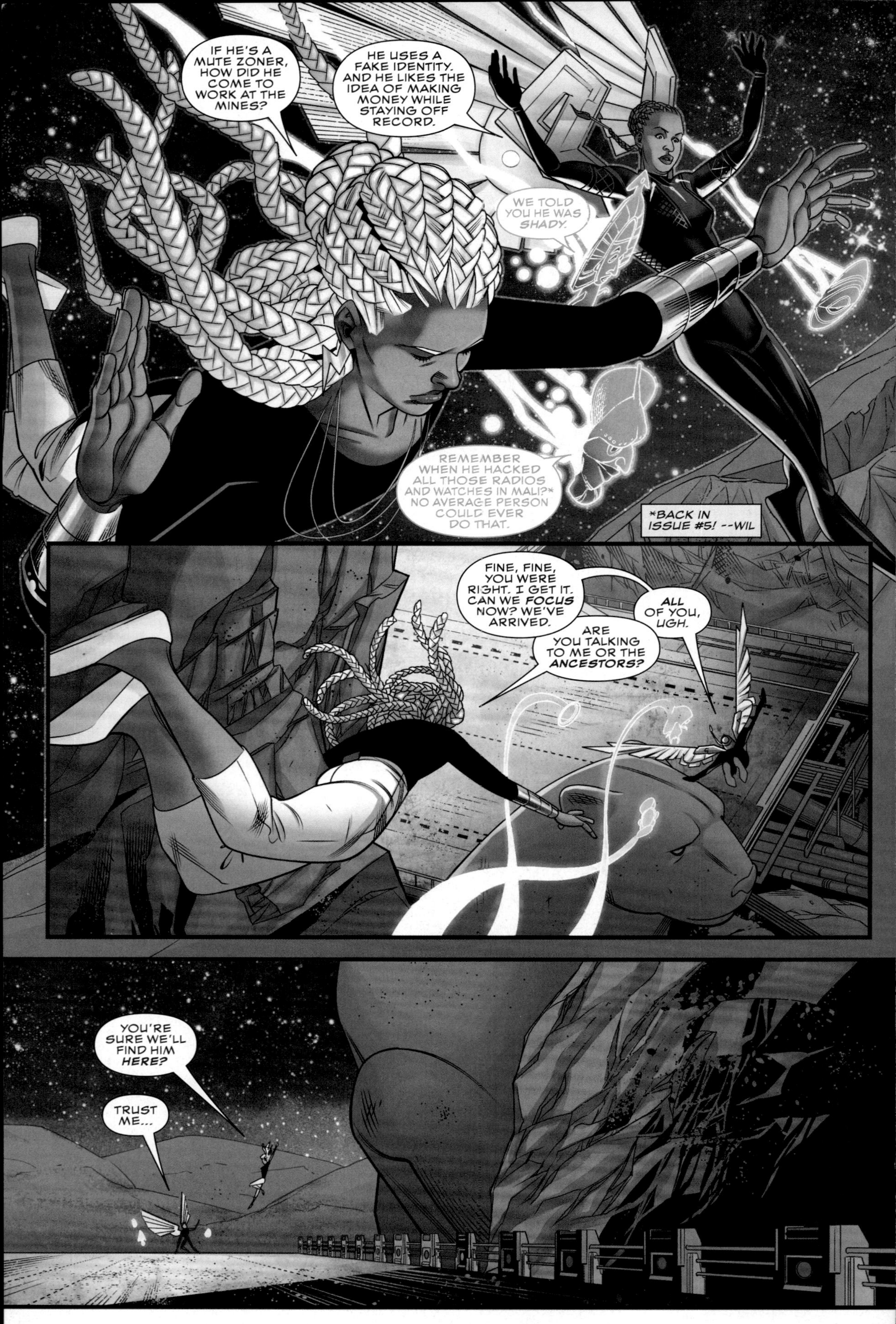

IF HE'S A MUTE ZONER, HOW DID HE COME TO WORK AT THE MINES?
HE USES A FAKE IDENTITY. AND HE LIKES THE IDEA OF MAKING MONEY WHILE STAYING OFF RECORD.
WE TOLD YOU HE WAS SHADY.
REMEMBER WHEN HE HACKED ALL THOSE RADIOS AND WATCHES IN MALI?* NO AVERAGE PERSON COULD EVER DO THAT.
*BACK IN ISSUE #5! --WIL
FINE, FINE, YOU WERE RIGHT. I GET IT. CAN WE FOCUS NOW? WE'VE ARRIVED.
ALL OF YOU, UGH.
ARE YOU TALKING TO ME OR THE ANCESTORS?
YOU'RE SURE WE'LL FIND HIM HERE?
TRUST ME...

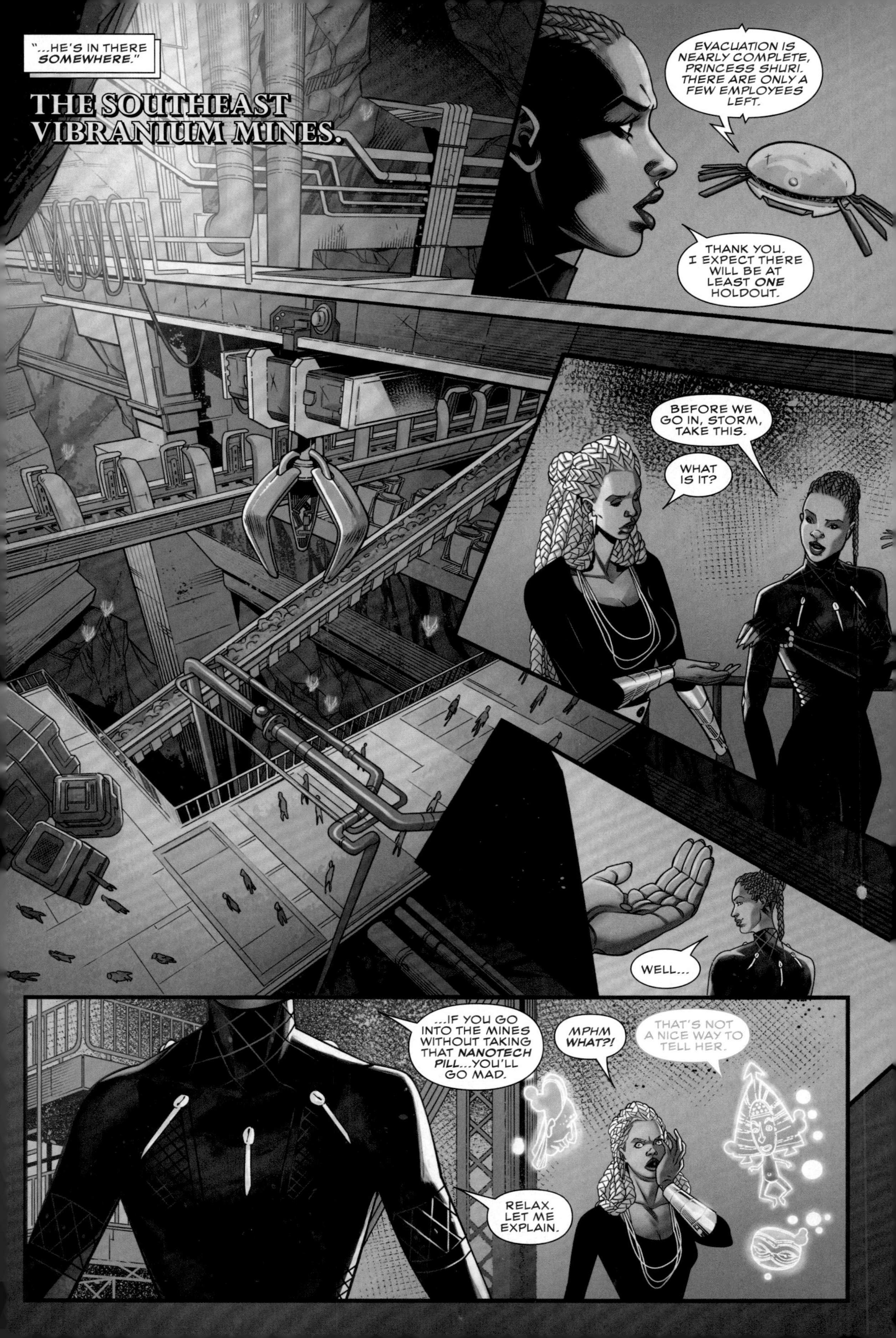
"...HE'S IN THERE SOMEWHERE."
THE SOUTHEAST VIBRANIUM MINES.
EVACUATION IS NEARLY COMPLETE, PRINCESS SHURI. THERE ARE ONLY A FEW EMPLOYEES LEFT.
THANK YOU. I EXPECT THERE WILL BE AT LEAST ONE HOLDOUT.
BEFORE WE GO IN, STORM, TAKE THIS.
WHAT IS IT?
WELL...
...IF YOU GO INTO THE MINES WITHOUT TAKING THAT NANOTECH PILL...YOU'LL GO MAD.
MPHM WHAT?!
THAT'S NOT A NICE WAY TO TELL HER.
RELAX. LET ME EXPLAIN.

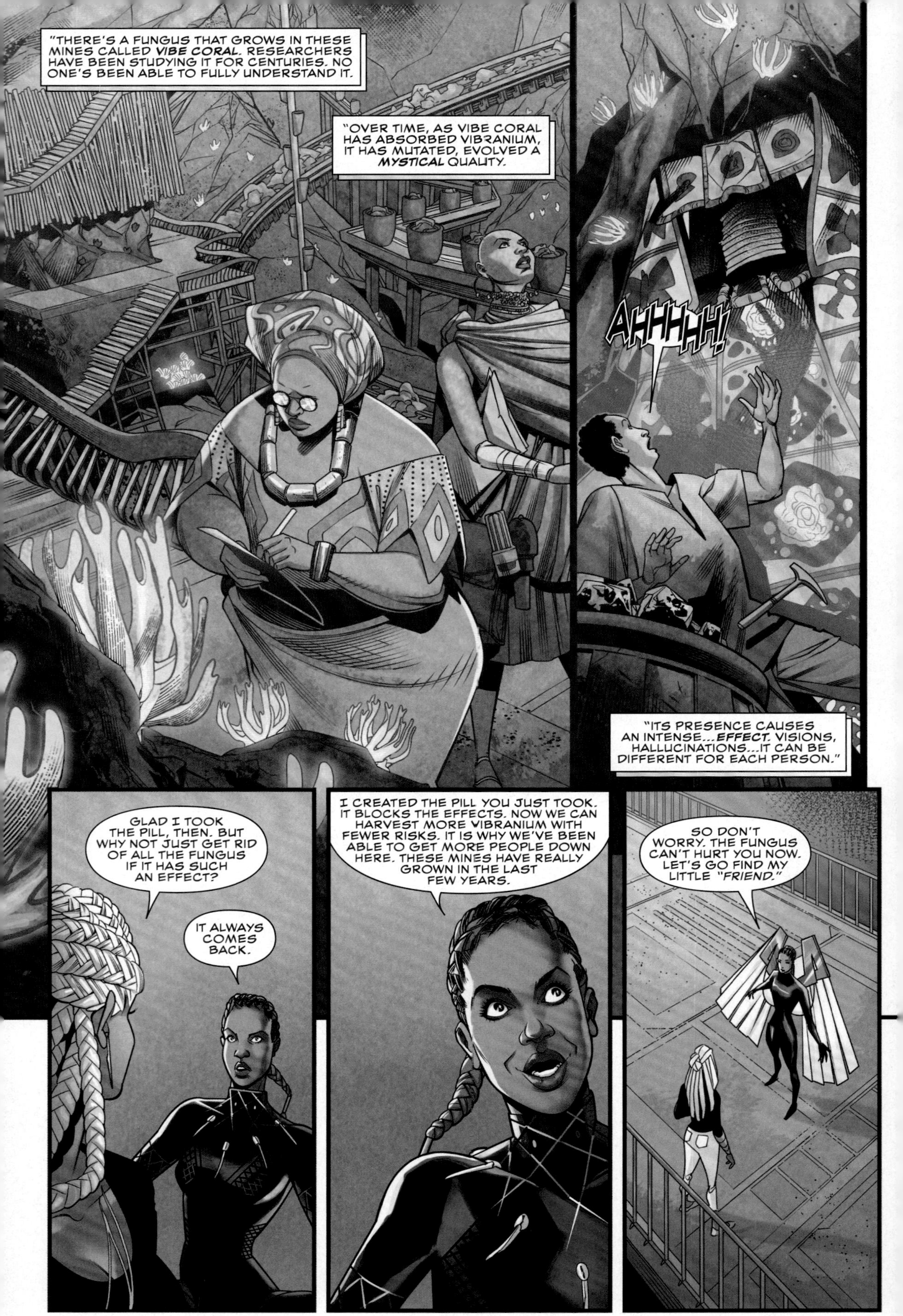
"THERE'S A FUNGUS THAT GROWS IN THESE MINES CALLED VIBE CORAL. RESEARCHERS HAVE BEEN STUDYING IT FOR CENTURIES. NO ONE'S BEEN ABLE TO FULLY UNDERSTAND IT.
"OVER TIME, AS VIBE CORAL HAS ABSORBED VIBRANIUM, IT HAS MUTATED, EVOLVED A MYSTICAL QUALITY.
AHHHHH!
"ITS PRESENCE CAUSES AN INTENSE... EFFECT. VISIONS, HALLUCINATIONS...IT CAN BE DIFFERENT FOR EACH PERSON."
GLAD I TOOK THE PILL, THEN. BUT WHY NOT JUST GET RID OF ALL THE FUNGUS IF IT HAS SUCH AN EFFECT?
IT ALWAYS COMES BACK.
I CREATED THE PILL YOU JUST TOOK. IT BLOCKS THE EFFECTS. NOW WE CAN HARVEST MORE VIBRANIUM WITH FEWER RISKS. IT IS WHY WE'VE BEEN ABLE TO GET MORE PEOPLE DOWN HERE. THESE MINES HAVE REALLY GROWN IN THE LAST FEW YEARS.
SO DON'T WORRY. THE FUNGUS CAN'T HURT YOU NOW. LET'S GO FIND MY LITTLE "FRIEND."

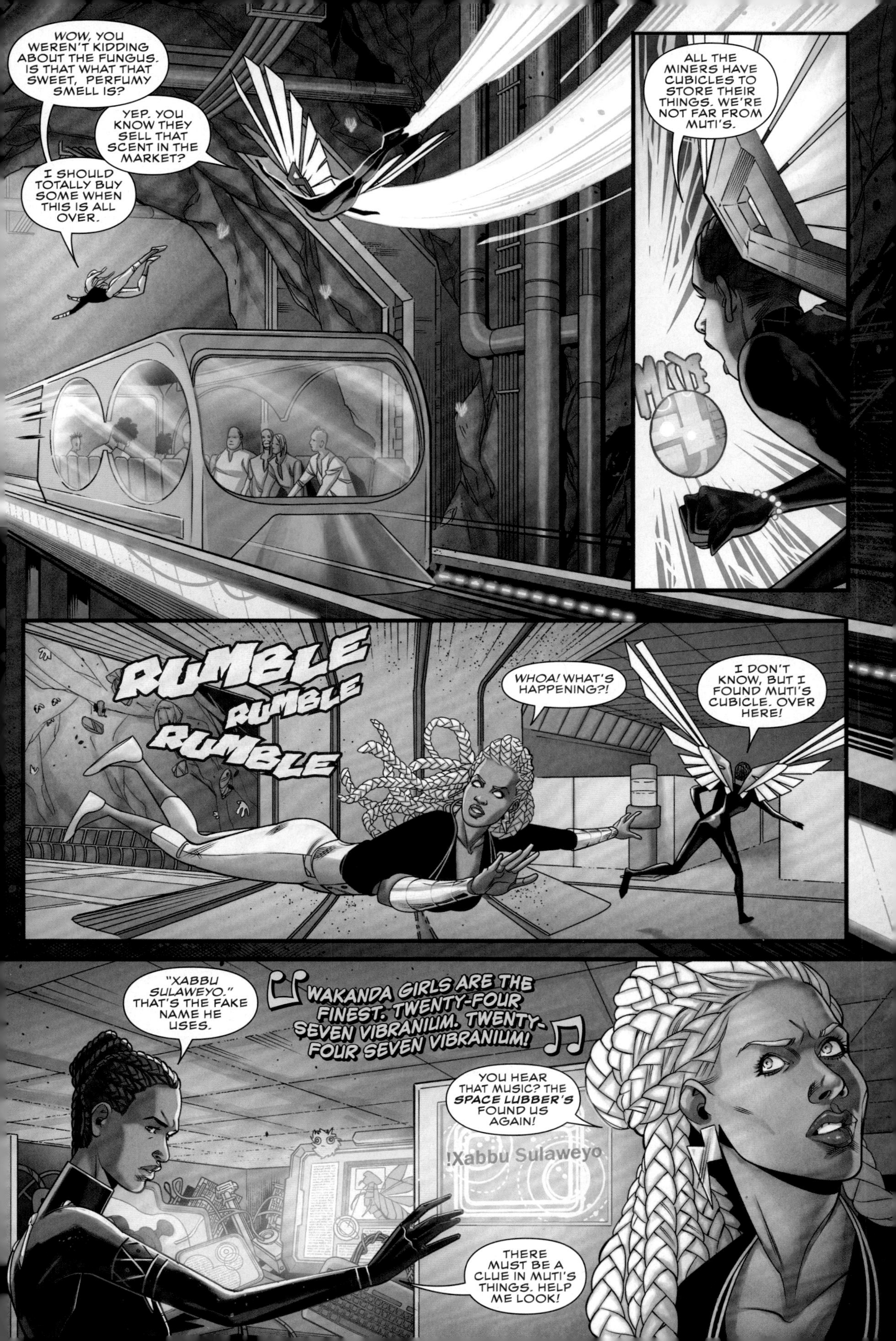
WOW, YOU WEREN'T KIDDING ABOUT THE FUNGUS. IS THAT WHAT THAT SWEET, PERFUMY SMELL IS?
YEP. YOU KNOW THEY SELL THAT SCENT IN THE MARKET?
I SHOULD TOTALLY BUY SOME WHEN THIS IS ALL OVER.
ALL THE MINERS HAVE CUBICLES TO STORE THEIR THINGS. WE'RE NOT FAR FROM MUTI'S.
RUMBLE RUMBLE RUMBLE
WHOA! WHAT'S HAPPENING?!
I DON'T KNOW, BUT I FOUND MUTI'S CUBICLE. OVER HERE!
"XABBU SULAWEYO." THAT'S THE FAKE NAME HE USES.
WAKANDA GIRLS ARE THE FINEST. TWENTY-FOUR SEVEN VIBRANIUM. TWENTY-FOUR SEVEN VIBRANIUM!
YOU HEAR THAT MUSIC? THE SPACE LUBBER'S FOUND US AGAIN!
!Xabbu Sulaweyo
THERE MUST BE A CLUE IN MUTI'S THINGS. HELP ME LOOK!

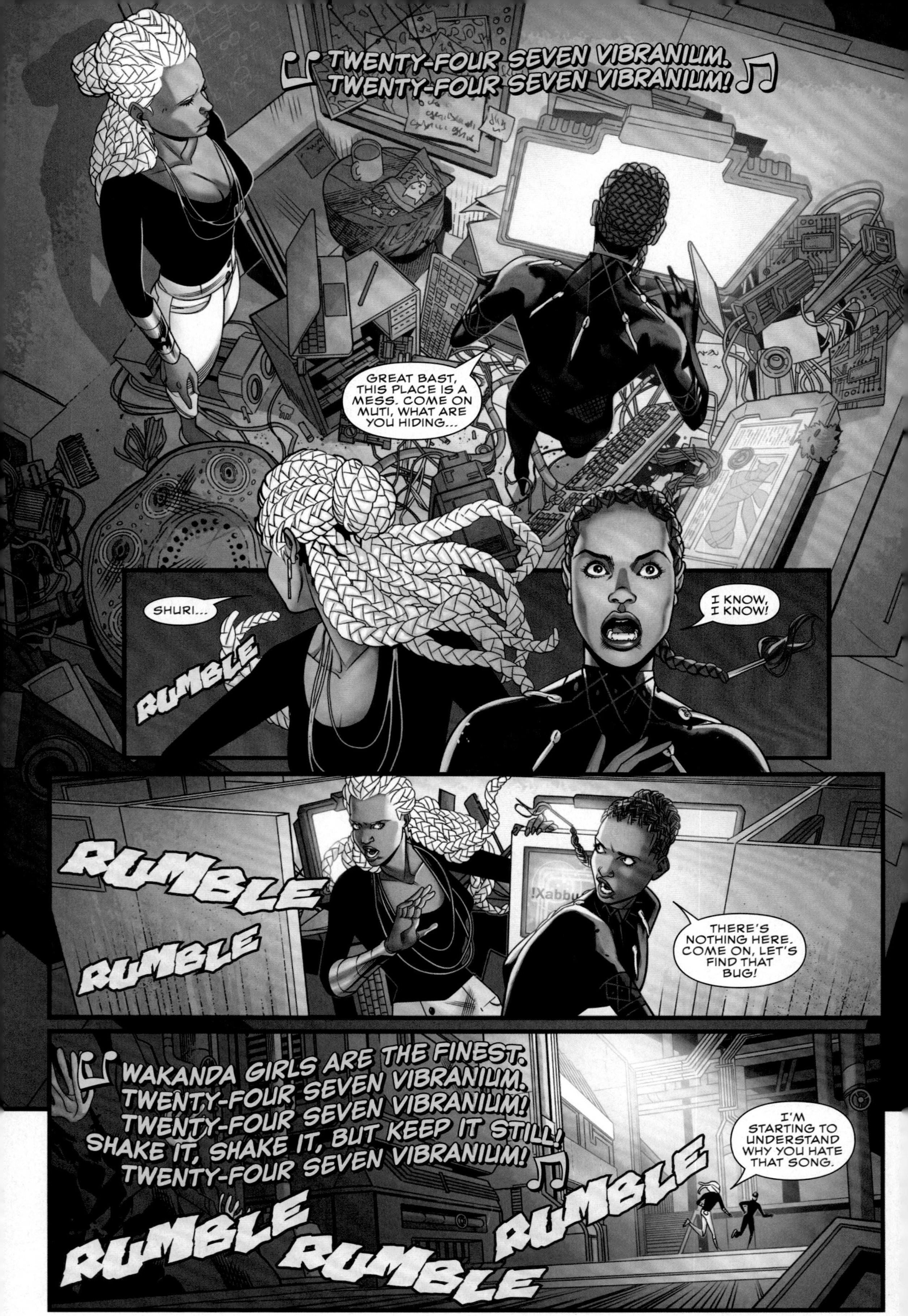
TWENTY-FOUR SEVEN VIBRANIUM. TWENTY-FOUR SEVEN VIBRANIUM!
GREAT BAST, THIS PLACE IS A MESS. COME ON MUTI, WHAT ARE YOU HIDING...
SHURI...
RUMBLE
I KNOW, I KNOW!
RUMBLE
RUMBLE
!Xabbu
THERE'S NOTHING HERE. COME ON, LET'S FIND THAT BUG!
WAKANDA GIRLS ARE THE FINEST. TWENTY-FOUR SEVEN VIBRANIUM. TWENTY-FOUR SEVEN VIBRANIUM! TWENTY-FOUR SEVEN VIBRANIUM! SHAKE IT, SHAKE IT, BUT KEEP IT STILL! TWENTY-FOUR SEVEN VIBRANIUM! TWENTY-FOUR SEVEN VIBRANIUM!
I'M STARTING TO UNDERSTAND WHY YOU HATE THAT SONG.
RUMBLE
RUMBLE
RUMBLE

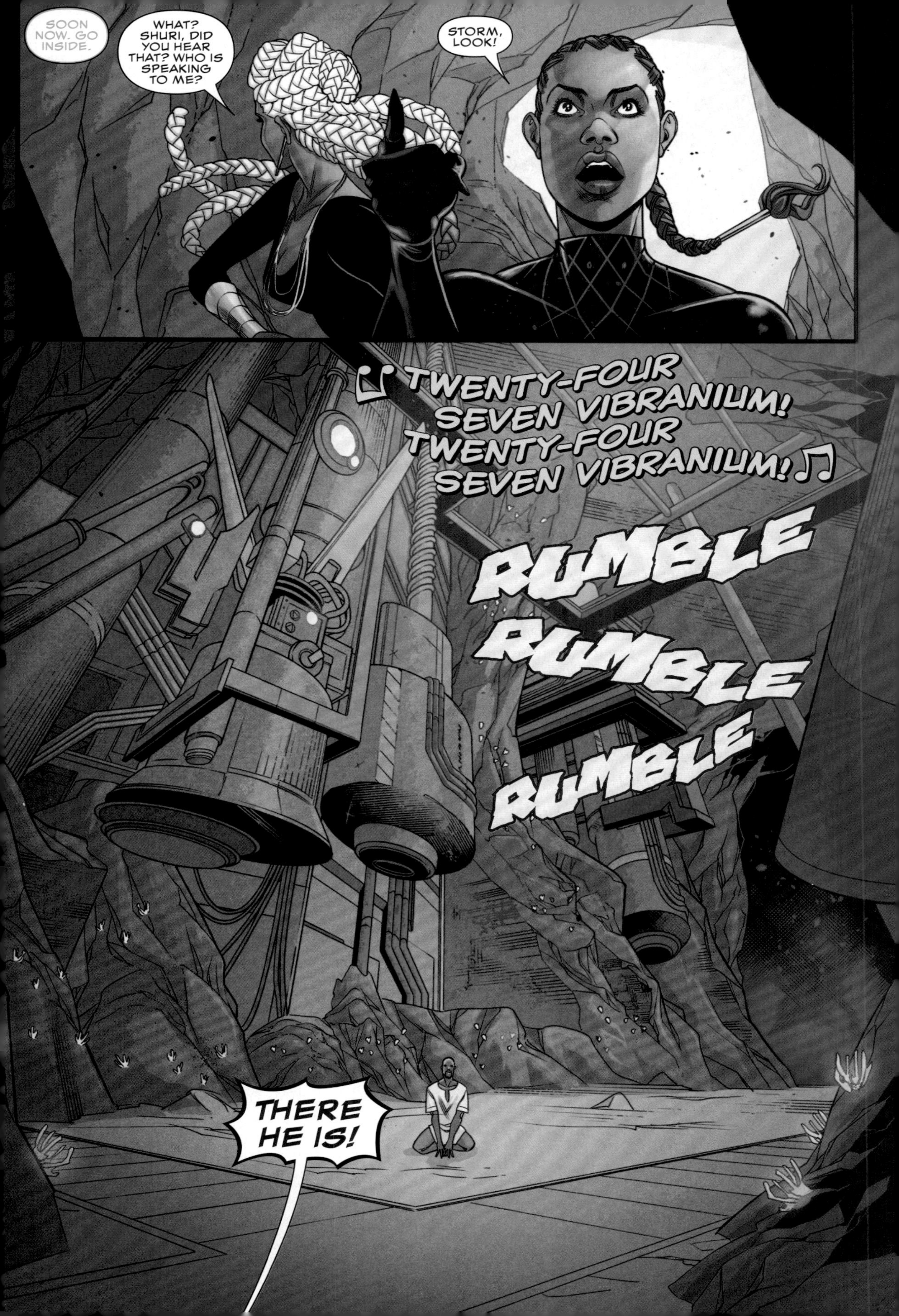
SOON NOW. GO INSIDE.
WHAT? SHURI, DID YOU HEAR THAT? WHO IS SPEAKING TO ME?
STORM, LOOK!
♫ TWENTY-FOUR SEVEN VIBRANIUM! TWENTY-FOUR SEVEN VIBRANIUM! ♫
RUMBLE RUMBLE RUMBLE
THERE HE IS!

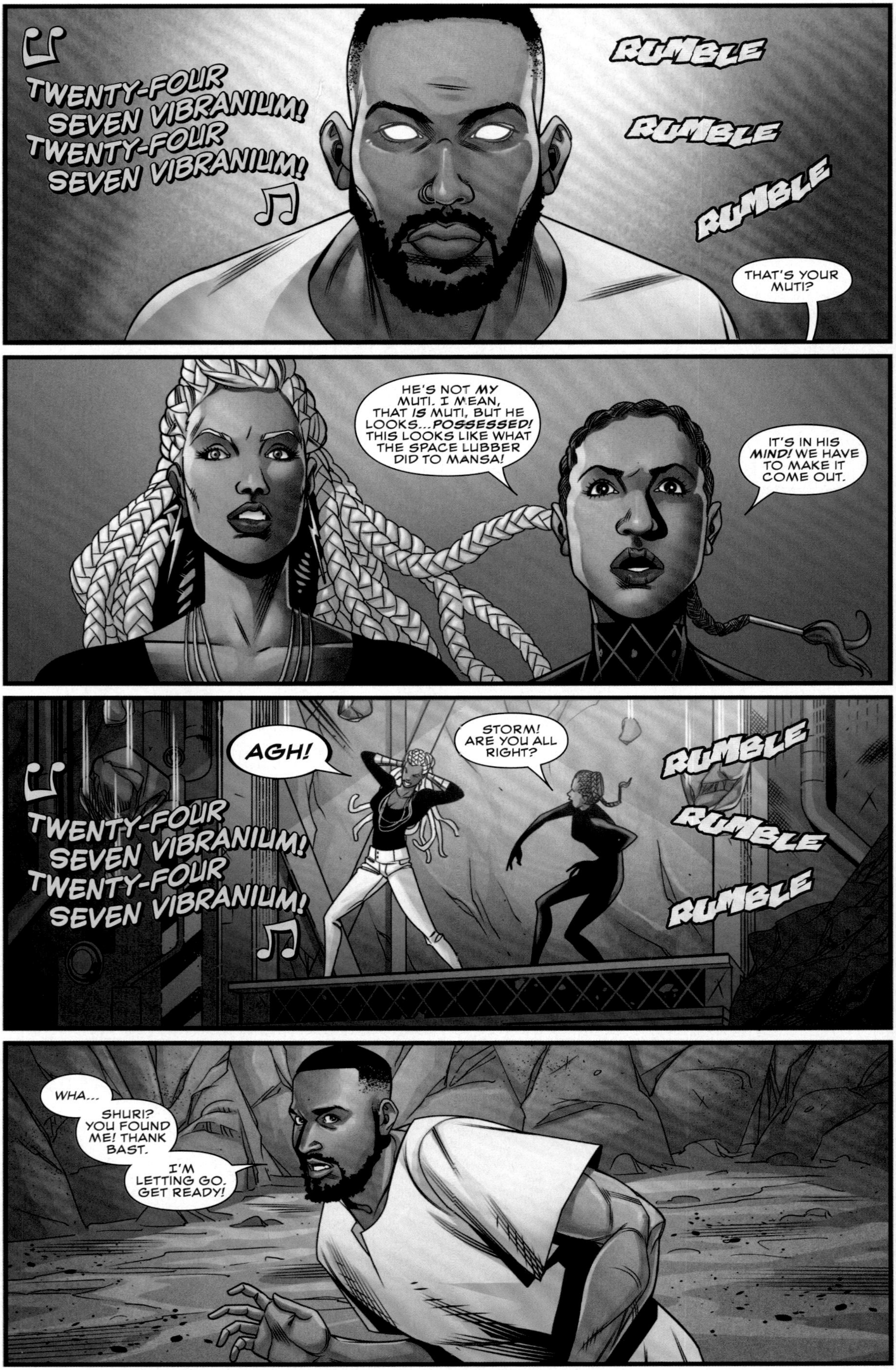
TWENTY-FOUR SEVEN VIBRANIUM! TWENTY-FOUR SEVEN VIBRANIUM!
RUMBLE
RUMBLE
RUMBLE
THAT'S YOUR MUTI?
HE'S NOT MY MUTI. I MEAN, THAT IS MUTI, BUT HE LOOKS...POSSESSED! THIS LOOKS LIKE WHAT THE SPACE LUBBER DID TO MANSA!
IT'S IN HIS MIND! WE HAVE TO MAKE IT COME OUT.
TWENTY-FOUR SEVEN VIBRANIUM! TWENTY-FOUR SEVEN VIBRANIUM!
AGH!
STORM! ARE YOU ALL RIGHT?
RUMBLE
RUMBLE
RUMBLE
WHA...
SHURI? YOU FOUND ME! THANK BAST.
I'M LETTING GO. GET READY!

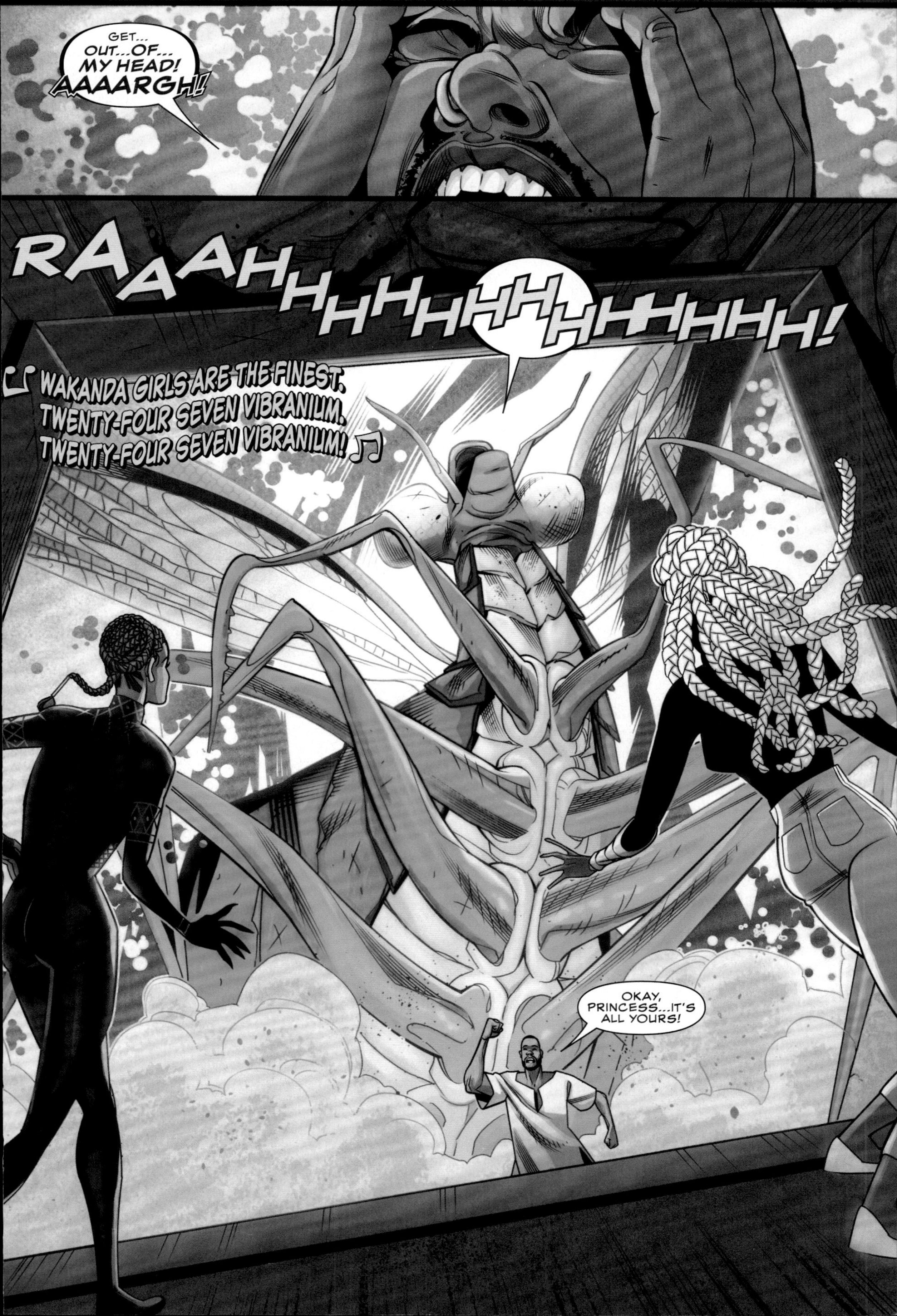
GET... OUT...OF... MY HEAD! AAAARGH!
RAAAHHHHHHHHHHHHH!
♫ WAKANDA GIRLS ARE THE FINEST. TWENTY-FOUR SEVEN VIBRANIUM. TWENTY-FOUR SEVEN VIBRANIUM! ♫
OKAY, PRINCESS...IT'S ALL YOURS!

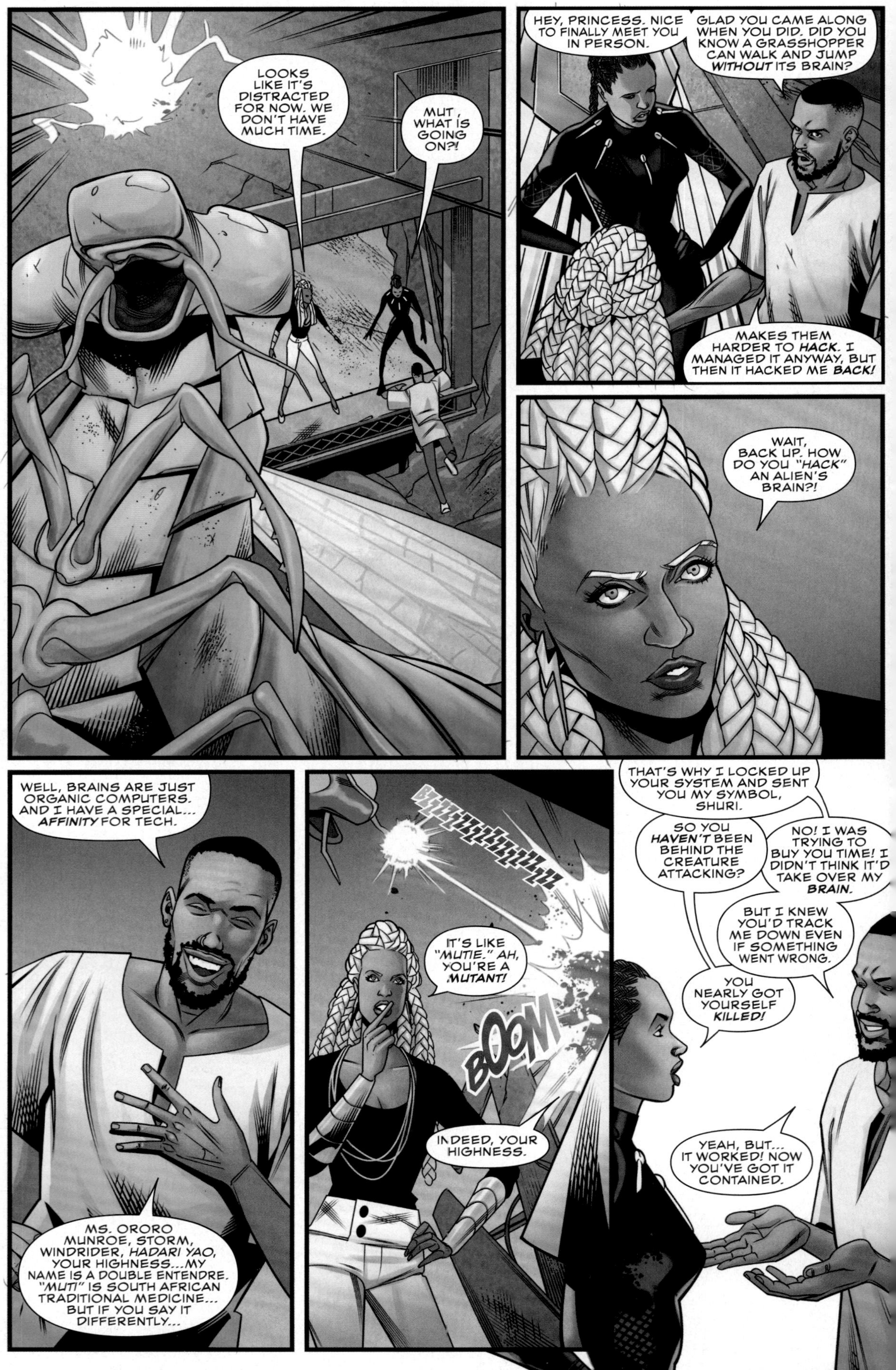
LOOKS LIKE IT'S DISTRACTED FOR NOW. WE DON'T HAVE MUCH TIME.
MUT, WHAT IS GOING ON?!
HEY, PRINCESS. NICE TO FINALLY MEET YOU IN PERSON.
GLAD YOU CAME ALONG WHEN YOU DID. DID YOU KNOW A GRASSHOPPER CAN WALK AND JUMP WITHOUT ITS BRAIN?
MAKES THEM HARDER TO HACK. I MANAGED IT ANYWAY, BUT THEN IT HACKED ME BACK!
WAIT, BACK UP. HOW DO YOU "HACK" AN ALIEN'S BRAIN?!
WELL, BRAINS ARE JUST ORGANIC COMPUTERS. AND I HAVE A SPECIAL... AFFINITY FOR TECH.
MS. ORORO MUNROE, STORM, WINDRIDER, HADARI YAO, YOUR HIGHNESS...MY NAME IS A DOUBLE ENTENDRE. "MUTI" IS SOUTH AFRICAN TRADITIONAL MEDICINE... BUT IF YOU SAY IT DIFFERENTLY...
BZZZZZZZZZZZZZZZ
IT'S LIKE "MUTIE." AH, YOU'RE A MUTANT!
BOOM
INDEED, YOUR HIGHNESS.
THAT'S WHY I LOCKED UP YOUR SYSTEM AND SENT YOU MY SYMBOL, SHURI.
SO YOU HAVEN'T BEEN BEHIND THE CREATURE ATTACKING?
NO! I WAS TRYING TO BUY YOU TIME! I DIDN'T THINK IT'D TAKE OVER MY BRAIN.
BUT I KNEW YOU'D TRACK ME DOWN EVEN IF SOMETHING WENT WRONG.
YOU NEARLY GOT YOURSELF KILLED!
YEAH, BUT... IT WORKED! NOW YOU'VE GOT IT CONTAINED.

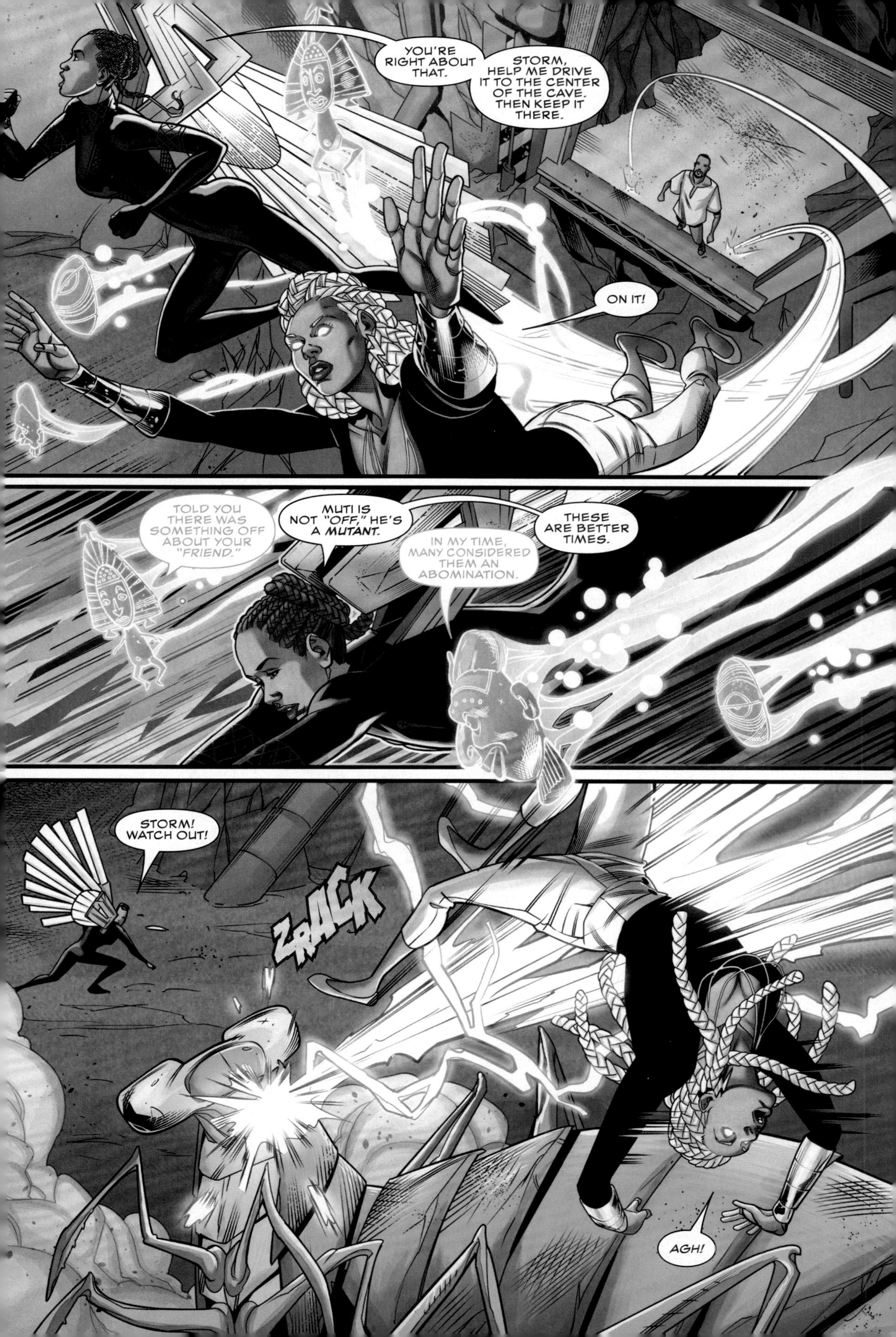

YOU'RE RIGHT ABOUT THAT.
STORM, HELP ME DRIVE IT TO THE CENTER OF THE CAVE. THEN KEEP IT THERE.
ON IT!
TOLD YOU THERE WAS SOMETHING OFF ABOUT YOUR "FRIEND."
MUTI IS NOT "OFF," HE'S A MUTANT.
IN MY TIME, MANY CONSIDERED THEM AN ABOMINATION.
THESE ARE BETTER TIMES.
STORM! WATCH OUT!
ZRACK
AGH!

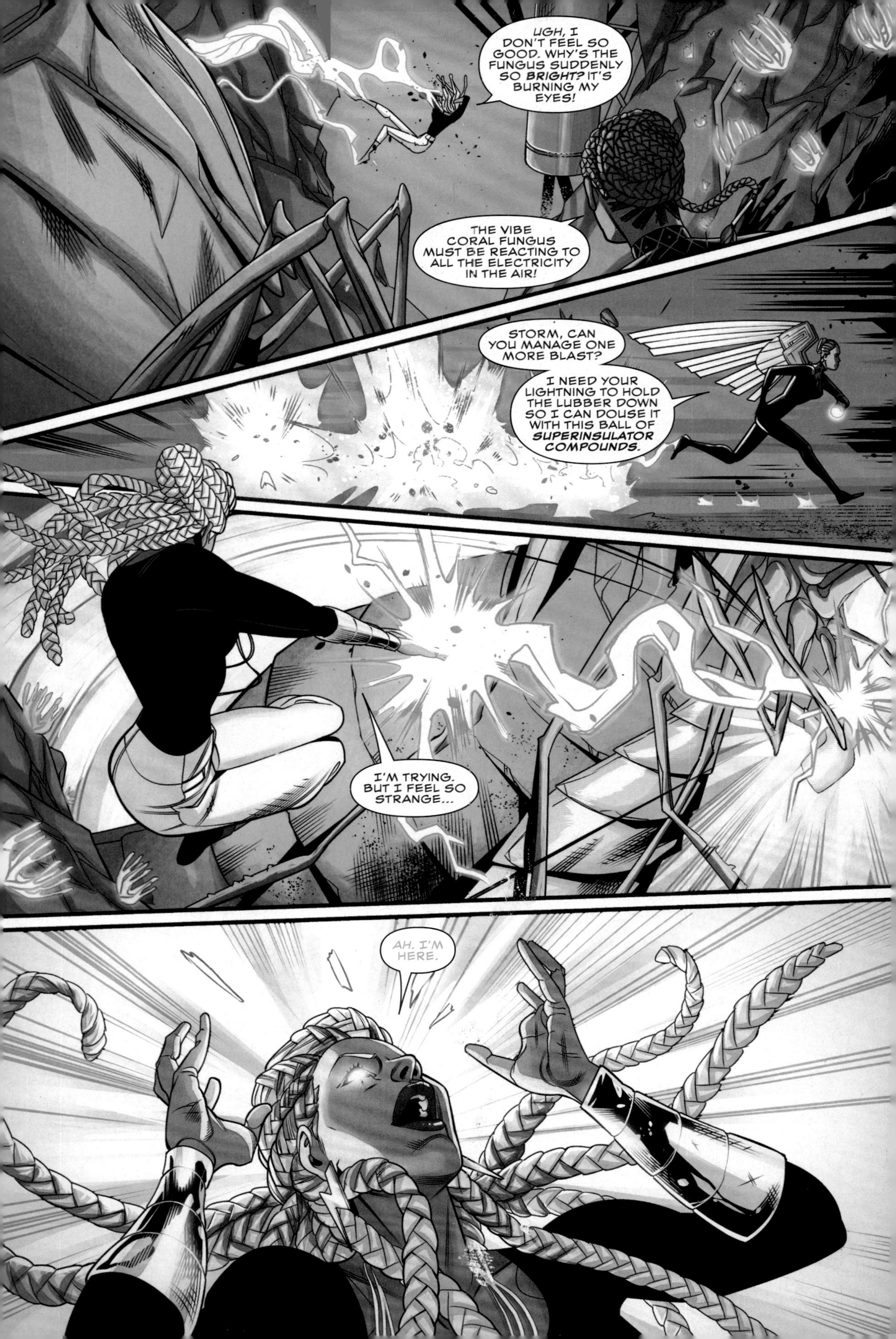
UGH, I DON'T FEEL SO GOOD. WHY'S THE FUNGUS SUDDENLY SO BRIGHT? IT'S BURNING MY EYES!
THE VIBE CORAL FUNGUS MUST BE REACTING TO ALL THE ELECTRICITY IN THE AIR!
STORM, CAN YOU MANAGE ONE MORE BLAST?
I NEED YOUR LIGHTNING TO HOLD THE LUBBER DOWN SO I CAN DOUSE IT WITH THIS BALL OF SUPERINSULATOR COMPOUNDS.
I'M TRYING. BUT I FEEL SO STRANGE...
AH. I'M HERE.

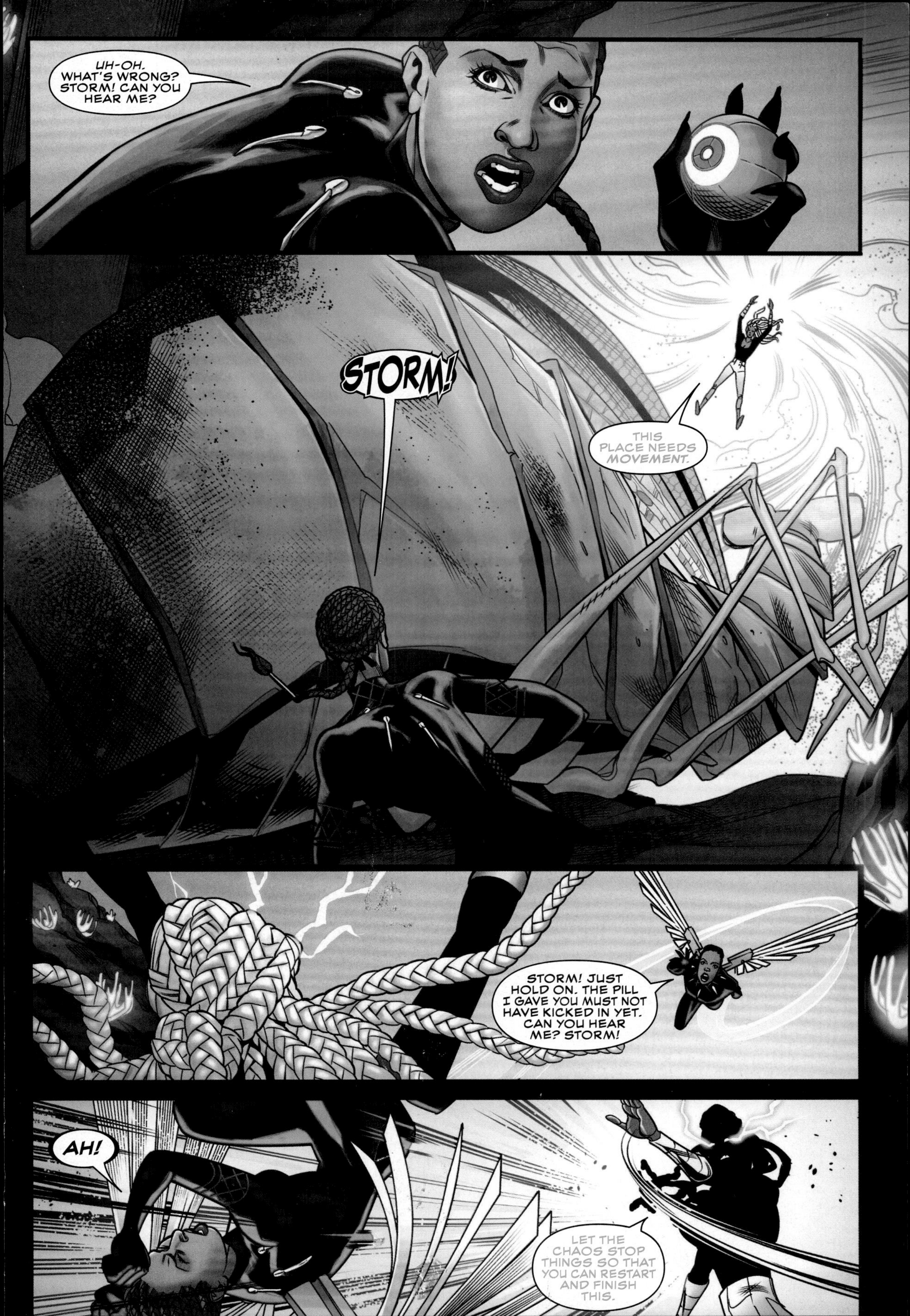
UH-OH. WHAT'S WRONG? STORM! CAN YOU HEAR ME?
STORM!
THIS PLACE NEEDS MOVEMENT.
STORM! JUST HOLD ON. THE PILL I GAVE YOU MUST NOT HAVE KICKED IN YET. CAN YOU HEAR ME? STORM!
AH!
LET THE CHAOS STOP THINGS SO THAT YOU CAN RESTART AND FINISH THIS.

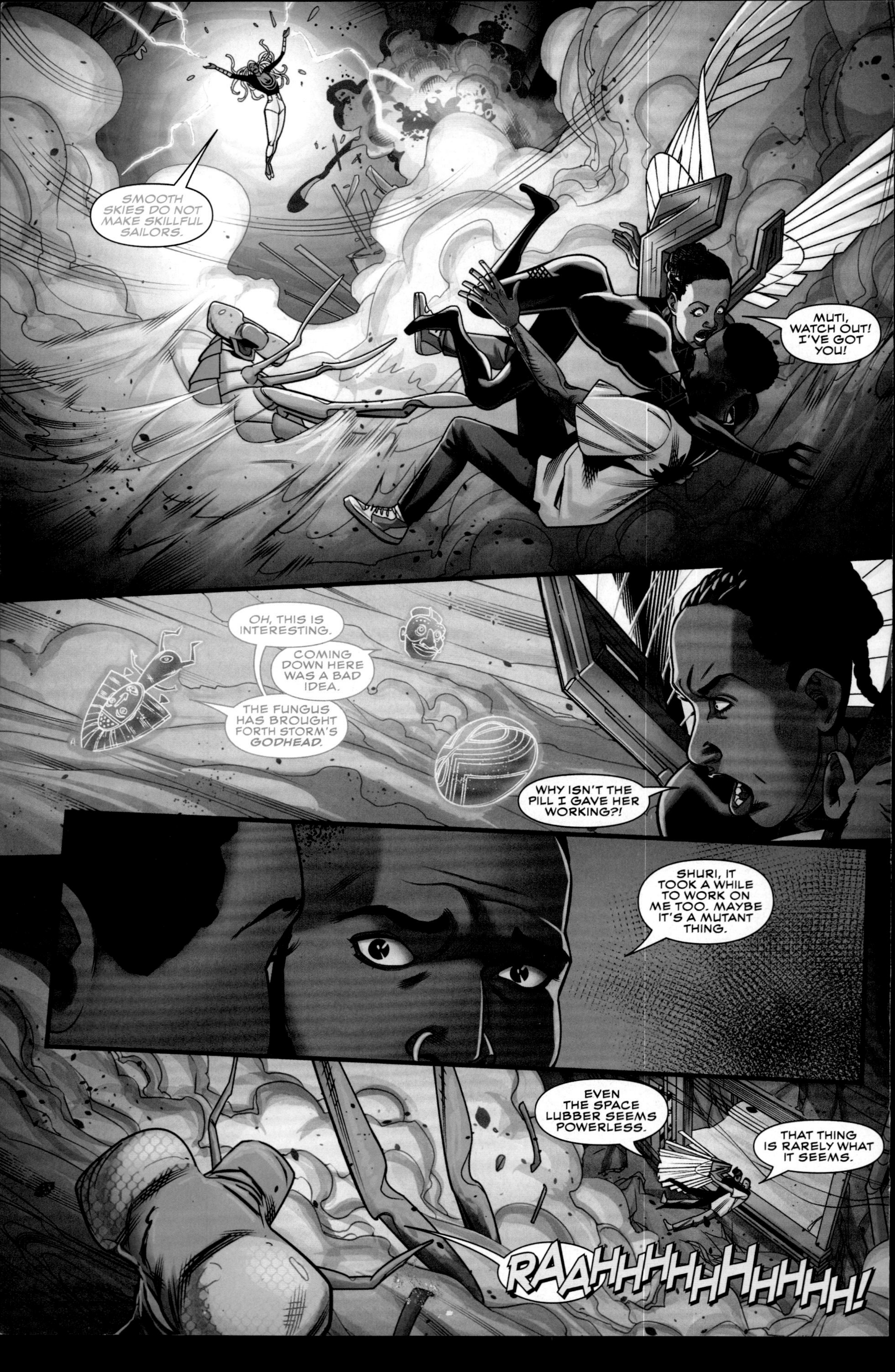
SMOOTH SKIES DO NOT MAKE SKILLFUL SAILORS.
MUTI, WATCH OUT! I'VE GOT YOU!
OH, THIS IS INTERESTING.
COMING DOWN HERE WAS A BAD IDEA.
THE FUNGUS HAS BROUGHT FORTH STORM'S *GODHEAD*.
WHY ISN'T THE PILL I GAVE HER WORKING?!
SHURI, IT TOOK A WHILE TO WORK ON ME TOO. MAYBE IT'S A MUTANT THING.
EVEN THE SPACE LUBBER SEEMS POWERLESS.
THAT THING IS RARELY WHAT IT SEEMS.
RAAHHHHHHHHHHH!

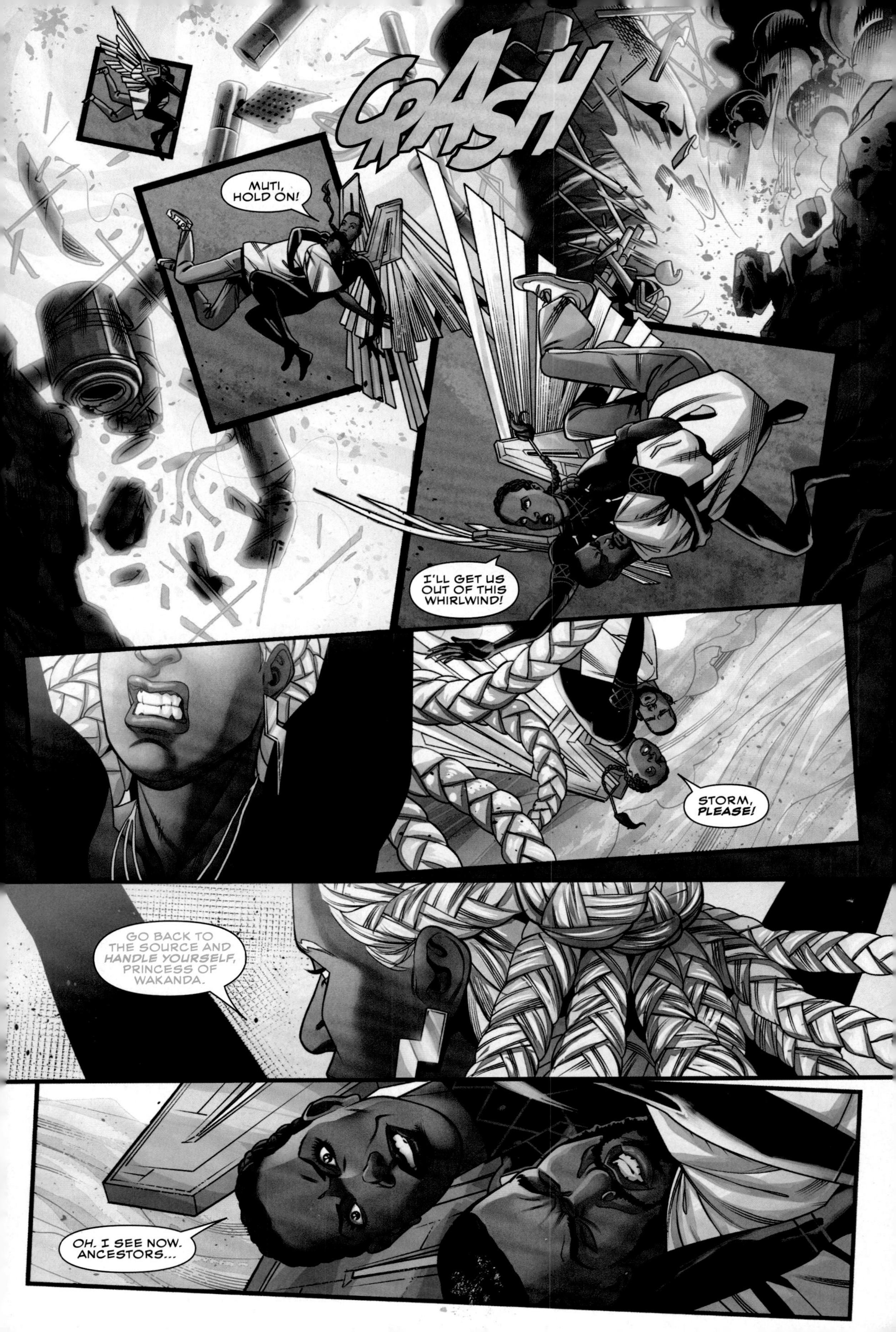
CRASH
MUTI, HOLD ON!
I'LL GET US OUT OF THIS WHIRLWIND!
STORM, PLEASE!
GO BACK TO THE SOURCE AND HANDLE YOURSELF, PRINCESS OF WAKANDA.
OH. I SEE NOW. ANCESTORS...

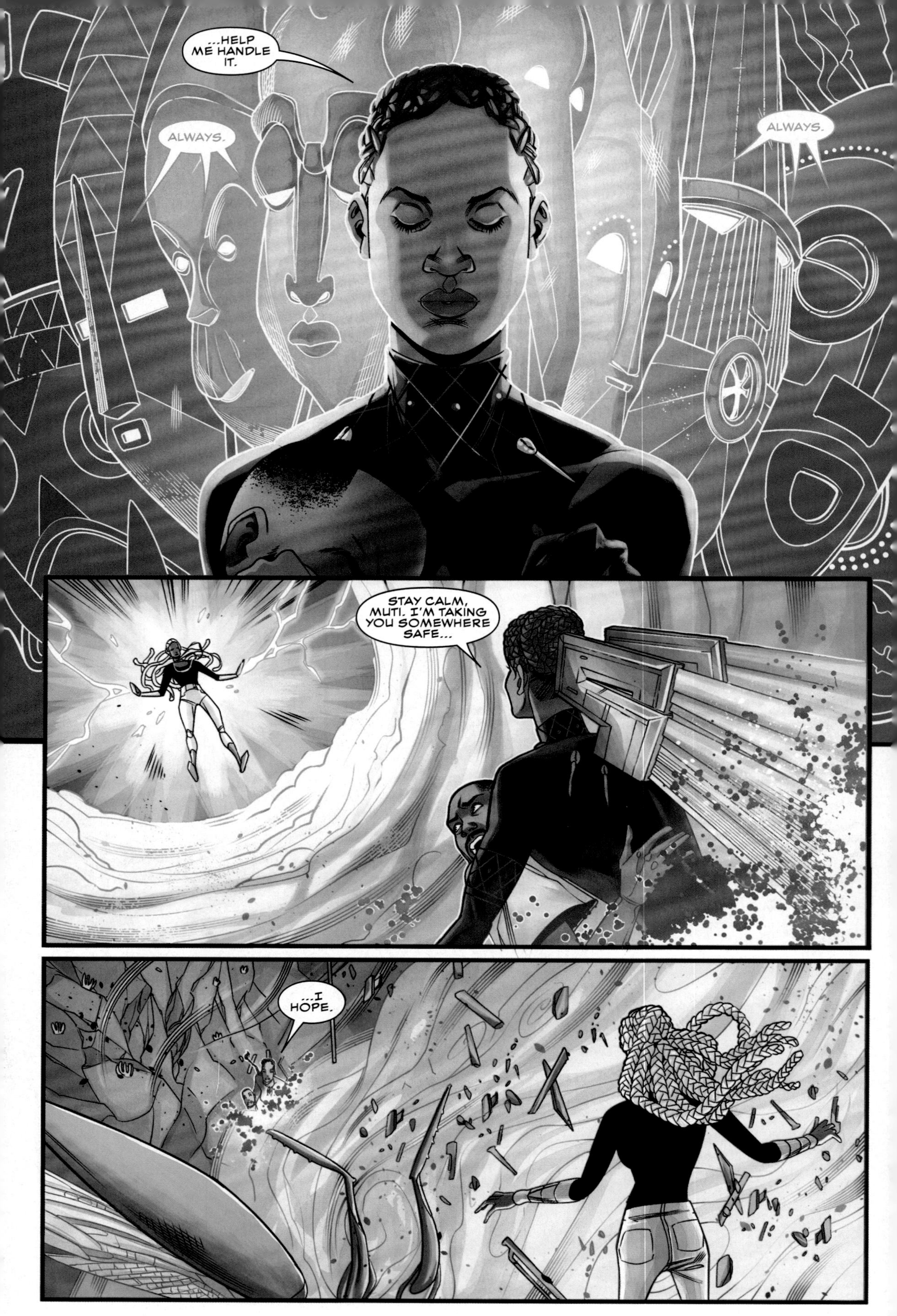
...HELP ME HANDLE IT.
ALWAYS.
ALWAYS.
STAY CALM, MUTI. I'M TAKING YOU SOMEWHERE SAFE...
...I HOPE.

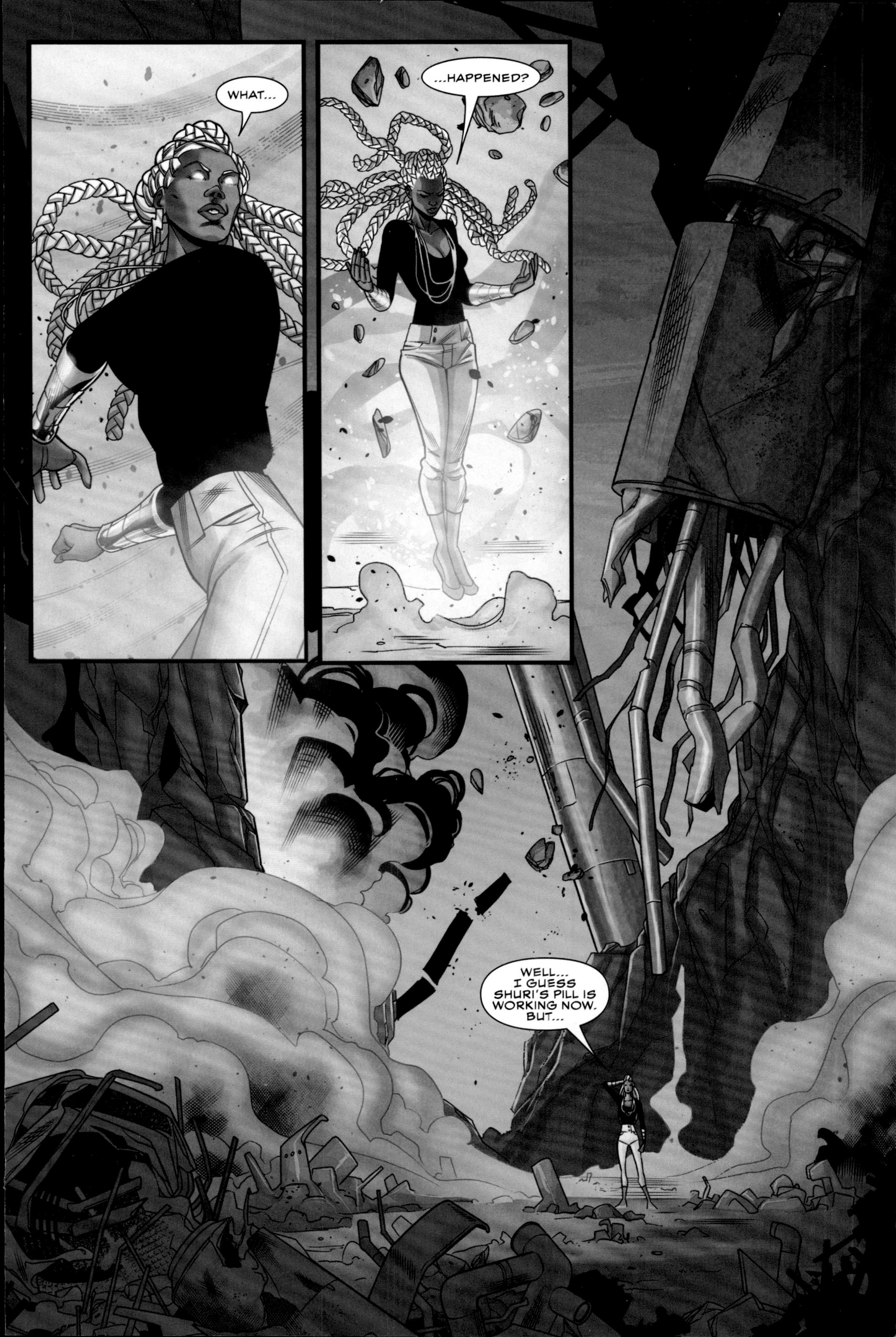
WHAT...
...HAPPENED?
WELL... I GUESS SHURI'S PILL IS WORKING NOW. BUT...

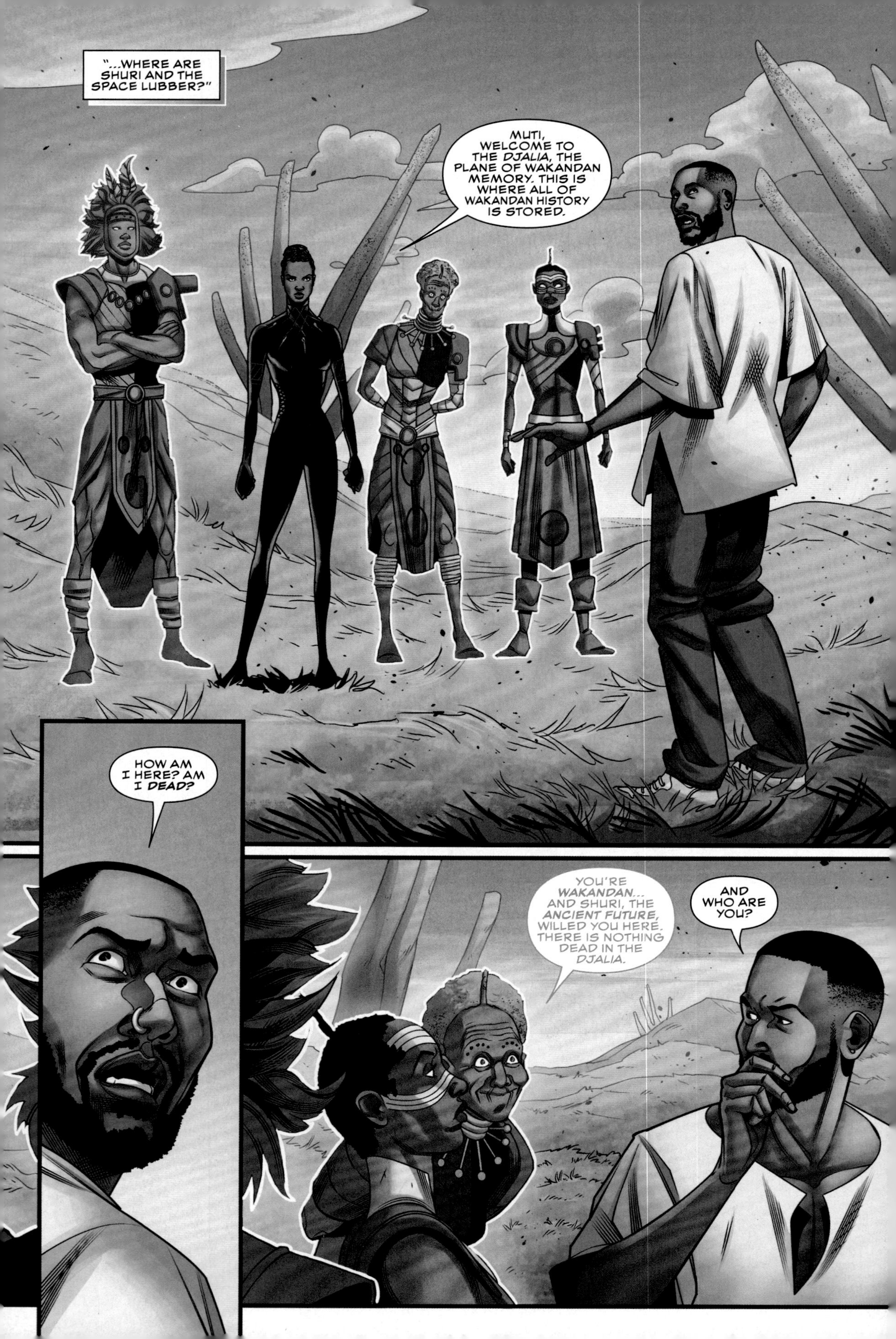
"...WHERE ARE SHURI AND THE SPACE LUBBER?"
MUTI, WELCOME TO THE DJALIA, THE PLANE OF WAKANDAN MEMORY. THIS IS WHERE ALL OF WAKANDAN HISTORY IS STORED.
HOW AM I HERE? AM I DEAD?
YOU'RE WAKANDAN... AND SHURI, THE ANCIENT FUTURE, WILLED YOU HERE. THERE IS NOTHING DEAD IN THE DJALIA.
AND WHO ARE YOU?

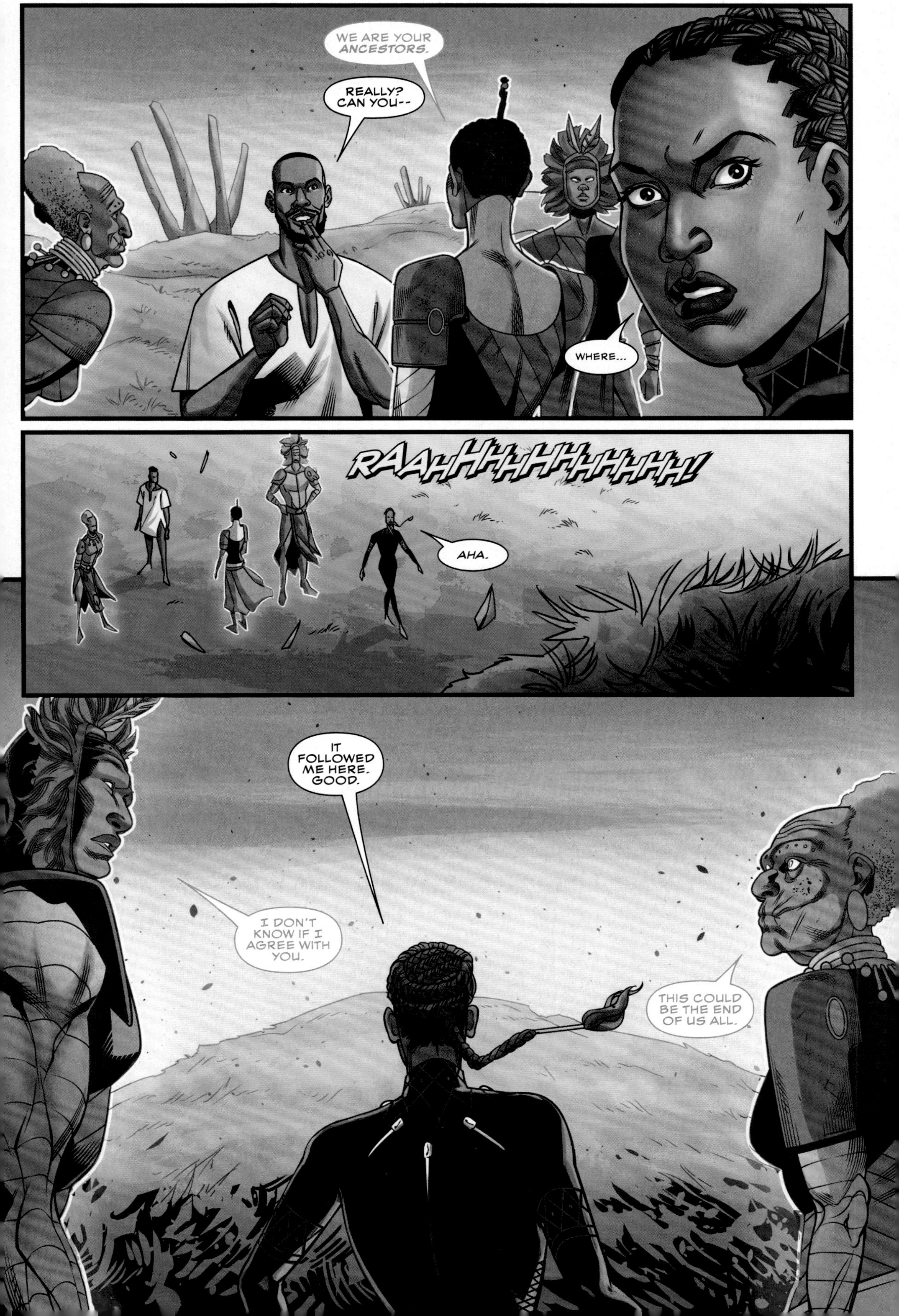
WE ARE YOUR ANCESTORS.
REALLY? CAN YOU--
WHERE...
RAAHHHHHHHHHHH!
AHA.
IT FOLLOWED ME HERE. GOOD.
I DON'T KNOW IF I AGREE WITH YOU.
THIS COULD BE THE END OF US ALL.

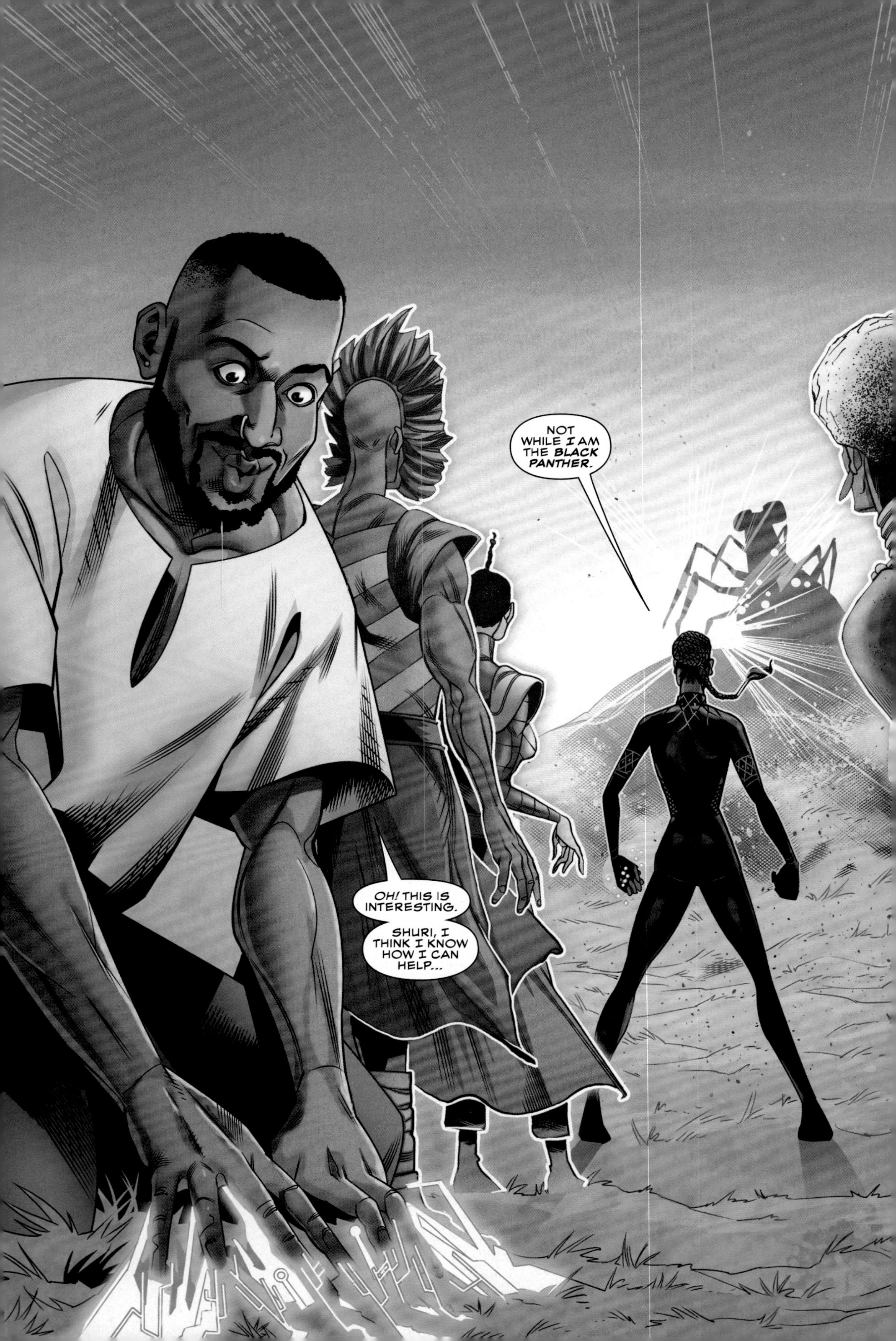
NOT WHILE I AM THE BLACK PANTHER.
OH! THIS IS INTERESTING.
SHURI, I THINK I KNOW HOW I CAN HELP...

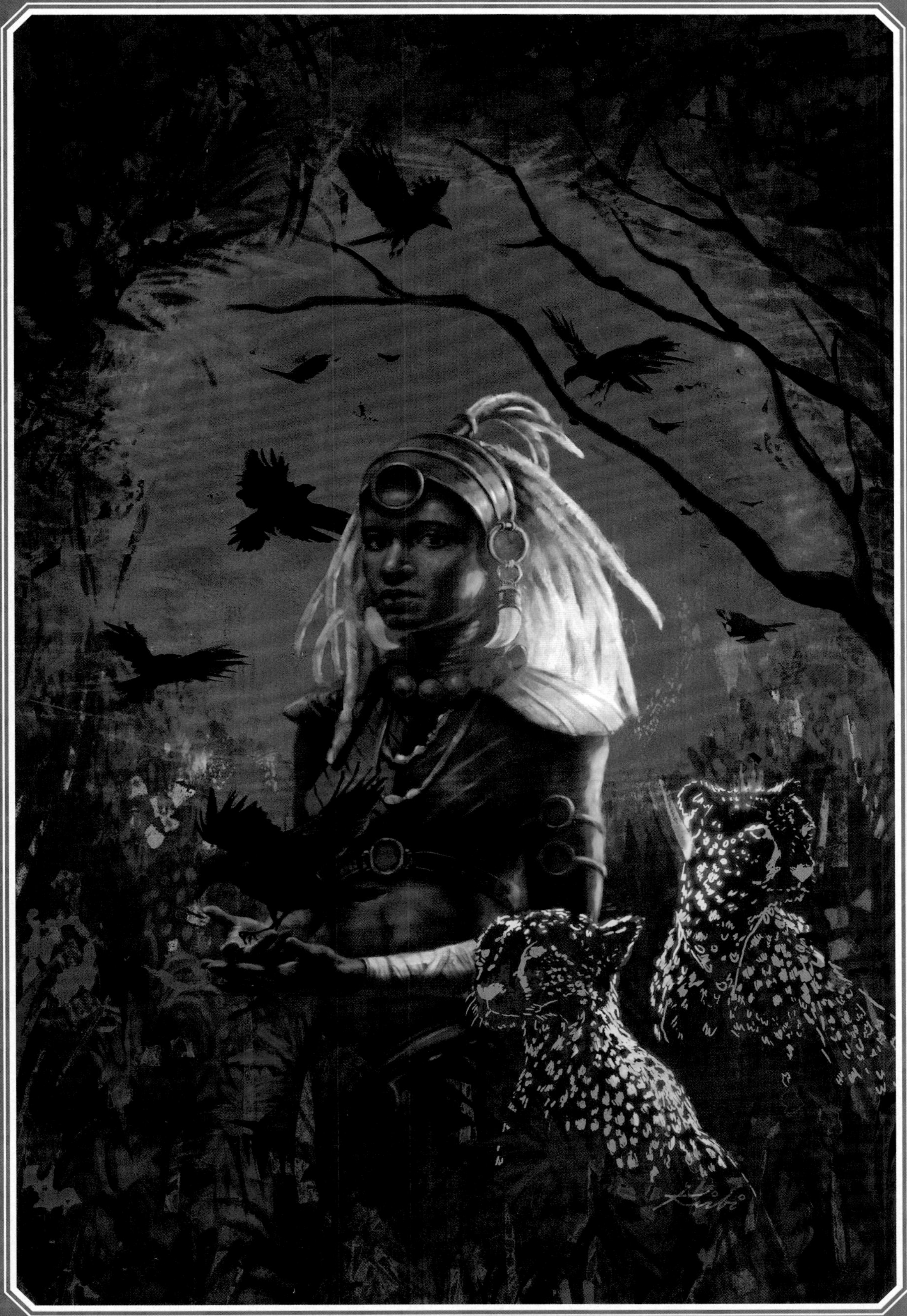

10 – LIVING MEMORY

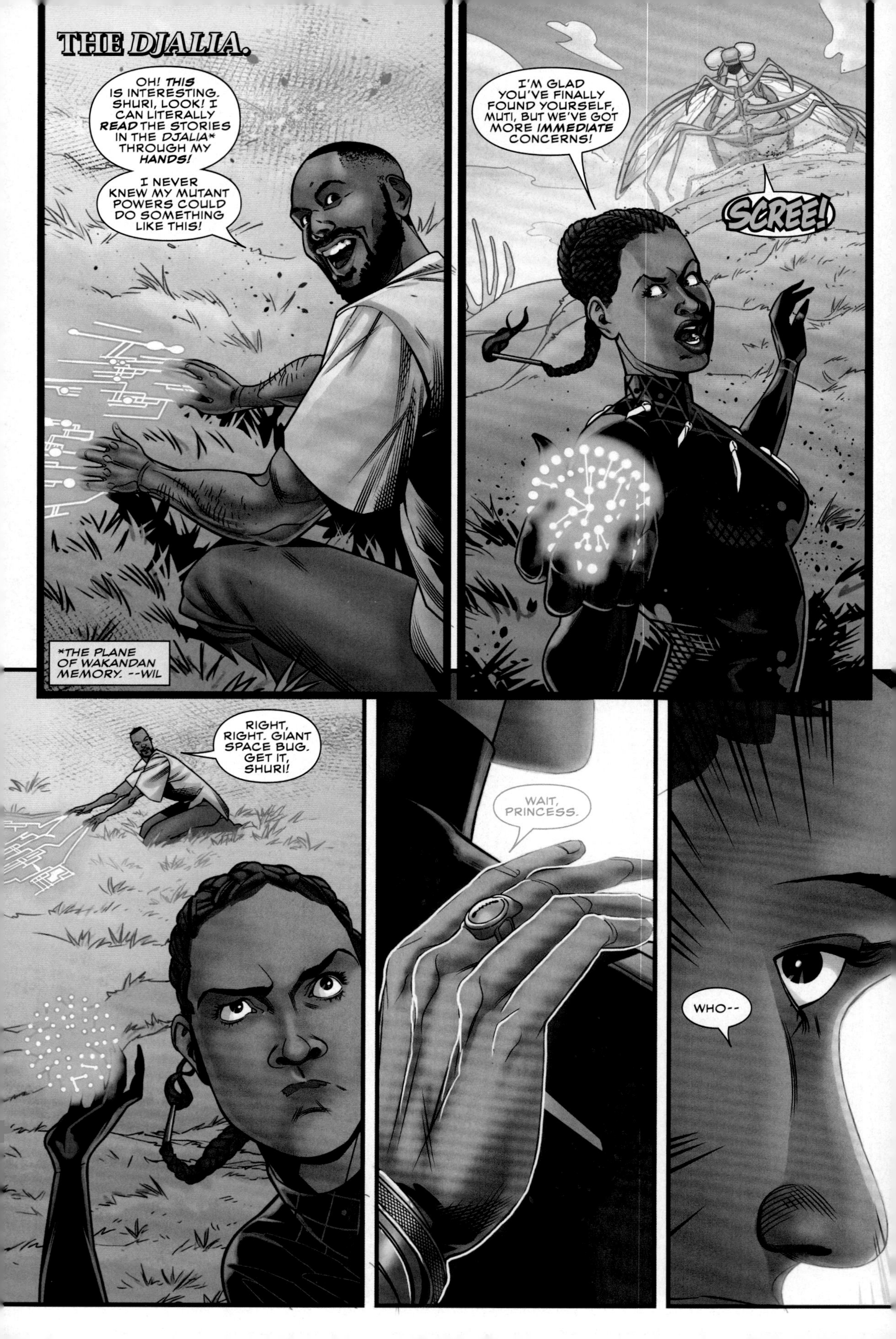
THE DJALIA.
OH! THIS IS INTERESTING. SHURI, LOOK! I CAN LITERALLY READ THE STORIES IN THE DJALIA* THROUGH MY HANDS!
I NEVER KNEW MY MUTANT POWERS COULD DO SOMETHING LIKE THIS!
*THE PLANE OF WAKANDAN MEMORY. --WIL
I'M GLAD YOU'VE FINALLY FOUND YOURSELF, MUTI, BUT WE'VE GOT MORE IMMEDIATE CONCERNS!
SCREE!
RIGHT, RIGHT. GIANT SPACE BUG. GET IT, SHURI!
WAIT, PRINCESS.
WHO--

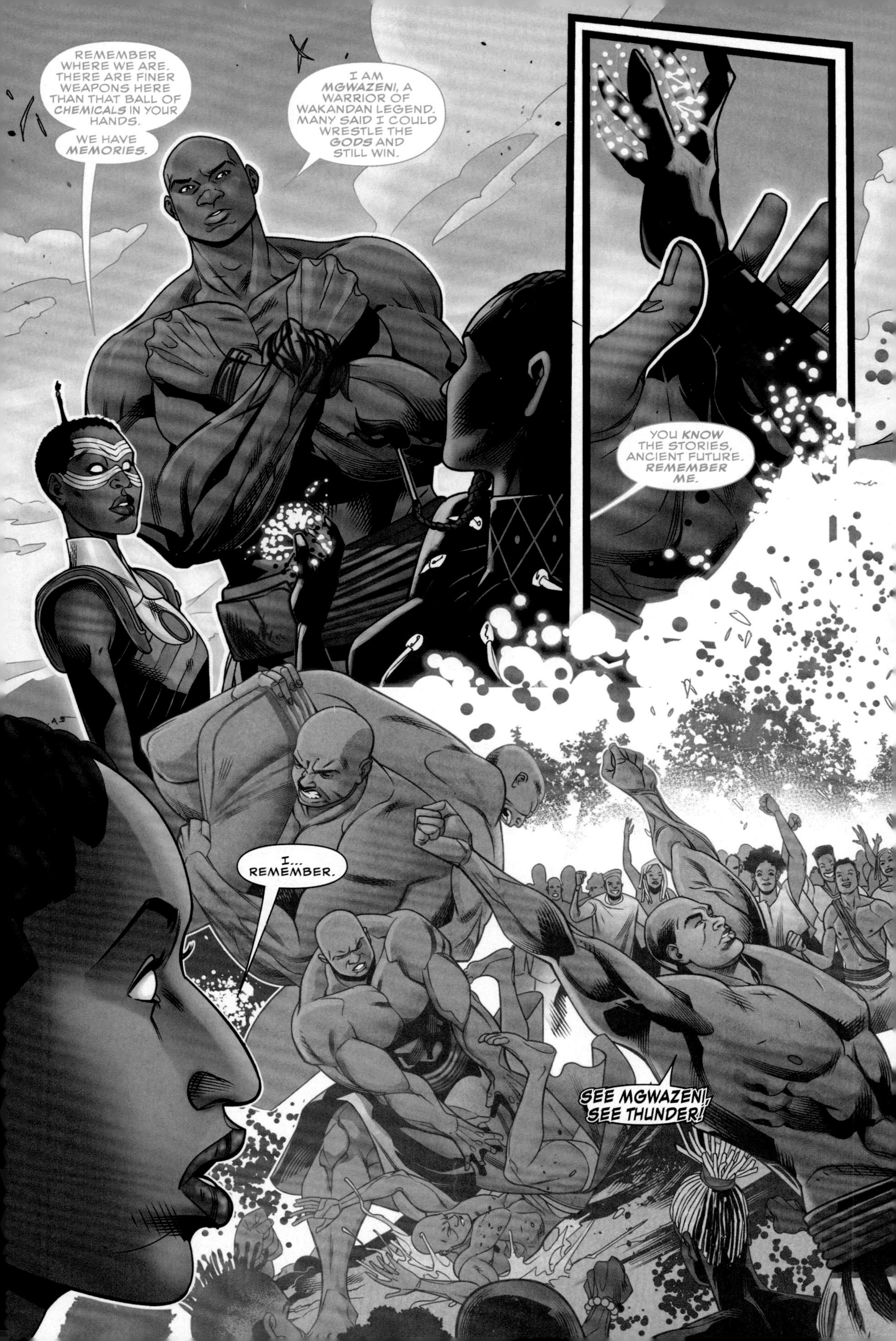
REMEMBER WHERE WE ARE. THERE ARE FINER WEAPONS HERE THAN THAT BALL OF CHEMICALS IN YOUR HANDS.
WE HAVE MEMORIES.
I AM MGWAZENI, A WARRIOR OF WAKANDAN LEGEND. MANY SAID I COULD WRESTLE THE GODS AND STILL WIN.
YOU KNOW THE STORIES, ANCIENT FUTURE. REMEMBER ME.
I... REMEMBER.
SEE MGWAZENI, SEE THUNDER!

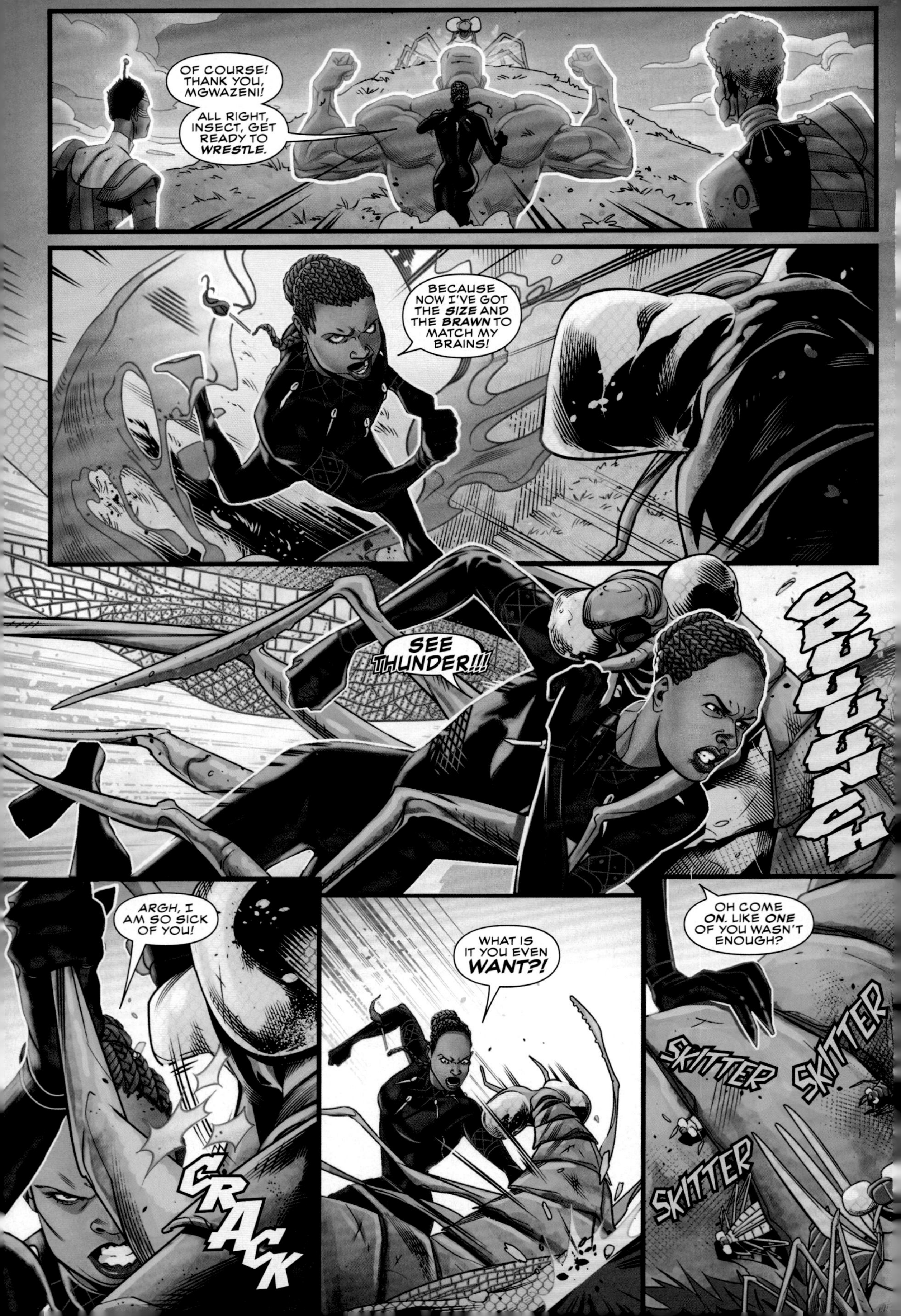
OF COURSE! THANK YOU, MGWAZENI!
ALL RIGHT, INSECT, GET READY TO WRESTLE.
BECAUSE NOW I'VE GOT THE SIZE AND THE BRAWN TO MATCH MY BRAINS!
SEE THUNDER!!!
ARGH, I AM SO SICK OF YOU!
CRACK
WHAT IS IT YOU EVEN WANT?!
OH COME ON. LIKE ONE OF YOU WASN'T ENOUGH?
SKITTER
SKITTER
SKITTER

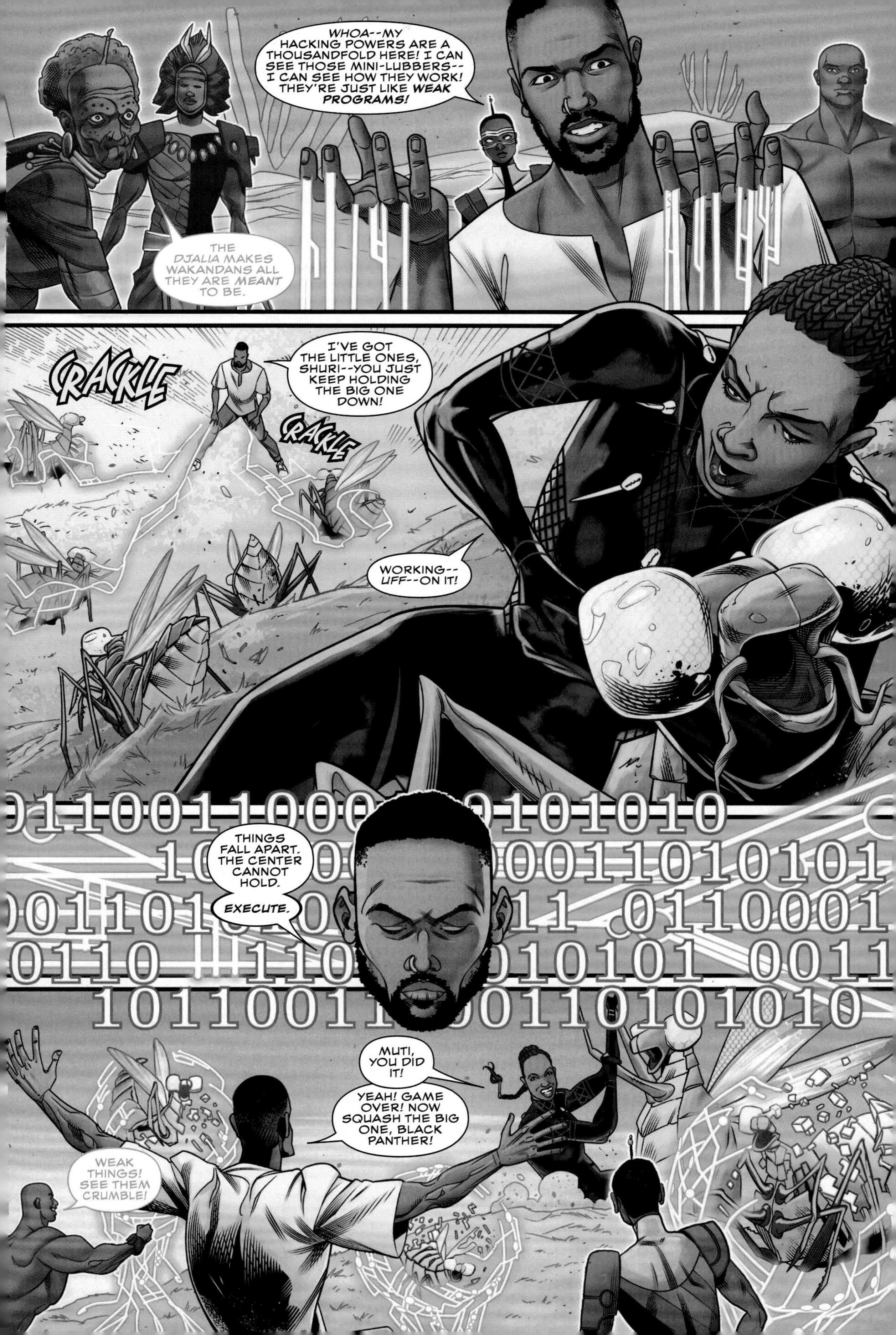
WHOA--MY HACKING POWERS ARE A THOUSANDFOLD HERE! I CAN SEE THOSE MINI-LUBBERS--I CAN SEE HOW THEY WORK! THEY'RE JUST LIKE WEAK PROGRAMS!
THE DJALIA MAKES WAKANDANS ALL THEY ARE MEANT TO BE.
CRACKLE
I'VE GOT THE LITTLE ONES, SHURI--YOU JUST KEEP HOLDING THE BIG ONE DOWN!
CRACKLE
WORKING--UFF--ON IT!
THINGS FALL APART. THE CENTER CANNOT HOLD.
EXECUTE.
MUTI, YOU DID IT!
YEAH! GAME OVER! NOW SQUASH THE BIG ONE, BLACK PANTHER!
WEAK THINGS! SEE THEM CRUMBLE!

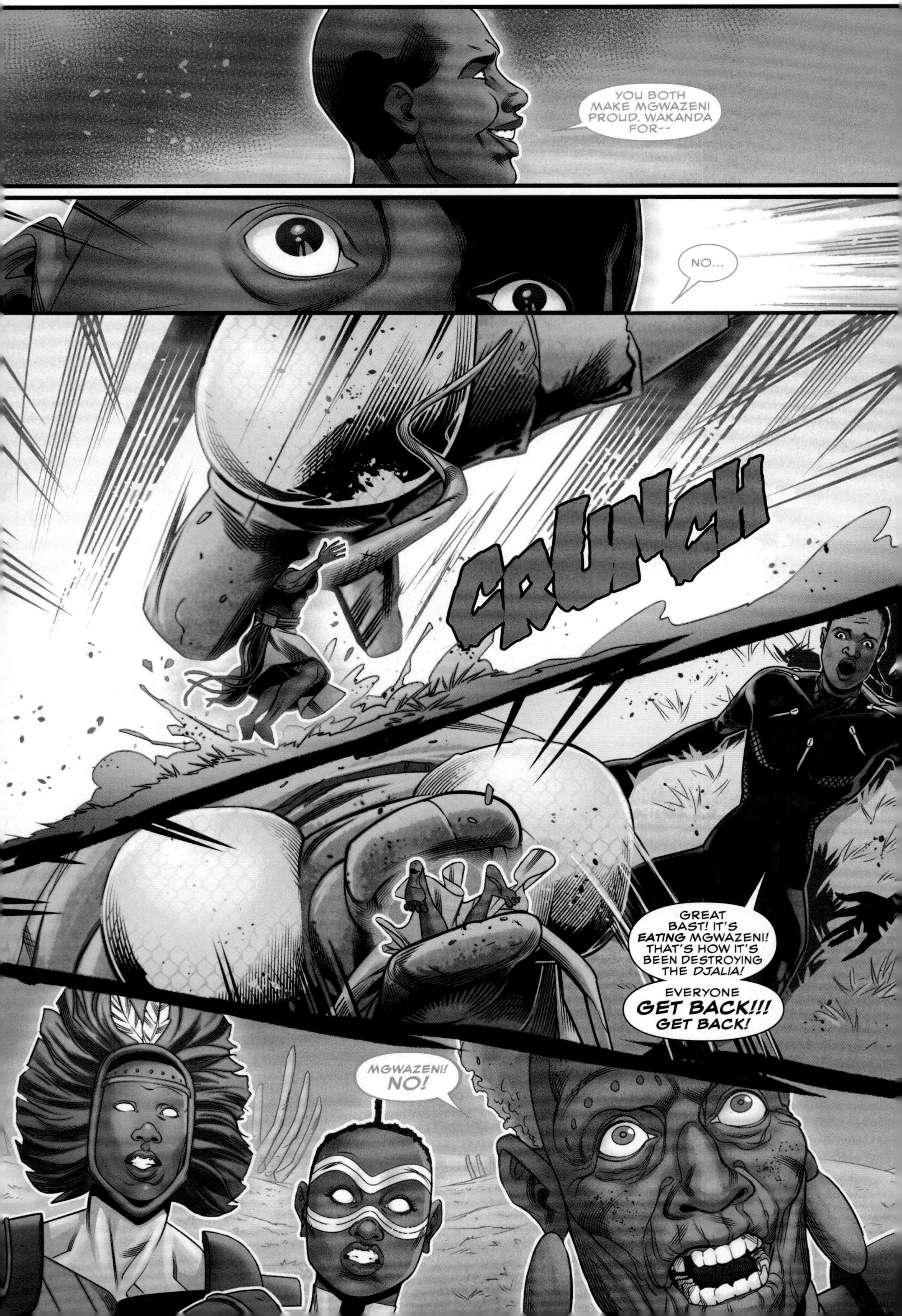
YOU BOTH MAKE MGWAZENI PROUD. WAKANDA FOR--
NO...
CRUNCH
GREAT BAST! IT'S EATING MGWAZENI! THAT'S HOW IT'S BEEN DESTROYING THE DJALIA!
EVERYONE GET BACK!!! GET BACK!
MGWAZENI! NO!

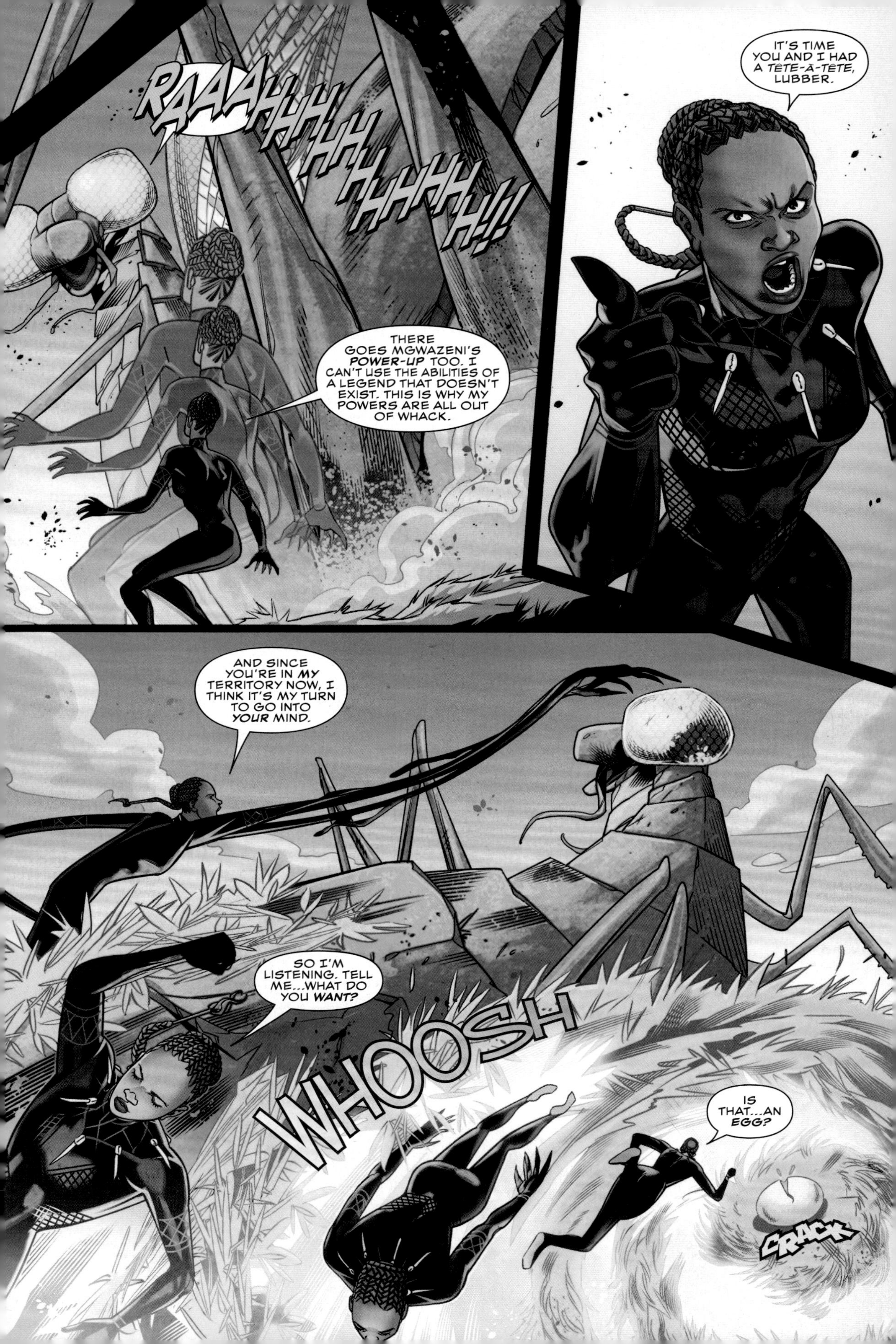
RAAAHHHHHHHHHHH!!!
THERE GOES MGWAZENI'S POWER-UP TOO. I CAN'T USE THE ABILITIES OF A LEGEND THAT DOESN'T EXIST. THIS IS WHY MY POWERS ARE ALL OUT OF WHACK.
IT'S TIME YOU AND I HAD A TÊTE-À-TÊTE, LUBBER.
AND SINCE YOU'RE IN MY TERRITORY NOW, I THINK IT'S MY TURN TO GO INTO YOUR MIND.
SO I'M LISTENING. TELL ME...WHAT DO YOU WANT?
WHOOSH
IS THAT...AN EGG?
CRACK

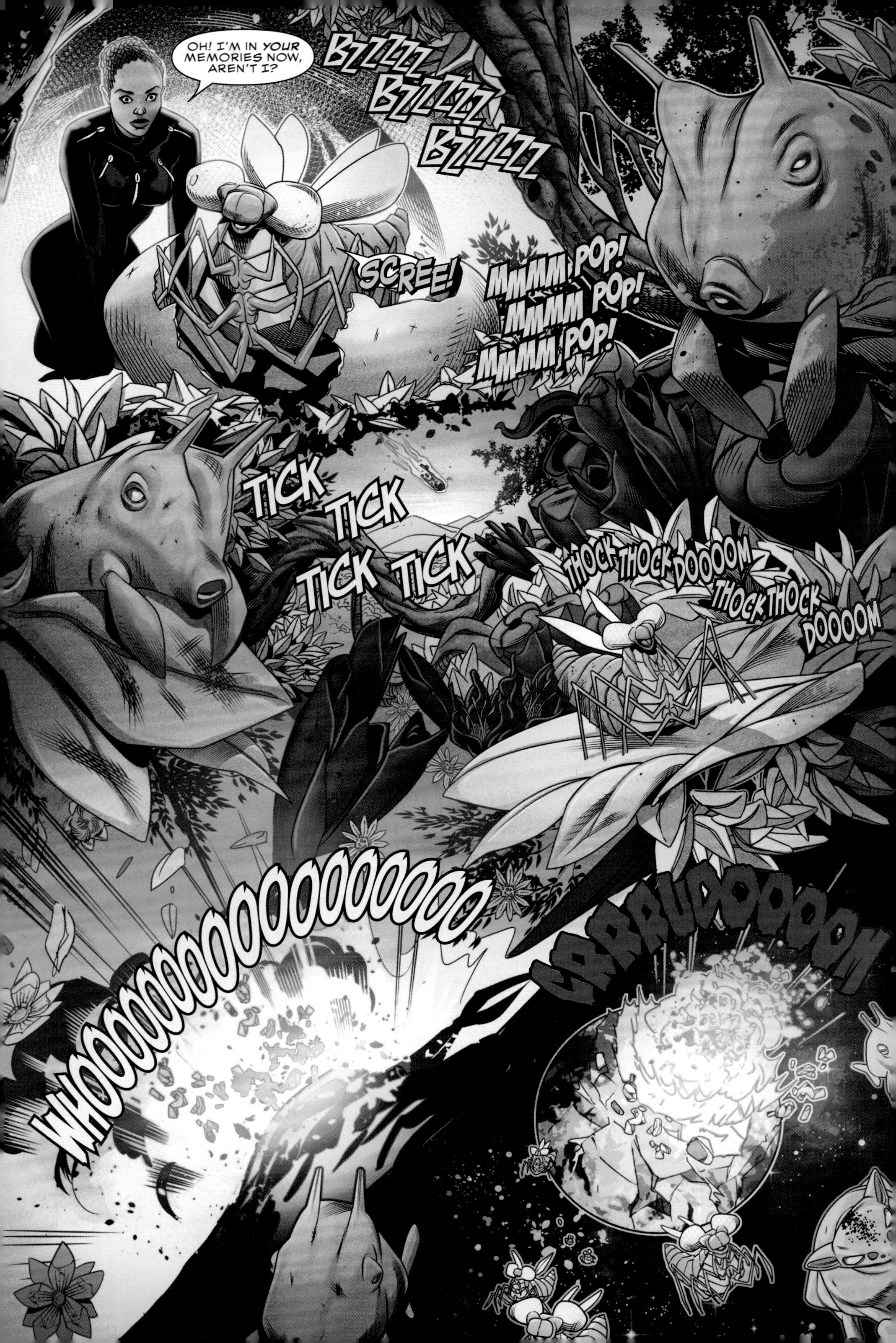
OH! I'M IN YOUR MEMORIES NOW, AREN'T I?
BZZZZZ BZZZZZ BZZZZZ
SCREE!
MMMM POP! MMMM POP! MMMM POP!
TICK TICK TICK TICK
THOCK THOCK DOOOOM THOCK THOCK DOOOOM
WHOOOOOOOOOOOOOOOOOO
GRRRUDOOOOOM

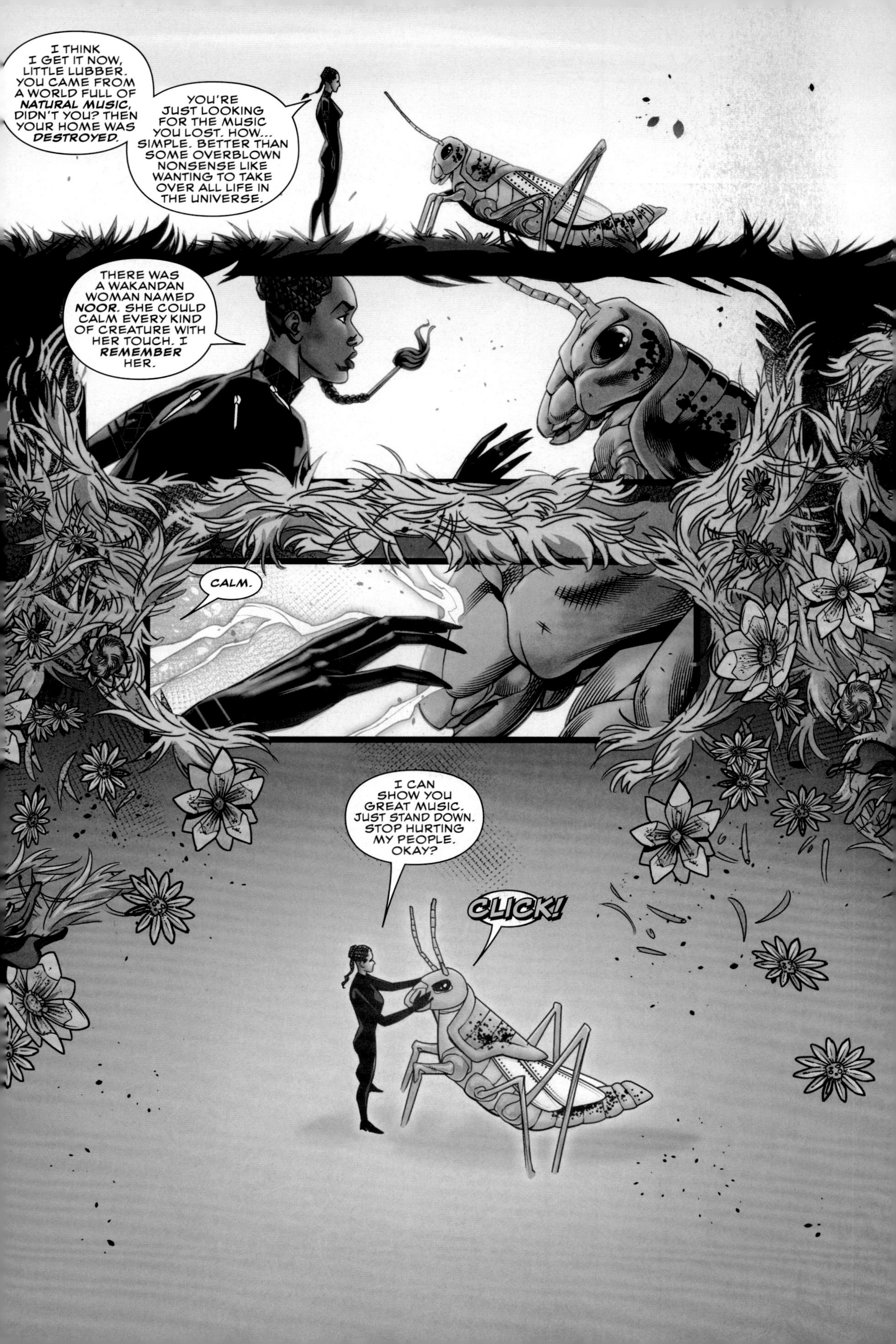
I THINK I GET IT NOW, LITTLE LUBBER. YOU CAME FROM A WORLD FULL OF NATURAL MUSIC, DIDN'T YOU? THEN YOUR HOME WAS DESTROYED.
YOU'RE JUST LOOKING FOR THE MUSIC YOU LOST. HOW... SIMPLE. BETTER THAN SOME OVERBLOWN NONSENSE LIKE WANTING TO TAKE OVER ALL LIFE IN THE UNIVERSE.
THERE WAS A WAKANDAN WOMAN NAMED NOOR. SHE COULD CALM EVERY KIND OF CREATURE WITH HER TOUCH. I REMEMBER HER.
CALM.
I CAN SHOW YOU GREAT MUSIC. JUST STAND DOWN. STOP HURTING MY PEOPLE. OKAY?
CLICK!

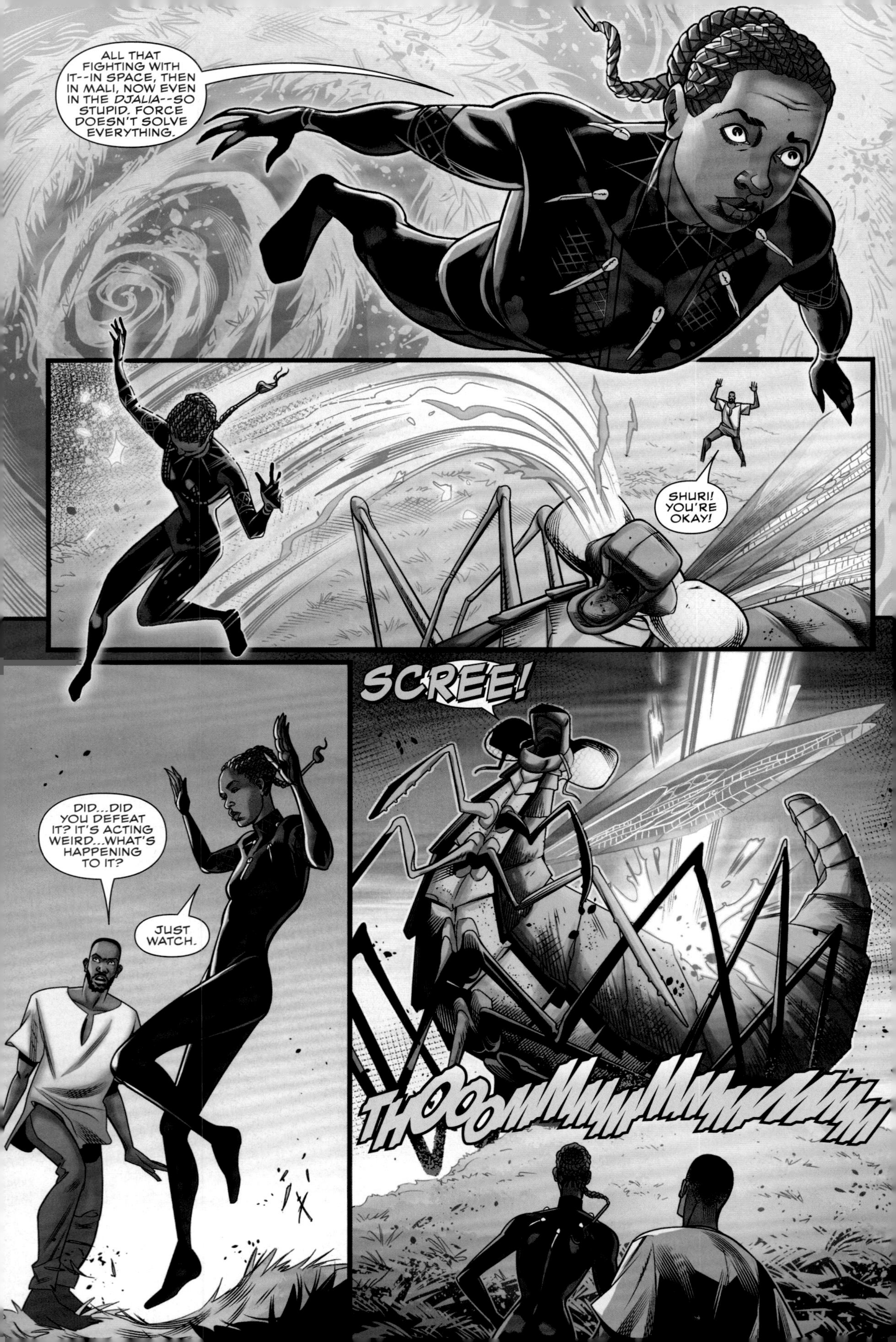
ALL THAT FIGHTING WITH IT--IN SPACE, THEN IN MALI, NOW EVEN IN THE *DJALIA*--SO STUPID. FORCE DOESN'T SOLVE EVERYTHING.
SHURI! YOU'RE OKAY!
DID...DID YOU DEFEAT IT? IT'S ACTING WEIRD...WHAT'S HAPPENING TO IT?
JUST WATCH.
SCREE!
THOOOOMMMMMMMMMMM

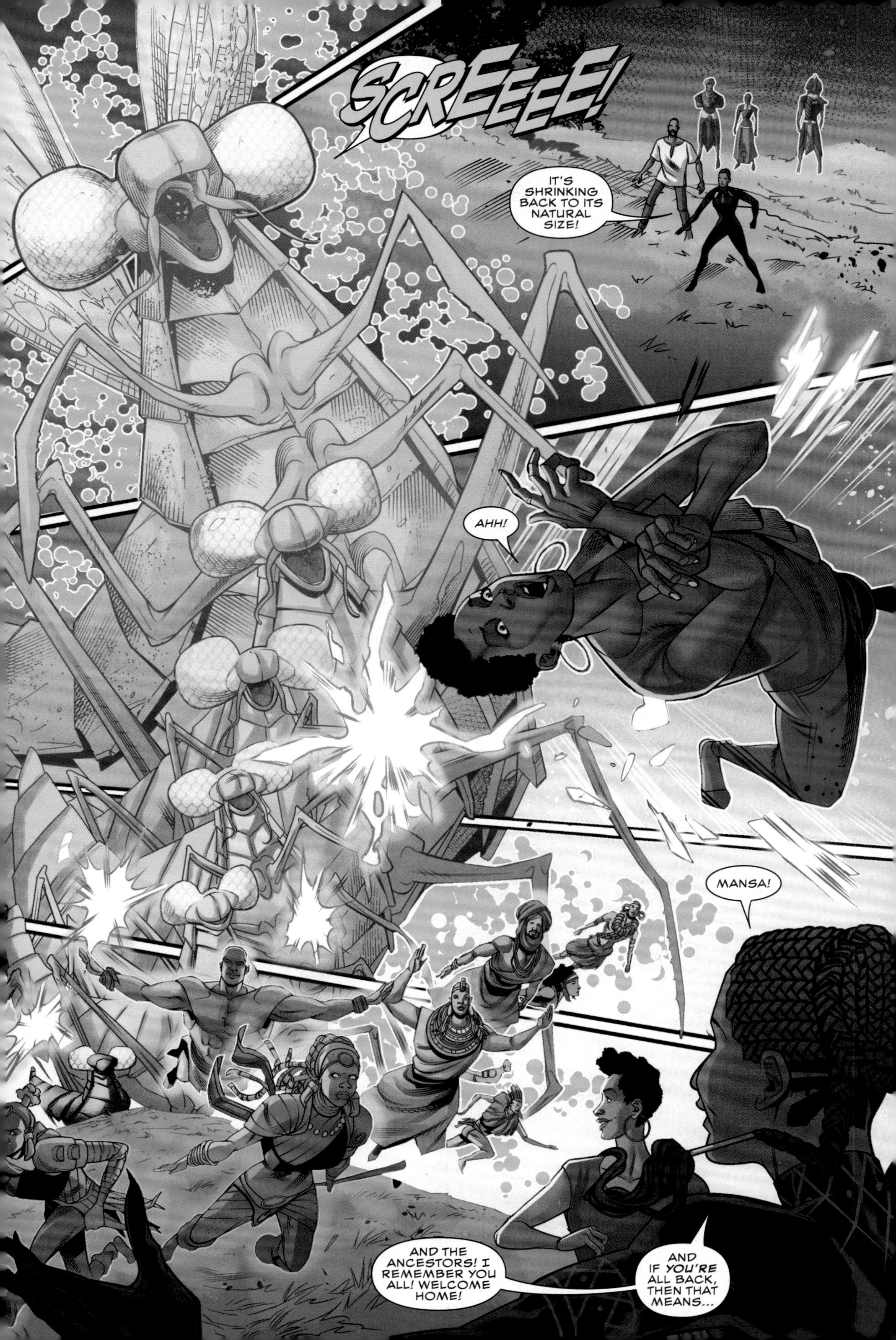
SCREEEEE!
IT'S SHRINKING BACK TO ITS NATURAL SIZE!
AHH!
MANSA!
AND THE ANCESTORS! I REMEMBER YOU ALL! WELCOME HOME!
AND IF YOU'RE ALL BACK, THEN THAT MEANS...

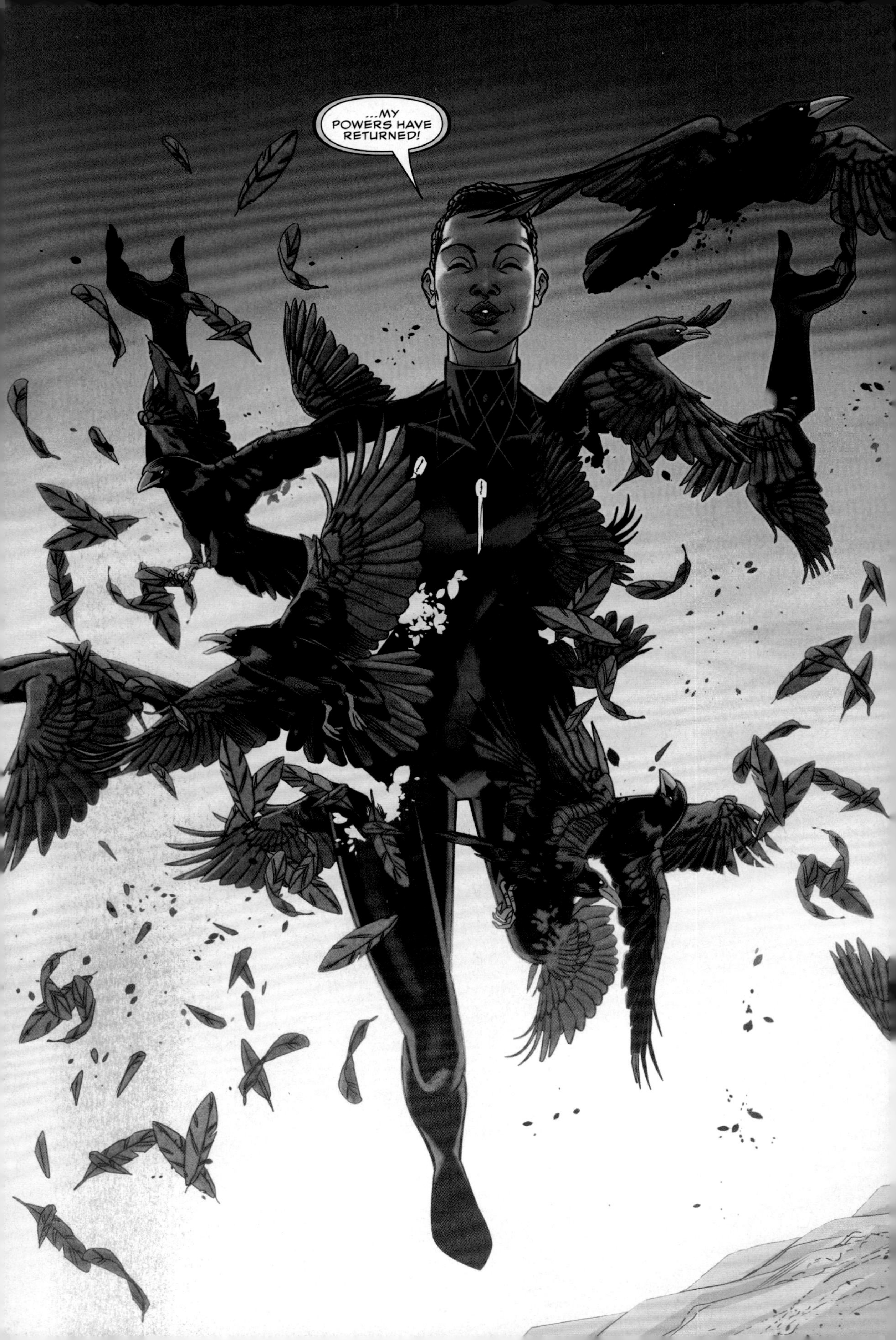
...MY POWERS HAVE RETURNED!

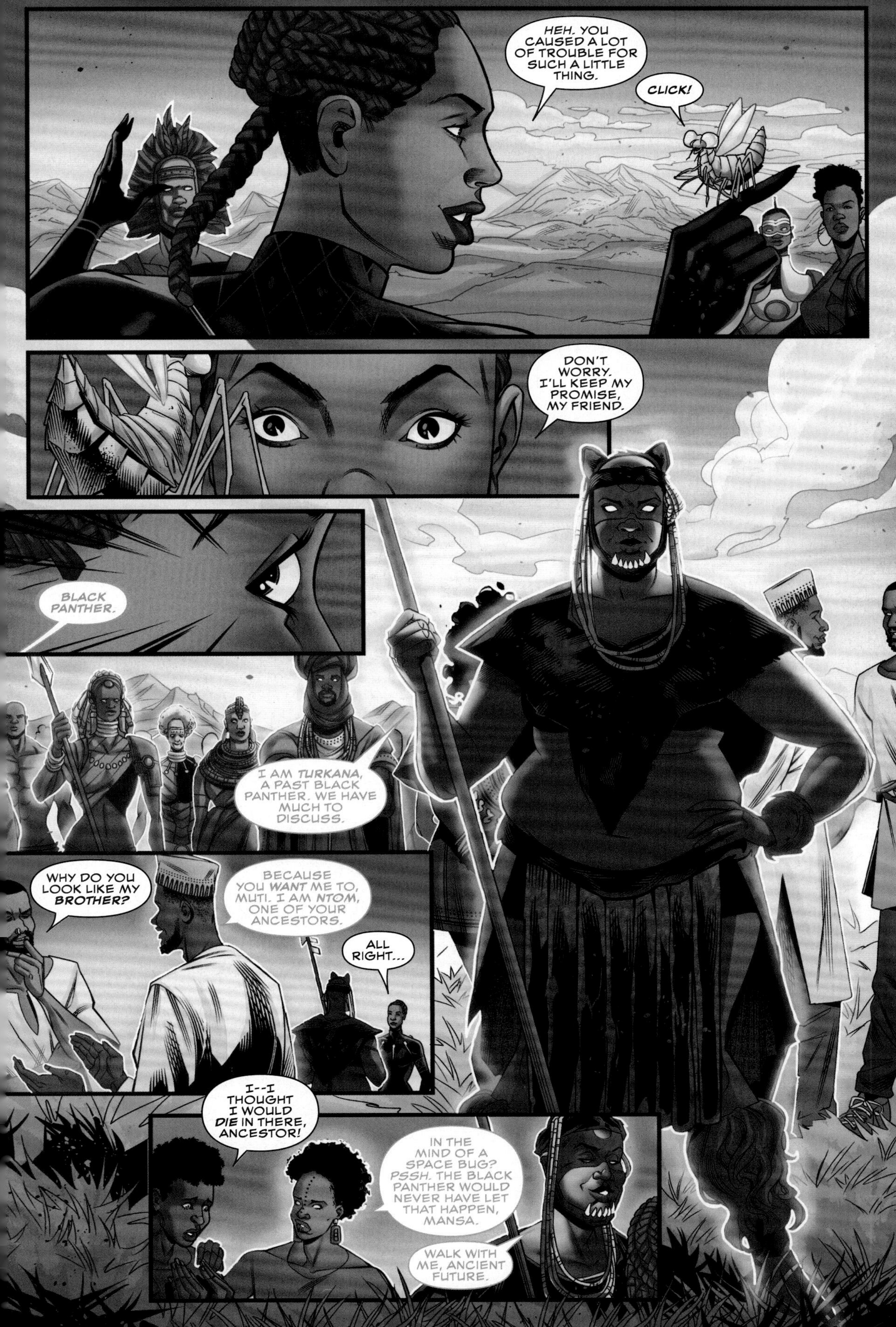

HEH. YOU CAUSED A LOT OF TROUBLE FOR SUCH A LITTLE THING.
CLICK!
DON'T WORRY. I'LL KEEP MY PROMISE, MY FRIEND.
BLACK PANTHER.
I AM TURKANA, A PAST BLACK PANTHER. WE HAVE MUCH TO DISCUSS.
WHY DO YOU LOOK LIKE MY BROTHER?
BECAUSE YOU WANT ME TO, MUTI. I AM NTOM, ONE OF YOUR ANCESTORS.
ALL RIGHT...
I--I THOUGHT I WOULD DIE IN THERE, ANCESTOR!
IN THE MIND OF A SPACE BUG? PSSH. THE BLACK PANTHER WOULD NEVER HAVE LET THAT HAPPEN, MANSA.
WALK WITH ME, ANCIENT FUTURE.

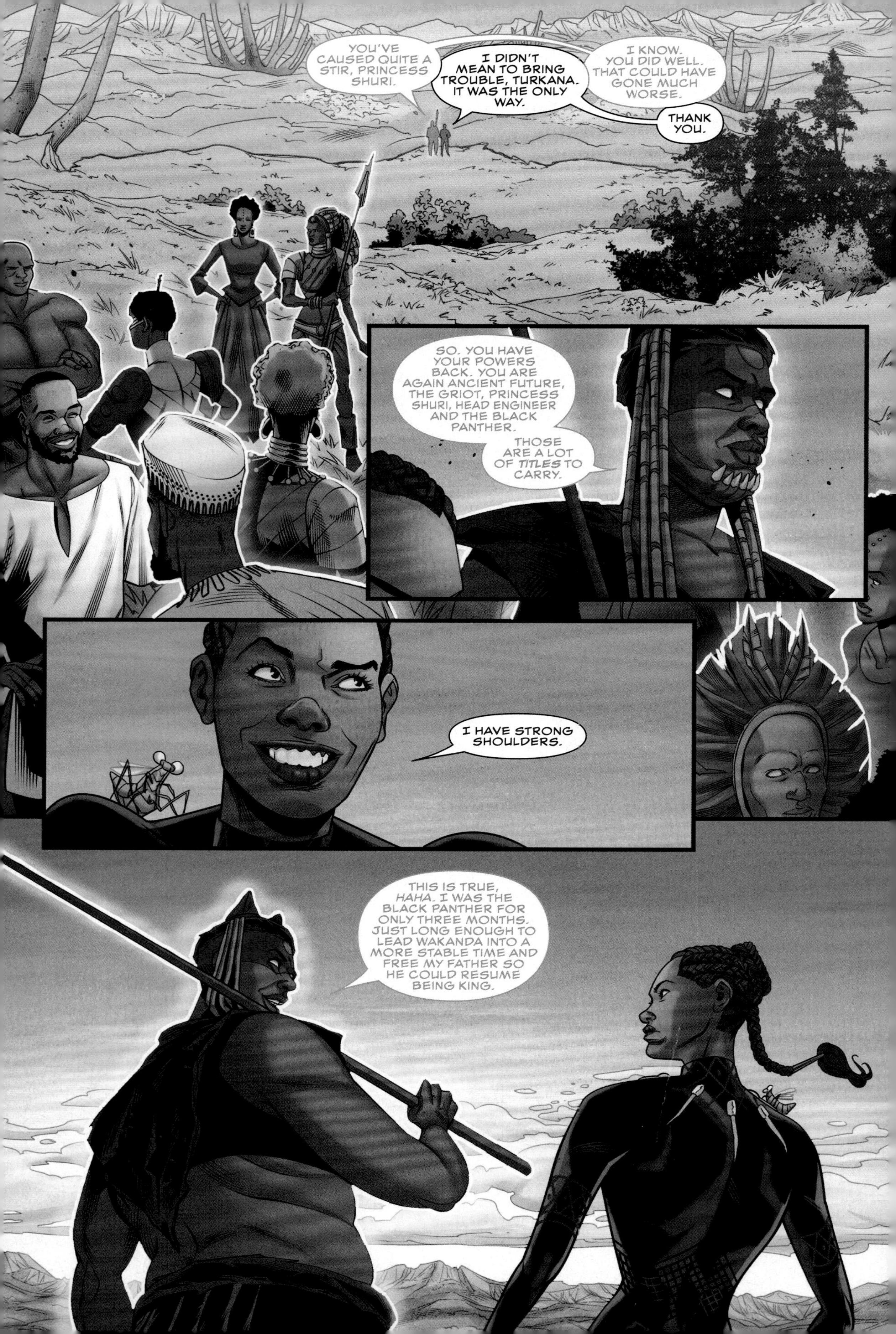
YOU'VE CAUSED QUITE A STIR, PRINCESS SHURI.
I DIDN'T MEAN TO BRING TROUBLE, TURKANA. IT WAS THE ONLY WAY.
I KNOW. YOU DID WELL. THAT COULD HAVE GONE MUCH WORSE.
THANK YOU.
SO. YOU HAVE YOUR POWERS BACK. YOU ARE AGAIN ANCIENT FUTURE, THE GRIOT, PRINCESS SHURI, HEAD ENGINEER AND THE BLACK PANTHER.
THOSE ARE A LOT OF TITLES TO CARRY.
I HAVE STRONG SHOULDERS.
THIS IS TRUE, HAHA. I WAS THE BLACK PANTHER FOR ONLY THREE MONTHS. JUST LONG ENOUGH TO LEAD WAKANDA INTO A MORE STABLE TIME AND FREE MY FATHER SO HE COULD RESUME BEING KING.

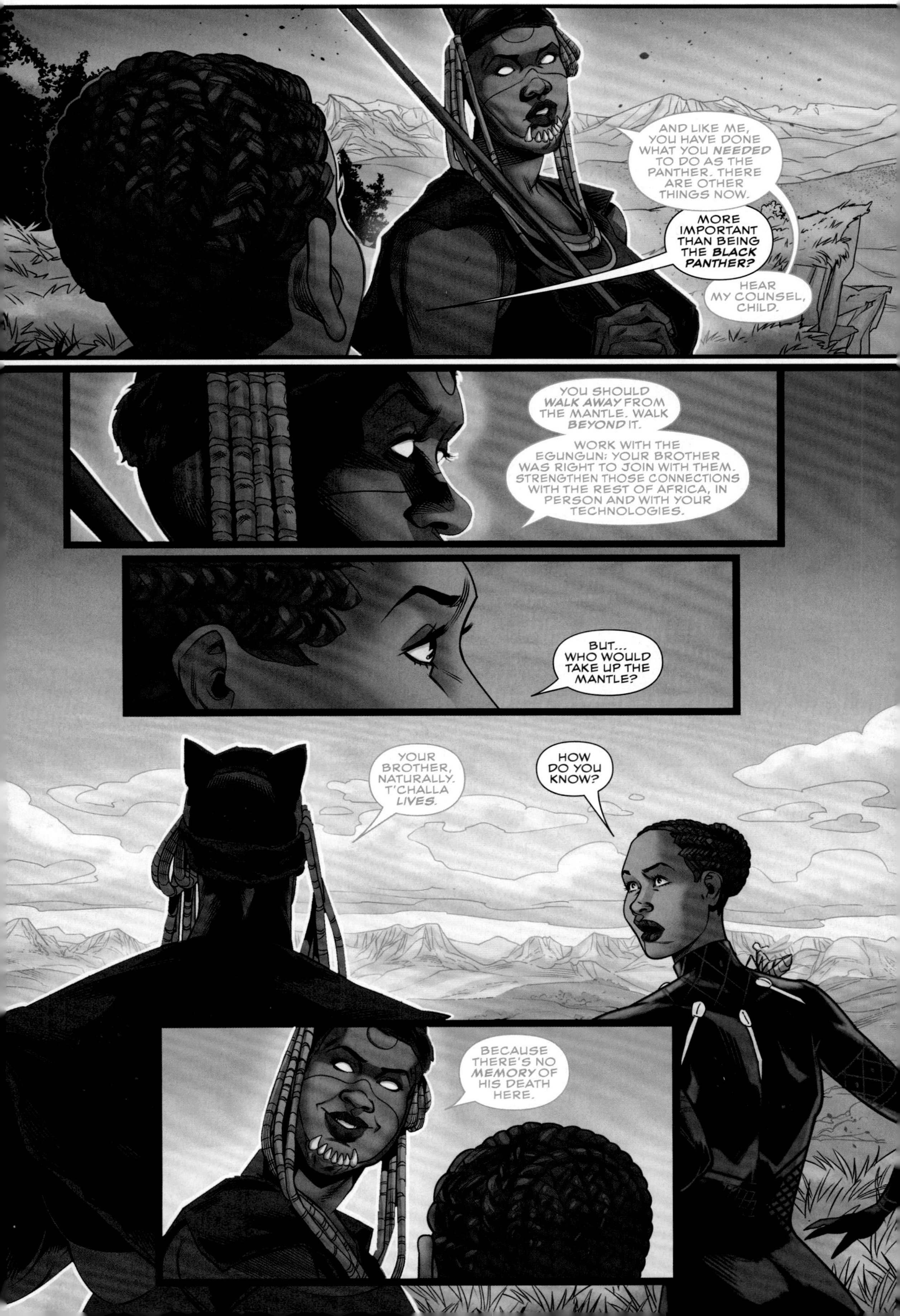

AND LIKE ME, YOU HAVE DONE WHAT YOU NEEDED TO DO AS THE PANTHER. THERE ARE OTHER THINGS NOW.
MORE IMPORTANT THAN BEING THE BLACK PANTHER?
HEAR MY COUNSEL, CHILD.
YOU SHOULD WALK AWAY FROM THE MANTLE. WALK BEYOND IT.
WORK WITH THE EGUNGUN; YOUR BROTHER WAS RIGHT TO JOIN WITH THEM. STRENGTHEN THOSE CONNECTIONS WITH THE REST OF AFRICA, IN PERSON AND WITH YOUR TECHNOLOGIES.
BUT... WHO WOULD TAKE UP THE MANTLE?
YOUR BROTHER, NATURALLY. T'CHALLA LIVES.
HOW DO YOU KNOW?
BECAUSE THERE'S NO MEMORY OF HIS DEATH HERE.

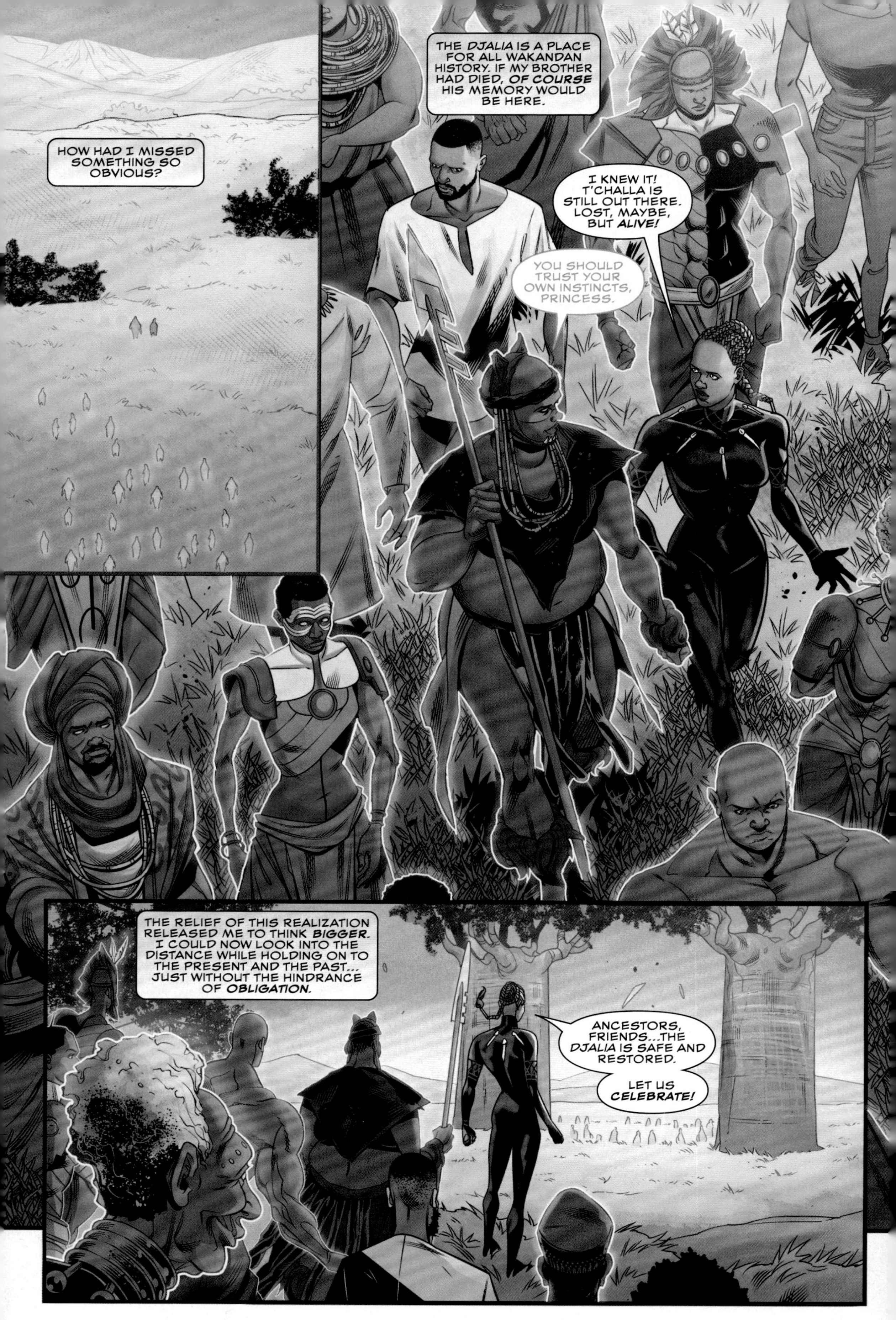
HOW HAD I MISSED SOMETHING SO OBVIOUS?
THE DJALIA IS A PLACE FOR ALL WAKANDAN HISTORY. IF MY BROTHER HAD DIED, OF COURSE HIS MEMORY WOULD BE HERE.
I KNEW IT! T'CHALLA IS STILL OUT THERE. LOST, MAYBE, BUT ALIVE!
YOU SHOULD TRUST YOUR OWN INSTINCTS, PRINCESS.
THE RELIEF OF THIS REALIZATION RELEASED ME TO THINK BIGGER. I COULD NOW LOOK INTO THE DISTANCE WHILE HOLDING ON TO THE PRESENT AND THE PAST... JUST WITHOUT THE HINDRANCE OF OBLIGATION.
ANCESTORS, FRIENDS...THE DJALIA IS SAFE AND RESTORED.
LET US CELEBRATE!

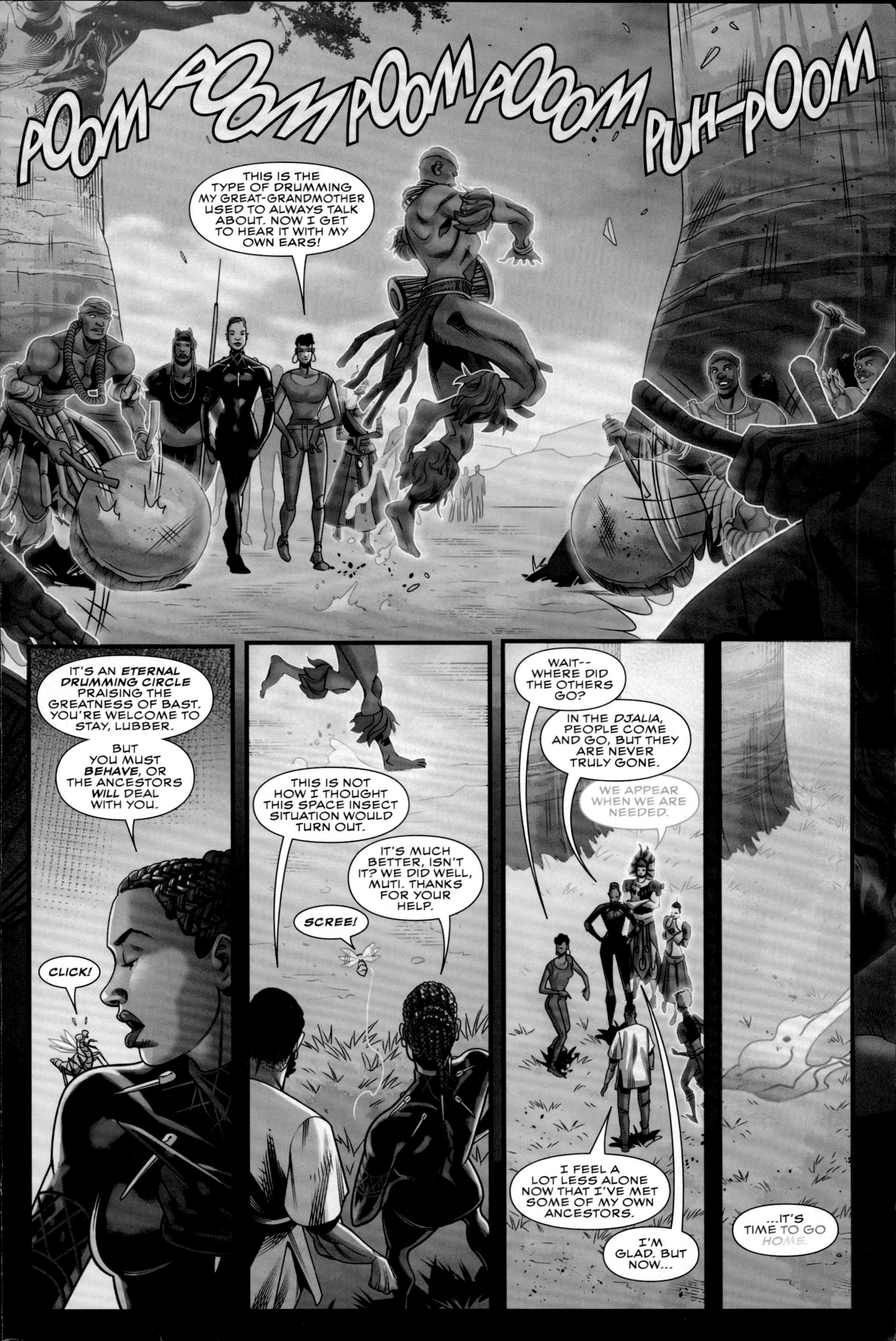
POOM POOM POOM POOOM PUH-POOM
THIS IS THE TYPE OF DRUMMING MY GREAT-GRANDMOTHER USED TO ALWAYS TALK ABOUT. NOW I GET TO HEAR IT WITH MY OWN EARS!
IT'S AN ETERNAL DRUMMING CIRCLE PRAISING THE GREATNESS OF BAST. YOU'RE WELCOME TO STAY, LUBBER.
BUT YOU MUST BEHAVE, OR THE ANCESTORS WILL DEAL WITH YOU.
CLICK!
THIS IS NOT HOW I THOUGHT THIS SPACE INSECT SITUATION WOULD TURN OUT.
IT'S MUCH BETTER, ISN'T IT? WE DID WELL, MUTI. THANKS FOR YOUR HELP.
SCREE!
WAIT-- WHERE DID THE OTHERS GO?
IN THE DJALIA, PEOPLE COME AND GO, BUT THEY ARE NEVER TRULY GONE.
WE APPEAR WHEN WE ARE NEEDED.
I FEEL A LOT LESS ALONE NOW THAT I'VE MET SOME OF MY OWN ANCESTORS.
I'M GLAD. BUT NOW...
...IT'S TIME TO GO HOME.

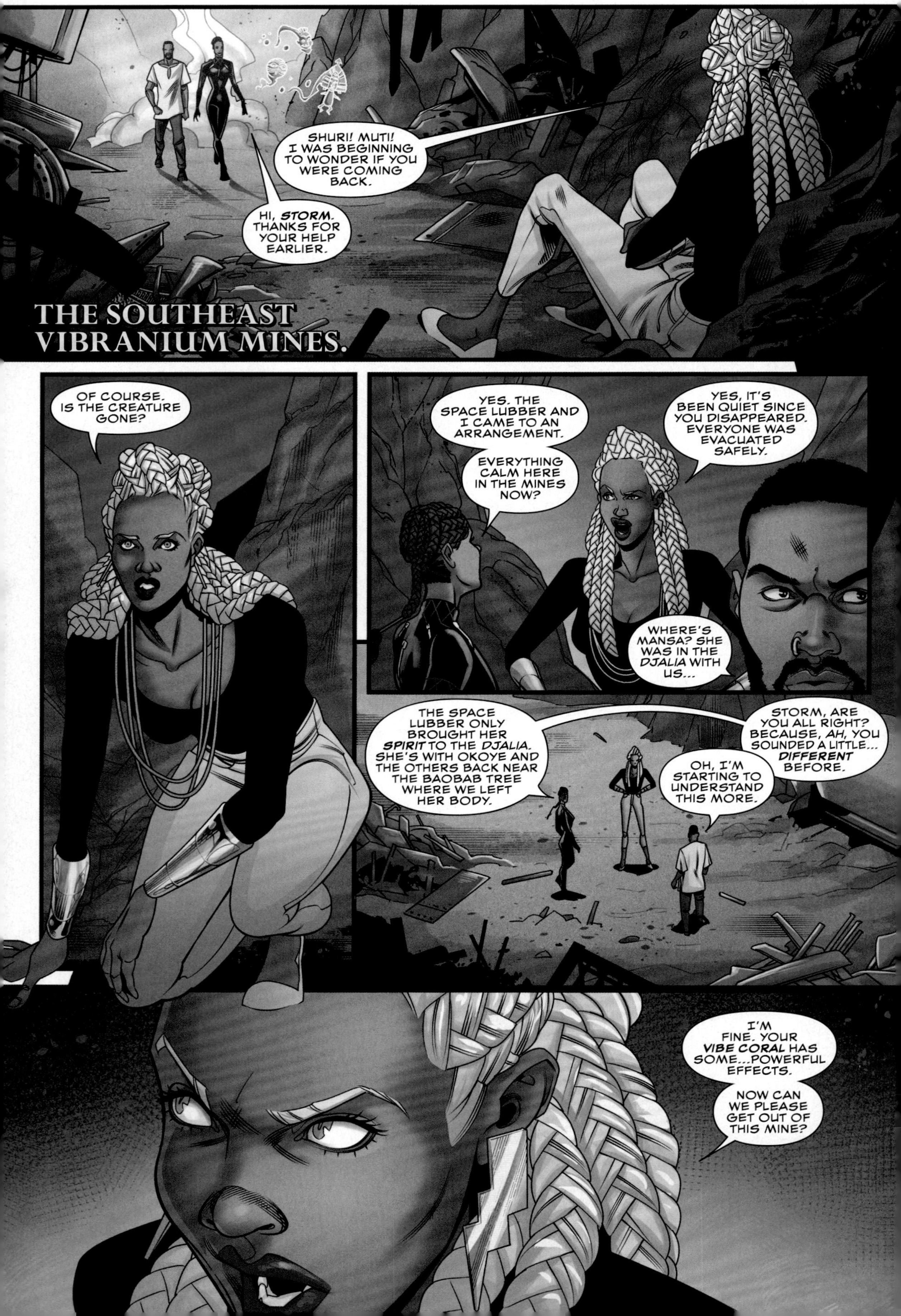

THE SOUTHEAST VIBRANIUM MINES.
SHURI! MUTI! I WAS BEGINNING TO WONDER IF YOU WERE COMING BACK.
HI, STORM. THANKS FOR YOUR HELP EARLIER.
OF COURSE. IS THE CREATURE GONE?
YES. THE SPACE LUBBER AND I CAME TO AN ARRANGEMENT.
EVERYTHING CALM HERE IN THE MINES NOW?
YES, IT'S BEEN QUIET SINCE YOU DISAPPEARED. EVERYONE WAS EVACUATED SAFELY.
WHERE'S MANSA? SHE WAS IN THE DJALIA WITH US...
THE SPACE LUBBER ONLY BROUGHT HER SPIRIT TO THE DJALIA. SHE'S WITH OKOYE AND THE OTHERS BACK NEAR THE BAOBAB TREE WHERE WE LEFT HER BODY.
STORM, ARE YOU ALL RIGHT? BECAUSE, AH, YOU SOUNDED A LITTLE... DIFFERENT BEFORE.
OH, I'M STARTING TO UNDERSTAND THIS MORE.
I'M FINE. YOUR VIBE CORAL HAS SOME...POWERFUL EFFECTS.
NOW CAN WE PLEASE GET OUT OF THIS MINE?

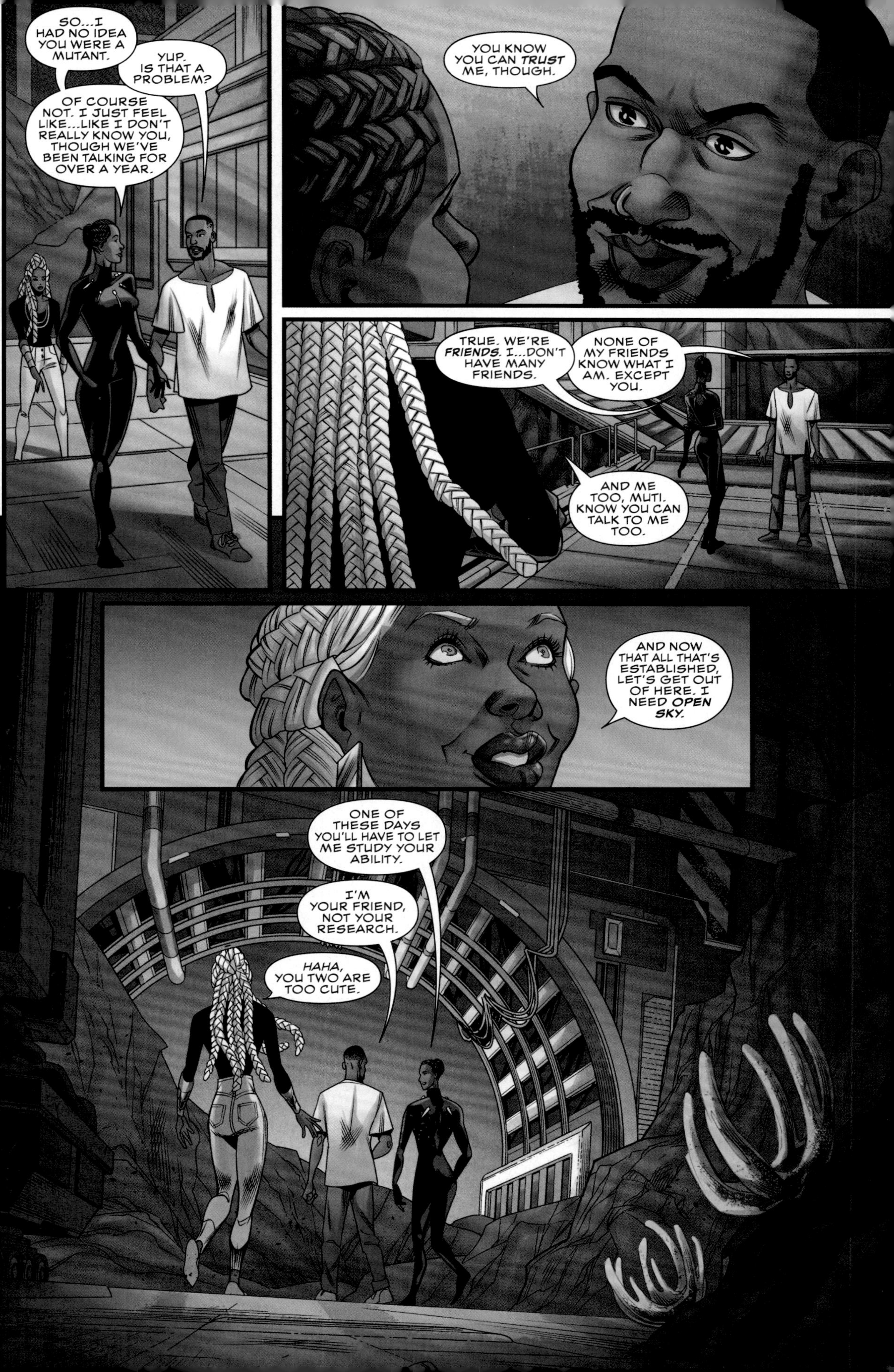

SO...I HAD NO IDEA YOU WERE A MUTANT.
YUP. IS THAT A PROBLEM?
OF COURSE NOT. I JUST FEEL LIKE...LIKE I DON'T REALLY KNOW YOU, THOUGH WE'VE BEEN TALKING FOR OVER A YEAR.
YOU KNOW YOU CAN TRUST ME, THOUGH.
TRUE. WE'RE FRIENDS. I...DON'T HAVE MANY FRIENDS.
NONE OF MY FRIENDS KNOW WHAT I AM. EXCEPT YOU.
AND ME TOO, MUTI. KNOW YOU CAN TALK TO ME TOO.
AND NOW THAT ALL THAT'S ESTABLISHED, LET'S GET OUT OF HERE. I NEED OPEN SKY.
ONE OF THESE DAYS YOU'LL HAVE TO LET ME STUDY YOUR ABILITY.
I'M YOUR FRIEND, NOT YOUR RESEARCH.
HAHA, YOU TWO ARE TOO CUTE.

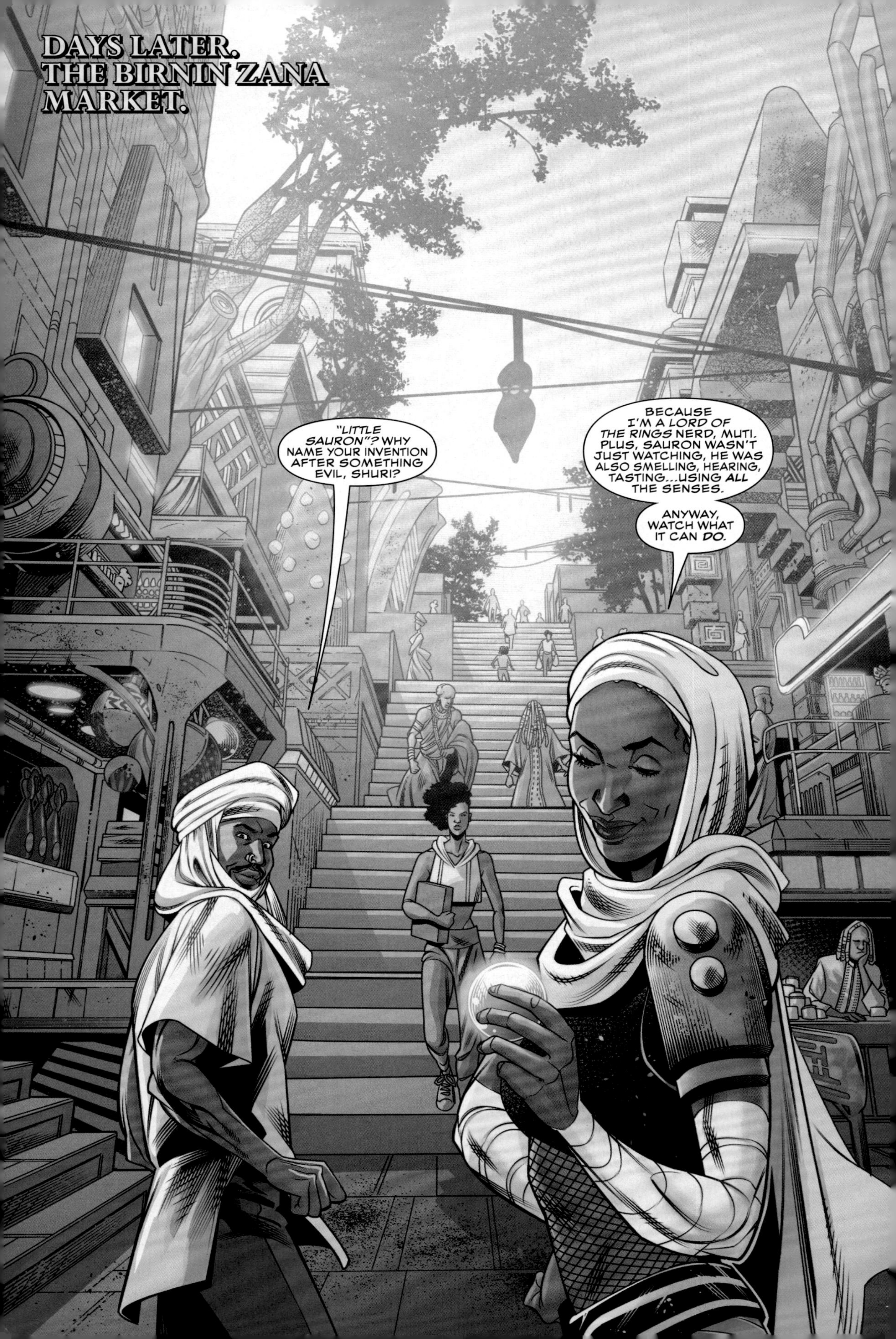
DAYS LATER. THE BIRNIN ZANA MARKET.
"LITTLE SAURON"? WHY NAME YOUR INVENTION AFTER SOMETHING EVIL, SHURI?
BECAUSE I'M A LORD OF THE RINGS NERD, MUTI. PLUS, SAURON WASN'T JUST WATCHING, HE WAS ALSO SMELLING, HEARING, TASTING...USING ALL THE SENSES.
ANYWAY, WATCH WHAT IT CAN DO.

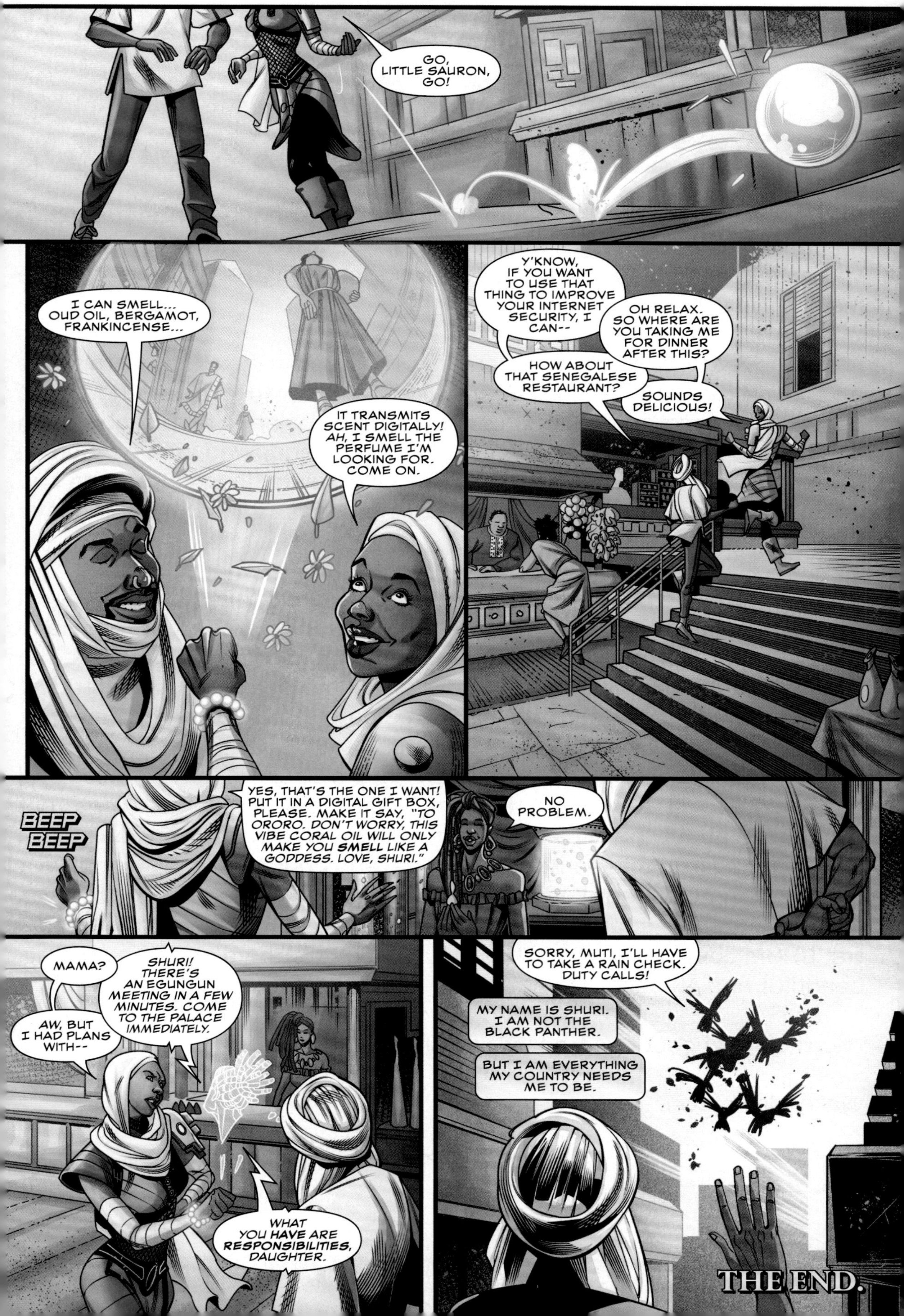
GO, LITTLE SAURON, GO!
I CAN SMELL... OUD OIL, BERGAMOT, FRANKINCENSE...
IT TRANSMITS SCENT DIGITALLY! AH, I SMELL THE PERFUME I'M LOOKING FOR. COME ON.
Y'KNOW, IF YOU WANT TO USE THAT THING TO IMPROVE YOUR INTERNET SECURITY, I CAN--
OH RELAX. SO WHERE ARE YOU TAKING ME FOR DINNER AFTER THIS?
HOW ABOUT THAT SENEGALESE RESTAURANT?
SOUNDS DELICIOUS!
BEEP BEEP
YES, THAT'S THE ONE I WANT! PUT IT IN A DIGITAL GIFT BOX, PLEASE. MAKE IT SAY, "TO ORORO. DON'T WORRY, THIS VIBE CORAL OIL WILL ONLY MAKE YOU SMELL LIKE A GODDESS. LOVE, SHURI."
NO PROBLEM.
MAMA?
SHURI! THERE'S AN EGUNGUN MEETING IN A FEW MINUTES. COME TO THE PALACE IMMEDIATELY.
AW, BUT I HAD PLANS WITH--
WHAT YOU HAVE ARE RESPONSIBILITIES, DAUGHTER.
SORRY, MUTI, I'LL HAVE TO TAKE A RAIN CHECK. DUTY CALLS!
MY NAME IS SHURI. I AM NOT THE BLACK PANTHER.
BUT I AM EVERYTHING MY COUNTRY NEEDS ME TO BE.
THE END.

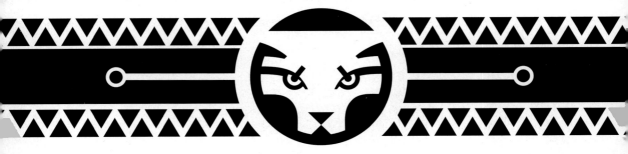

And so we leave Shuri here...for now. At a Wakandan perfume shop in the market, wiser, stronger, touched by space travel, and with a new and very interesting friend. They say that important things always begin in the market. We will see.

I've looooved writing Shuri's adventures. I knew from the start that this was a perfect fit for me. Shuri is gutsy, ambitious, and drawn to the sciences by a curious, interrogative nature. She's struggling to balance familial obligation and a need for independence. She's also been endowed with beautifully awesome abilities after dying. In a way, I can relate (long story). She and I didn't agree on everything (example: Shuri doesn't like bugs and I love them), but we made a good team.

There were some narrative things I set out to do in this arc, and I think I accomplished them. Aside from just allowing Shuri to go out there and BE Shuri (the princess, the engineer, the leader, the girl), I also wanted to reintroduce Wakanda to Africa and plant some seeds for that budding relationship with Shuri at the helm. This came in the shape of the *Egungun*.

Also, it was a heck of a challenge merging the Shuri from the comics and the Shuri from the film, and that challenge was one of the things that excited me about this project. I didn't get the balance right immediately. I remember some of my earlier ideas for her and how much they didn't work (and how my wonderful editors firmly but kindly let me know). However, when I found the equilibrium, we all knew it was just right. Sam Spratt's first SHURI cover concretized this new fusion, and there she was—strong, beautiful, and African.

I don't care for goodbyes, so let's do an "Until next time."

Wakanda Forever.

Nnedimma Nkemdili Okorafor
Flossmoor, IL
June 25, 2019

Send your emails to **mheroes@marvel.com** and mark them "okay to print."

PAGE NINETEEN

This is a detailed splash page. We are back in the same market as in that early scene in issue #1, this time in the perfume section at the bottom of a hill. The perfume section of the market is mostly on this hill -- Shuri and Muti stand together at the bottom of it. Shuri is wearing a hood (as she did in issue #1) to hide her identity. Muti is wearing a Tuareg-style face veil, just because he's Muti.

Shuri is carrying her same digitized ball from that #1 scene – "Little Sauron," which can spy on things down to the smell. She holds it to her chest.

We are directly in front of them.

All around them are people selling things in glass vials. This is a very detailed panel of colors, shiny perfume and scented oil bottles and people dressed in Wakandan attire. There are trees growing in the market, too, so this place isn't outside of nature, it's woven into it. There are birds perched on the top of booths and flying by, a cicada zooming by, etc. Shuri stands in the center, looking at us, holding Little Sauron.

DIALOGUE/MUTI: "Little Sauron"? Why name it after

something evil?

DIALOGUE/SHURI: Because I'm a Lord of the Rings nerd. Plus, Sauron wasn't just *watching*, he was also smelling, hearing, tasting…all the senses. Anyway, watch.

NNEDI OKORAFOR
#10, PAGE 19 SCRIPT

RACHAEL STOTT
#10, PAGE 19 ART

PAGE EIGHTEEN

PANEL 1 (ROW 1)

Shuri and Muti walk side by side through the mines. Storm is walking behind them, pensive and looking up at the vastness of the mines.

DIALOGUE/SHURI: So, Muti, you're a mutant?

DIALOGUE/MUTI: Yup. Is that a problem?

DIALOGUE/SHURI: No…I just feel like…like I don't really know you.

PANEL 2 (ROW 1)

Close on Muti.

DIALOGUE/MUTI: You know you can trust me, though.

PANEL 3 (ROW 2)

They've stopped and are looking at each other, somewhat close. Storm stands behind them with her arms across her chest. She's smirking.

DIALOGUE/SHURI: True. I can. We're friends. I don't have many friends.

DIALOGUE/MUTI: None of my friends know what I am. Except you.

PANEL 4 (ROW 2)

Close on Storm. This is a small panel.

DIALOGUE/STORM: Now that that's established, let's get out of here. I need open sky.

PANEL 5 (ROW 3)

The point of view is from behind them as they walk out of the mines, taking the long way since Muti can't fly. Storm walks behind them.

DIALOGUE/SHURI: One of these days you have to let me study your ability.

DIALOGUE/MUTI: I'm your friend, not your research.

DIALOGUE/STORM: Haha, you two are too cute.

NNEDI OKORAFOR
#10, PAGE 18 SCRIPT

RACHAEL STOTT
#10, PAGE 18 ART